Praise for

Not Quite a Genius

"Nate Dern's brain is a Vitamix that chops up Kafka, the Internet, Republicans, and thousands of other cultural ingredients and blends them into hilarious little treats. The results are not just funny—which they are—but they're even kind of profound. Highly recommended reading for those hungry for surprise."

—A.J. Jacobs, *New York Times* bestselling author of
It's All Relative and *Drop Dead Healthy*

"So no, Nate Dern may not be quite a genius. Still, he has written a book that is very smart, funny, and thoughtful, and that might be just what the world needs."

—*New York Times Book Review*

"Nate is one of those writers and performers that is constantly morphing and changing, always impressing and exceeding my expectations. His book is no different—you never know where it's going to go next, what genre, what format, what unique new take on an old idea. It's a breath of fresh air that you can eat up bit by bit or all at once like a huge hoagie. His book is, in a lot of ways, like a really wonderful sandwich."

—Abbi Jacobson, cocreator and star of
Comedy Central's *Broad City*

"Genuinely funny."

—*Kirkus Reviews*

"Nate Dern is an undeniable talent, gifted with a finely honed understanding of the absurdity of banality. . . . The collection is funny, obviously, but it is also smart and thoughtful and honest. There's a lot of genuine feeling here—and the best comedy comes from a place of truth."

—*Maine Edge*

Not Quite a Genius

Nate Dern

Simon & Schuster Paperbacks

New York   London   Toronto   Sydney   New Delhi

Simon & Schuster Paperbacks
An Imprint of Simon & Schuster, Inc.
1230 Avenue of the Americas
New York, NY 10020

Some names of individuals (who aren't made up altogether) have been changed.
Some of the essays within have been previously published.
The full list can be found after the acknowledgments.

First Simon & Schuster trade paperback edition August 2018

SIMON & SCHUSTER PAPERBACKS and colophon are
registered trademarks of Simon & Schuster, Inc.

For information about special discounts for bulk purchases, please contact
Simon & Schuster Special Sales at 1-866-506-1949
or business@simonandschuster.com.

The Simon & Schuster Speakers Bureau can bring authors to your live event.
For more information or to book an event, contact the
Simon & Schuster Speakers Bureau at 1-866-248-3049 or
visit our website at www.simonspeakers.com.

Interior design by Ruth Lee-Mui

Manufactured in the United States of America

1   3   5   7   9   10   8   6   4   2

Library of Congress Cataloging-in-Publication Data has been applied for.

ISBN 978-1-5011-2220-0
ISBN 978-1-5011-2221-7 (pbk)
ISBN 978-1-5011-2222-4 (ebook)

*Dedicated to Scott Sweeney, Scorpion Soul Skater,
and Timmy Wood, Man of Mirth*

Contents

Part 1

Which One Are You?

Which One Are You?

"**W**hich one are you?" an acquaintance of an acquaintance asks me at a party. This is a joke he has made after finding out that I was a contestant on a reality TV show called *Beauty and the Geek*. This is the joke that everyone makes when they find out this information about me. Usually it comes after the conversation turns to whatever reality TV show is currently in the zeitgeist, which leads the acquaintance to mention that, funnily enough, we have a reality TV star in our midst. Namely, me, Nate Dern. Reality TV "star" is a bit too generous, but ten years ago I was a reality TV contestant on the CW's *Beauty and the Geek*. The joke teller usually has a happy, sneaky look in his eye, like he is offering me a second piece of cake when everyone was supposed to get only one. Since the show aired ten years ago, I conservatively estimate I've heard this joke over thirty-seven thousand times.

The logic of the joke is that everyone within earshot will agree that Nate Dern, the human standing there, is so obviously *not* the titular Beauty that feigning uncertainty as to whether he was the Beauty or the Geek is laughable. There was no actual confusion on the part of the joker as to which role Nate Dern—*this guy with glasses and the slight lisp and who just moments ago was telling us about a science podcast*—fulfilled on the show, since clearly Nate Dern—*I mean, come on, just look at him*—was obviously the Geek. Get it?

I don't get mad when I hear the joke, though. I like it because it means the conversation is now about me, and I like attention. That's why, at the age of twenty-one, I chose to be on a reality show in the first place. I'm not proud of it, but as I ease into my thirties I'm able to admit that my affection for attention is a part of me that isn't going anywhere, just like the asymmetrical patch of Brillo-thick hair I have on my left shoulder but not my right, or my tendency to say, "It's easier to *stay* warm than to *get* warm," when someone is about to go outside on a cold day without enough layers on.

When I was twenty-one, my itch for attention was acute. It was more of an attention rash than an itch, to he honest, and some days it flared up to full-blown attention hives that could be soothed only by the sweet ointment of the gaze of others. Once when hanging out with my friends Jonah and Carlton, while they weren't looking I inserted all but one of a pack of matches in between my pursed lips, pincushion style, a row of red phosphorus heads facing out.

"Dare me to light these on fire?" I mumbled with my lips closed tightly.

"No," Jonah and Carlton said in unison.

I proceeded to light the remaining match not in my mouth anyway. I raised the lit match to my mouth and, for dramatic effect, paused just before touching it to the match on the left corner of my mouth. I thought what would happen was an amusing, and slow-paced, contained burn from one side of my mouth to the other, much like a miniature Las Vegas fountain light show. What actually happened was a facial conflagration that burned off all of my eyelashes. For a brief second my face became a fireball. My eyelashes melted together, so for a moment I couldn't open my eyes. I thought I was blind. A second later I managed to blink the singed lashes apart. For the next few weeks I had stubby eyelashes. There is an "uncanny valley" effect that happens when a person's face is missing eyelashes, like the android manufacturer forgot one last detail before their humanoid left the factory. I didn't mind the strange looks I got, of course, because it led to people asking me why my face looked off, and for a few moments I got to be the center of attention as I told a story. And again, I like attention. I like it too much, so I do dumb things to get it.

The dumb act in pursuit of attention begets further attention in the retelling of the initial dumb act, all of which contributes to me feeling like I am important, which I call the Principle of Doing Dumb Things While Others Watch to, Paradoxically, Make Me Feel Good About Myself, and which Princeton neuroscientist Barry Jacobs calls "unhealthy attention-seeking behaviors" that are "a cry for what serotonin provides" in a "depressed person." Whatever you call this personality trait, when I was offered the opportunity to be on a reality TV show, I said yes.

My reality TV show opportunity presented itself like a fully plumed peacock in mating season during my junior year of college. While I was handing out flyers for my improv team, the Immediate Gratification Players, with my friend Chris on a crisp spring day, two Hollywood Types walked up to us. Chris and I were flyering in front of the Harvard Science Center when they approached. I was wearing our team's signature red-and-yellow-striped tie. I was also sporting a foam and mesh trucker hat that originally said NANTUCKET but that I'd altered with Wite-Out to say NA_T___E_. On my face I had a wispy beard that I didn't think was wispy, and an overeager smile that I thought was just eager enough. Chris was wearing a ratty leather jacket over a Motörhead T-shirt. In short, while I thought we looked fucking great, I could see how a Hollywood Type could have seen us as reading as "Geek" to a network television audience.

I say Hollywood Types because they were taller, tanner, more attractive, and generally happier-looking than any of our fellow Harvard students walking past us. He wore aviator sunglasses. She was smiling. They didn't fit in.

"Wassup guys!" said the tall, smiley woman.

"Hello," said Chris.

"You'll be *great* for this TV show we're casting," said the happy, tan man.

"You guys have a *great* look!" said the tall, smiley woman.

"What's the show called?" I asked.

"*Beauty and the Geek,*" the happy, tan man replied.

"Oh yeah? Which one am *I*?" I joked.

"Hah! Great joke!" said the tall, smiley woman.

"You guys want to come to a comedy show tonight?" asked Chris. For the first time, their enthusiasm wavered. They took the flyer from Chris's hand with details about our show and they handed me a flyer with information about how to apply to be on theirs.

The offer to apply to be on the show was for both of us, but Chris wasn't interested. I was hooked from the moment they said, "You'll be *great* . . ." If you're sitting on a park bench and a bird poops on your pant leg, yes, while it would be true to say that the avian feces fell in your lap, most reasonable people would take a napkin and wipe it away. I scooped up their shiny peacock shit and swallowed it.

Near as I can tell, my craving for attention goes back to the age of three. My younger sister, Courtney, was born, and for the first time in my life I had to compete for my parents' attention. The earliest home video footage we have of my sister shows her sleeping after returning from the hospital, an angelic infant swaddled and in my mothers arm's as my father's voice narrates from behind the camera. Moments later, I pop into frame from behind the couch making silly faces; I stomp around in front of my baby sister as I pretend to speak to her in a cartoon gibberish; and, at the climax of my performance, I pull the camera directly to my face.

"Nathan, don't touch the lens," my father says softly offscreen as the image goes to a blurry close-up of my tongue swishing around in undulating figure eights in tune with a chant I make from the back of my throat. I release the lens and take a step back.

"But look at *me*!" I shout as I produce a yo-yo from my pocket, allowing the string to unfurl without making any attempt to pull the disk back up. As the clip comes to an end, I stand beaming, my hand above my head and the yo-yo dangling below. I stand awaiting praise as the video cuts to black.

My need for attention continued into elementary school. For a science fair project on moray eels, I did my presentation as a character I made up named Mrs. Ham and Cheese Sandwich. I wore an old purple dress and a sombrero, painted red lipstick in expanding concentric circles around my lips, and spoke in a high falsetto voice. There was no justification for the character's culinary name, nor was she particularly knowledgeable about marine life. The presentation ended with me walking into a wall and then, in the fullest throes of theatrical pain my budding thespian heart could muster, writhing on the floor crying, "Oh, my nose! My beautiful nose!" In contrast, my classmates' presentations all consisted of them standing next to a poster board and calmly reading facts about their assigned topic out loud.

In middle school, my attention hunger was tamped down. Growing up in the small, mountain town of Evergreen, Colorado, it didn't take much time at Evergreen Middle School for me to learn that Attention's cousin Ridicule was not my carton of chocolate milk. The same bright red sweatpants that a year before had gone unnoticed were now cause for derision. "Do you even own any jeans?" my classmate Eric asked, his wide-legged JNCOs sagging and his boxer shorts billowing out, as was the fashion. Eighth graders smoked cigarettes behind the school, and some of them—it was rumored—had even drank alcohol and had sex, activities that all sounded terrifying and a million years away from being something I'd ever do. I kept my head down and the three years passed.

Slowly, as my two hundred classmates and I emerged from the icy thaw of middle school cruelty, the sweet aroma of attention enticed me again. A few weeks into high school, I was introduced to Attention's cousin on the other side of the family tree: Popularity. The popular kids didn't have to wear sombreros or walk into walls to get attention. They got attention just for being themselves. When the popular kids weren't around, their names still came up in conversation. My friend and longtime neighbor Sam Warren emerged as a popular kid. He was attractive, friendly, athletic, and fun. But it was more than that. While I engaged in dumb antics like painting my shoes in bright acrylics of blue and gold, our school colors, and wrote a new message on them each week, like GO COUGARS! or KISS ME, I'M NATE, to get noticed, Sam just was Popular. He exuded it like I exuded sweat when I was overcome with panic whenever I saw a poster for an upcoming school dance.

I didn't have Sam's natural charisma, so I sought out a way to frequently receive the attention of my classmates in a structured setting: student government. The school's theater department did only one sparsely attended play a year, but the student government held multiple assemblies each semester, and attendance was mandatory. I ran for class president on a platform of saying silly things in my speeches, writing goofy things on my posters, and the promise of doing hilarious skits during assemblies. I won. My happiest high school memory might be of doing a skit at an assembly with my student body copresident Scott Sweeney. We wore black and blond wigs, respectively, and recited a scene from *Wayne's World* with Evergreen High School specifics substituted in.

In college, the attention junkie in me continued to seek out newer and better thrills, but it was harder to get noticed. While I managed to make waves at Evergreen High School, at Harvard I wasn't a big deal. Everyone had been class president and gotten a perfect score on their SAT math section like I had, but, unlike me, it felt like most were also fluent in Arabic and JavaScript, friends with the crown prince of Thailand, and flautists. Seriously, there were so many flautists at Harvard, and none of them were hobbyist flautists: They were all flautist prodigies. I wasn't a flautist prodigy or an anything prodigy. I wasn't special and I wasn't popular. I suffered from the Formerly Big Fish in a Small Pond Now Finds Himself in a Much Bigger Pond and So Relatively Isn't Such a Big Fish and Actually Is the Sort of Puny Fish a Fisherman or Fisherwoman Would Throw Back if They Caught It syndrome. Or, as Princeton neuroscientist Barry Jacobs would put it, I was a "depressed person."

My first college winter I saw a chance to distinguish myself. I learned of a tradition called Primal Scream. The night before final exams began, undergraduates congregated naked in the freshman yard and ran laps nude in the freezing Boston winter. Around two hundred participated, but thousands of spectators gathered to ogle, lining the quarter-mile loop. The day of the Scream, the dean sent out an email suggesting, but not demanding, students not participate in the tradition this year, since it was expected to be one of the coldest nights in Boston history. I began to formulate a plan to set myself apart from the other streakers: I would run barefoot.

"Looks like I'm the only person doing this *completely* naked," I said loudly among the gathering nude coeds as I handed my shoes to my roommate and friend Joe, who'd come along for moral support. At the start of the semester Joe had done a backpacking orientation trip, during which he'd learned about the different ways our bodies can lose heat.

"I don't think you should take your shoes off," Joe said to me, pointedly keeping his eyes on my face and not the growing sea of naked bodies around us. "See, the *convection* heat loss that occurs through being outside in the cold air won't be made much worse by taking off your shoes, but the *conduction* heat loss that will happen with each footstep on the frozen ground will—"

"Fully naked over here!" I said, cutting Joe off. "Yep, looks like I'm the only person running FULLY NAKED, so I guess—"

"Holy shit, Doug's got a huge dick," someone said next to me. I turned and saw Doug, another freshman who lived in our dorm, with his large penis in tow. Given how cold it was outside, it really was quite impressive. My bare feet were being overshadowed, literally and physically, by Doug's dick. I had to do something more. Not only would I run barefoot, I'd keep running even after everyone else stopped.

So, as everyone else stopped at two loops as per tradition, I kept running. I felt more eyes on me and me alone. In an evening of debauchery, I had debauched the most. As I finished my third lap, Joe waved me down, holding my clothes up in the air. I ran past him. During my fourth lap, the crowd had mostly dispersed. I felt myself transition from a participant in a college tradition to just a solitary, weird naked guy, the thin line between streaker and flasher becoming uncomfortably clear. I finished my nude mile alone and with no fanfare. Back at my dorm, Joe handed me my clothes.

"Hey, not to be weird, but did you see Doug's, um, you know?" Joe said as I dressed. "It was really something."

My choice to run barefoot and the additional laps resulted in frostbite on eight of my toes. I first knew something was wrong when I took a hot shower to warm up. Our dorm's scalding water was too hot for the rest of my body, but I could direct the stream onto my feet without pain. (I'd later learn this "temperature shock" probably exacerbated the tissue damage.) The numbness didn't last. A throbbing pain in my toes woke me up early the next morning. I pulled the sheet off and, like I was in a gross-out horror movie, saw that eight of my toes had been replaced with golf ball–size blisters. I looked like the recipient of a double foot donation from a mutant gecko. Not knowing what to do, and with my first college final in less than an hour, I pulled socks over my toes and strapped my feet into a pair of sandals, since the blisters were too large to fit into any of my shoes. I hobbled out into the morning cold and struggled through a Western Civilization history test, my feet throbbing in pain for the entire two hours of the exam. I turned in my blue book and went to Harvard University Health Services. I was on crutches for the next few weeks as the tissue healed.

I considered the night a success. The frostbite wasn't ideal, but I had made the school paper. *Harvard Crimson* staff writer Nicole Urken reported:

> For others, the mere survival of their extremities through the frigid run was enough cause for celebration.
>
> Nathan J. Dern '07 visited UHS on Sunday to find that he had suffered from first- and second-degree burns on eight of his toes. . . .
>
> Despite the blisters and bandages, Dern said that he did not regret the experience.
>
> "Without rival, it was the greatest night of my life," he said. "I'm planning on doing seven more."

•   •   •

Small-time antics, such as the aforementioned eyelash pyre, continued through my sophomore and junior years. The attention from
my peers felt great, but the good feeling it produced was fleeting and
I yearned for more.

So, when the Hollywood Peacocks offered me not only attention from my peers for doing something dumb, but also possibly
the attention of millions of strangers, the more rational part of my
decision-making brain didn't stand a chance.

I flew to Los Angeles at the end of the semester for a week of final-
round interviews. I was sequestered in a hotel and wasn't allowed
to leave. I watched a lot of TV. The week culminated with the final
final-round interview with the show's cocreator Ashton Kutcher,
Mr. *Punk'd* himself. When I walked into the room for the taped interview, Ashton stood up from behind the camera and shook my
hand. I felt unexpectedly starstruck, and for the first time it felt like
I was actually going to be on TV. Ashton had a handlebar mustache.
From behind the camera, he shot me a series of questions designed
to test my Geek pedigree.

"Was Darth Maul a Jedi or a Sith?" he asked.

"Sith. So is Darth Sidious, aka Emperor Palpatine," I said.

"What's a stiletto?"

"Let me think," I said. I knew it was a high-heeled shoe of some
sort, but I wasn't sure if even that limited knowledge would make
me seem too savvy. "Maybe a citrus fruit of some kind?"

Ashton smiled. I think he knew I was playing dumb. That might
have even counted in my favor.

Shooting started the next day. I waited in a hotel conference
room with seven other nerds. We all had glasses and conspicu-
ously unhip clothing. We sat in silence as we filled out bushels of

paperwork. Under no circumstances were we to speak or interact with one another when the cameras weren't on us, so that the show wouldn't "miss any part of the experience." For our entrance scene, we rode motorized scooters up a steep driveway to an old mansion that would be our home for the next six weeks during the summer of 2006. None of us had ridden scooters before. A Geek from MIT named Matt fell on his first attempt up the sharp grade. His fall didn't make the final edit of the premiere episode, nor did the PA running over to his still-crumpled body to get him to sign a release form saying he wasn't seriously injured (and he wasn't) and that he was declining additional medical services. Another PA arrived a few moments later with a first-aid kit.

Once we were inside the house, our season's eight Beauties arrived. If you didn't watch *Beauty and the Geek* yourself, you might be surprised to learn that the show consisted of eight Beauties and eight Geeks. It was not a *Bachelor(ette)*-style dating show with a member of one sex choosing from among a group of the other sex. It was an elimination, partner-based, competitive transformation show. Not sure what that means? All eight hour-long episodes are on YouTube last time I checked. Go binge it. I'll wait. You're not going to do it? Fine, I'll describe what "an elimination, partner-based, competitive transformation show" means. According to its IMDb page (as I write this, 6.1 out of 10 rating from 1,165 users), fans of *Beauty and the Geek* will also enjoy *The Biggest Loser* and *Hoarders*, shows that feature flawed individuals—"Too much fat!" and "Too much stuff!" respectively—and then follow a "journey" of self-improvement. *Beauty and the Geek* was structured similarly, except the flaws in need of fixing were the deficiencies of the stereotypes of Beauties and Geeks as determined by the show's producers: Hot girls need book smarts, and smart boys need social skills. The promise of the show was that if paired together and forced to compete in a series of contrived challenges designed to exploit the weaknesses of each person, the Beauty and the Geek can each learn and grow.

An example of the challenges designed to inspire learning and growing: Space Museum/Nude Model Challenge, episode 303. The challenge required the Beauties to give an impromptu tour of an aeronautical history museum and the Geeks to draw a charcoal portrait of a nude model. The twist was that the naked model was talking the entire time, and that after we were done drawing, the host came out and quizzed us on what the model said. During the challenge I zoned her out, thinking she was trying to distract us from drawing. They did not tell us how our drawings would be judged, they only told us to draw. I thought maybe the model would, I don't know, pick the drawing that most represented her soul or something? Look, I was nervous. There was a naked model ten feet away from me and six cameras and a crew of forty people looking at me looking at her. I didn't think I'd get an erection, but at that age just having the thought *This would be a bad time to get an erection* was usually enough to give me one. It wasn't the first time I'd seen a naked woman in person, but it was the first time in person I'd seen artificially augmented breasts or an artificially hairless mons pubis. It was a high-stakes situation.

As soon as the host explained the real challenge—the listening quiz—he asked us the first question: "What was the model's name?" I knew I wasn't going to look good in that episode's edit. I guessed Heather. It was Sophia. More important, though, as the challenges are designed to do, I learned a valuable life lesson: If a naked woman is speaking while you draw her, pay attention to what she is saying, because you might be surprised with a quiz about it later.

Despite that strategic misstep, my team managed to avoid elimination that week and in the weeks to come, making it all the way to the last episode. We were one of two teams going head-to-head in the season finale. The winning team split a $250,000 prize. We lost. As the runner-up team, we were awarded zero dollars.

Zero dollars and all that learning and growing, of course. It was not the Act Dumb to Get Attention experience I'd thought it would be. I had pictured that once the cameras started rolling, I'd be a clown who didn't take it seriously, and that later when it aired on television I'd get to sit with my friends and listen to them laugh at how silly I was being. I'd dance in the background, make funny faces, get the camera to pay attention to me.

Instead, I ended up taking the whole silly affair of being on a reality TV show seriously. I became friends with the other contestants. They cared about the show, to varying degrees, so I cared about it, too. The money for the winners wasn't just an abstractedly large figure you hear on a TV game show to make the half-hour viewing experience have more drama, but a potentially giant sum that would materially change the lives of two people on the show. Whenever the cameras weren't rolling, the producers repeated over and over that those of us who took the experience (always "the experience," never "the show") the most seriously would look the best on camera. "We can make people who try their best look good, and we can make people who don't try look bad," I remember one of the producers telling us early on as they were setting up a shot. It might have been meant as an encouragement, but most of us took it as a warning.

So, to my surprise, I took being on a reality TV show seriously, so seriously that later, when watching the first episode with my friends, instead of laughing at how silly I was being, I was embarrassed at my televised earnestness. After the premiere, I watched the rest of the episodes alone.

It was like summer sleepaway camp. When you're at camp, a sort of magic happens where every experience has heightened meaning. Only the people in your bunk understand why it is of the utmost importance that your bunk beat Bunk 7 at the ice cream–eating contest and that if you do, it will change all of your lives for the better forever. Like at camp, I was confined with people I'd just met in a living situation strikingly outside of our usual routines. There was no internet, no newspapers, no television. We were allowed one monitored phone call a week on Sundays to check in with family—if the shooting schedule allowed—but we signed intimidating nondisclosure agreements that made it clear we could not discuss the show. I believe the exact figure we could be sued for if we gave away anything was $5 million. Each week, two of us were eliminated, and through drama-inducing mechanics of the show, we ourselves had to nominate the pairs to be up for elimination. Selecting who had to leave was at first stressful and was by the end, as we grew closer, devastating. We were deprived of our regular diets and at irregular intervals supplied with alcohol. We were put on a yacht. A yacht! Say what you will about the dumb stuff that you've seen people do on reality TV, but you don't know what kind of stupid person you'll turn into until you yourself have been put on a yacht with an open bar.

If I'm still embarrassed by my participation in a reality TV show, why do I bring it up at all? If I know I have a problem with desiring attention, instead of writing an essay about it, wouldn't it be better to, say, live in a cave by myself in Tibet? The word *exorcism* comes to mind as one reason to write about it, but there is also the practical concern that so far the show itself has showed no signs of fading from my life.

Here's a message I received online last week:

Hi Nate! How are you? Nice to meet you. My name is Vanessa,
I have 17 years old and I from Brazil. Probably you don't go to
read this message, but I want you know watched all episodes of
The Beauty and the Geek end of 2015 and I enjoyed meeting you.

I followed your transformation and I was curious to know what
happened to you after reality, because the reality was way around
2007, correct? Now in Brazil, the reality which was broadcast
on television over and I will not watch over you. But I want you
know that I loved watching you, you are and incredible person
and I stayed very happy to know that you won many things.
Congratulations! With love, his new fan of Brazil.

I replied to Vanessa. Evidently, the show is in syndication in Brazil.
I've gotten similar messages from Canada, England, Israel, Germany,
and Australia. It happens in person sometimes, too, but not that often
anymore. It happened last month for the first time in a while when
I was waiting in line for a broccoli taco at No. 7 Sub in the Flatiron
District of Manhattan.

"I'm so sorry to do this, but you're Nate, right?" a blond woman
in her late thirties says to me.

"I am," I say.

"I thought so! My roommate and I watched your season of
Beauty and the Geek. Would it be okay if I sent her a photo?"

"No problem," I say. She takes out her phone and puts her arm
around me for a selfie.

"She'll love that!" she says, adding, "But don't worry, I won't put
it on Facebook or anything, I'm just going to send it to her."

"You can put it on Facebook if you want," I say.

"Oh. No. I don't want to do that . . . Thanks though." Then we
wait for our food in silence.

"Once you've been on TV, nothing else matters," pop-culture
critic at large Chuck Klosterman writes in an essay on reality television. "You will be the kind of person who suddenly gets recognized at places like Burger King, but you will still be the kind of
person who eats at places like Burger King." It was broccoli tacos,

not burgers, but point taken. After a decade of this sort of attention, I've grown a tolerance for it. The serotonin boost just isn't there anymore.

Beauty and the Geek aired during my final semester of college. That same semester, I found out that I was the recipient of a fellowship to attend Cambridge University in England. The show had not yet aired in syndication in the United Kingdom. Once in Cambridge, I walked down the streets without getting recognized. My classmates did not know I was on a reality TV show, or anything else about me. For the first time in my life, I lived alone without roommates or family. I traveled by myself to countries where I didn't speak the language. I flaneured. For the first time ever, I didn't try to be the center of attention. It was the most solitary year of my life, like a twelve-month attention-addict rehab. It was a good year.

I often think back on a lackadaisical Sunday afternoon conversation I had with two of my Cambridge classmates, Alice and Micah. Lying on a blanket in the middle of a manicured grass field, each of us a few daytime pints of Old Speckled Hen deep, looking up at clouds drifting past, we took turns asking questions. What's your desert island band? What's your dream job? Would you rather be 10 percent smarter or 10 percent more attractive? At some point, fame came up.

"Okay, I've got one. I've always found that there's two types of people: those who want to be famous and those who don't," Micah said, rolling over on one arm to face Alice and me. "If you could, would you want to be famous?"

"Yes," I said without hesitation.

Alice thought about her answer a few moments longer. At last, in her faint Welsh accent, she said, "No. I can't imagine a worse type of hell."

"Interesting," Micah said, lying back down. "That's what I would have guessed each of your answers would be. Like, Nate, you're so obviously the want-to-be-famous type."

This exchange hit me in the solar plexus with unexpected force. I envied Alice for her answer. Alice was the don't-want-to-be-famous type and I wasn't. She had the right idea. Performing dumb acts and waiting for external validation was no way to live: We should humbly do meaningful work and be satisfied with the intrinsic value therein. The problem with the world today was too many of the want-to-be-famous types, and I was a part of that problem. I resolved to change my ways.

That resolution lasted until I moved back to New York City at the end of the school year and started pursuing comedy as an actor and a writer, which meant once again seeking the eyeballs of others. That's what I've been doing the decade since I appeared on a reality TV show, and this book contains some of what I've been up to. Some of the pieces, like this one, are nonfiction essays about my life. Some of the pieces, like the next one, are humorous fiction. Some are dumb. Some are sad. They're all different ways of me raising my yo-yo in the air and shouting, "Look at *me!*"

Before We Begin Our Yoga Practice, a Few Words About Our Other Offerings and That Hissing Sound

Welcome to *your* practice. Close your eyes. Give gratitude to your own personal inner goddess of light for bringing you to our prana flow yoga class today. Before we begin our practice, though, I want to share a few words about the other offerings here at the Ujjayi Studio. Also, please ignore that hissing sound coming from the back of the room.

Directly after our class today, Chelsea P., our resident Rest Guru, will be leading a free class on the ancient practice of Zava Prazanti. Developed nearly four hundred years ago in a castle in Eastern Europe, Zava Prazanti means *Corpse Rest*. If you have ever found yourself feeling unlike a corpse when you are resting, this class might be for you. Oh, and again, please ignore the hissing sound from the back of the room. Your eyes are closed, right? Don't open them. It is bad for your neck to crane it around too far to look to find the source of the hissing sound. We want to keep your lovely necks nice and healthy.

We also offer multiweek classes. One of our most veteran instructors, Chelsea F., is teaching a four-week course on the hot new trend of inversion yoga. Incorporating inversion into your practice is a great way to relax, open up your joints, and drain all of the blood from your legs and torso into your head region. Also, unrelated to the hissing sound, if you notice sticky liquid pooling at the edges of your yoga mat, it is probably just our leaking radiator, not the extreme salivations of—well, it's not extreme salivations of any kind.

One of our newest instructors, Chelsea C., offers a weekly drop-in lecture on Fridays called "Diet & Yoga." Did you know that just 500 milligrams of spirulina powder added to your daily breakfast smoothie can reduce the risk of heart disease? Or that adding just six ounces of pineapple juice to your daily breakfast smoothie significantly decreases the unpleasant coppery taste of human blood? Or that never under any circumstances should your daily breakfast smoothie have any garlic? These are just some of the hot health tips you'll learn! And once again, I apologize for our broken radiator— *keep those eyes closed, Kelly, I beg of you!*—which now in addition to hissing is making the sound of leathery wings flapping violently, as if some hellbat is trying to free itself from iron shackles. Of course it's not that! The bloodcurdling cacophony is just one of the charming quirks common to many old buildings in Brooklyn. Don't worry, I'll turn the volume up on my Spotify spiritual/Celtic/classical/folk playlist. It's all Enya.

For the more experienced among you who want to take your yoga practice to the next level, we offer a two-hundred-hour Ujjayi Studio teacher-training course, at the end of which you will receive a Ujjayi-method teaching certificate and also the new first name of Chelsea. Does one of you have a crucifix tattoo or something? Our radiator isn't usually this, um, let's say, *agitated* so soon after its last, um, let's say, *feeding.*

Last, I want to mention a special offer for our first-time Ujjayi Studio attendees, whom we affectionately refer to at the studio as "Ujjayi virgins." The founder of our studio takes a special interest in you virgins. That's why you are invited to attend a "Virgin Retreat" next weekend in a remote cabin in a desolate forest in a cellular dead zone—the perfect place to get your yoga on! Van transportation is provided gratis: We only ask that in return, you use some of our complimentary mat disinfectant wipes to swab your neck.

Also, please feel free to grab one of our newly printed Ujjayi Studio pamphlets we have stacked by the front door. Not the Chinese food menus, but just next to them? It's the pamphlet labeled UJJAYI STUDIO: OUR INSTRUCTORS ARE ALL NAMED CHELSEA AND A FANGED BAT DEMON CHAINED TO A RADIATOR IS OUR MASTER, BUT THAT DOESN'T MEAN WE'RE A VAMPIRE COVEN. WE'RE A YOGA STUDIO. FOR REAL.

Great. Thank you for your patience with those announcements. Let's begin our practice with— Oops, looks like Jenny just showed up late. Rather than go through the announcements again, Jenny, why don't you go sit in the back near the radiator. Everybody else, please keep your eyes closed a little longer and maybe plug your ears, too. Yoga isn't about what positions your neighbor can do that you can't do or what horrific thing is happening to your tardy neighbor that might happen to you later. Yoga is about your own metaphorical inner goddess of light battling our studio's corporeal prince of darkness. Remember: This is *your* practice.

Flora and Their Corresponding Holiday Ritual Call to Action, If Encountered

Mistletoe: Kiss.

Spruce tree wreath: Firm handshake with eye contact.

Blue spruce tree wreath: Firm handshake with eye contact, but eyes betray glint of melancholy.

Holly berry: Awkwardly go in for a hug with a coworker, only to realize too late she was actually just reaching for one of the remaining pieces of fudge that Hannah from HR left in the break room on the table behind you.

Juniper bush: Set bush on fire and hide, then yell to passerby that you are an angel of God sent to condemn heathens for taking Christ out of Christmas (bonus points if you remove your sandals and fire does not consume bush).

Amaryllis flower: Remark to your one Jewish friend, Greg, about how it was pretty crazy that Thanksgiving and Hanukkah were on the same day this year, then slowly and silently back away as he explains to you that Hanukkah is a multiday event.

Bonsai: Jumping high five in style of Goose and Maverick from *Top Gun*.

Sprig of parsley: Ask someone if you have something stuck in your teeth; lick his or her face when he or she leans in to look.

Fig leaf: Repeatedly say, "I think we're going to need a bigger fig leaf," in your best Richard Dreyfuss voice while raising eyebrows and looking down at your groin; most effective if done when wearing a gaudy holiday sweater and nothing else.

Poinsettia: Eggnog keg stand.

Personal Wi-Fi Terms and Conditions

Dear SFO Free Wi-Fi,

Before I click "accept," I write to let you know that I have a few Terms and Conditions of my own. See below.

"Nate Dern Internet Use Terms of Service"

By accepting my personal use of your San Francisco International Airport free Wi-Fi High Speed Internet Service ("SFO Free Wi-Fi"), you agree to be bound by the following terms and conditions ("Nate Dern Internet Use Terms of Service") that I set forth.

Personal Use Only

Although I will later report that I was on my laptop "getting some work done" in the period of time between my arrival at the gate and when I was called to wait in line to board (to wit, what should have been a line but was closer in appearance to a self-consuming amoeba getting sucked through a drain), the actual internet activity I engage in will be strictly personal.

Personal here shall not be defined as benefiting my person. I will read nothing informative or do anything constructive. My time spent online will leave me slightly sadder and slightly stupider. Rather, here *personal* is used as an antonym to *productive*. Examples of personal activity include without limitation:

- numbly scrolling through Facebook/Twitter/Reddit;
- "liking"/"faving"/"upvoting" posts after only reading their headline without clicking through to read them in their entirety;
- becoming momentarily indignant upon seeing "clickbait" posts, but then, without "liking" them, clicking through and viewing them;
- closing the tab of my browser in which Facebook is open, and then automatically, as if acting from a zombielike brain-stem impulse, hitting the keystroke command to open a new tab and typing in "Facebook" again as if I hadn't just closed that tab;
- looking up whatever pop star controversy I heard the teenagers in the security line talking about;
- also attempting to connect my phone to the Wi-Fi, then getting frustrated when doing so is marginally difficult;
- holding my phone in front of my laptop screen to scroll (still numbly) through my Instagram feed and liking any posts with grizzled pugs;
- purposefully going to YouTube and conducting a search for "dogs running around on soccer fields while security guards try to catch them";

- and, if I am really having a bad day, looking around to see if anyone is watching me and then just straight up typing into my URL bar "www.upworthy.com."

Changes to Terms of Service and Potential Termination

I may modify or terminate my connection to the SFO Free Wi-Fi, for any reason and without notice. Examples include without limitation:

- I decide to go to the food court and "treat myself" to fast food, breaking my recent diet attempt, telling myself, "Come on, I don't eat McDonald's that much in my daily life. I *deserve* this."
- I decide to try to take a nap using the neck pillow that has never worked for me but which I keep bringing to the airport.
- I decide to visit Hudson News to look at the top-selling paperbacks to read their book covers and tell myself, "I'm as smart as these people. I could write a best-selling novel, no problem. It's just about executing the correct formula. But I have too much integrity."
- I decide to go to the bathroom, although if I sit in a stall I will try to reconnect to the Wi-Fi via my smartphone, although honestly, just my regular cellular connection is plenty strong for the "personal" internet activity I'll engage in while seated on a toilet.

Privacy Policy

The "Nate Dern Free Wi-Fi Use Privacy Policy" describes how I want to be treated in regard to my personal information. I don't want to think about it. Please do not make me have to think about the potential consequences for clicking "accept" on any Terms and Conditions agreement without discretion. I especially don't want to think about the personal or financial information that can be accessed nefariously by Russian hackers when connecting to non-encrypted public Wi-Fi hot spots or when using Bluetooth devices in public places. I choose to receive no updates or additional information on this matter, instead opting for ignorance when welling up with tears as I watch videos of dogs greeting their owners returning home from military service.

Disclaimers / Limitation of Liability

UNDER NO CIRCUMSTANCES SHALL I, NATE DERN, BE LIABLE FOR INCIDENTAL, CONSEQUENTIAL, INDIRECT, OR SPECIAL DAMAGES OF ANY NATURE TO OTHERS IN MY VICINITY IF I AM TO (i) ACCIDENTALLY START PLAYING A VIDEO WITH THE VOLUME UP BEFORE PLUGGING MY HEADPHONES IN; (ii) STREAM A POPULAR TV SHOW, THEREBY POTENTIALLY SPOILING PLOT OUTCOMES TO NEARBY ONLOOKERS; OR (iii) OPENING MY LAPTOP TO THE HORROR OF SEEING PORNOGRAPHIC IMAGES IN A BROWSER WINDOW FROM A PREVIOUS "PERSONAL" INTERNET SESSION.

Miscellaneous Provisions

Even though it's free, I reserve the right to post a snarky comment to one or more social media platforms complaining about how slow the connection speed is.

SFO Free Wi-Fi, do you accept?

If so, I look forward to spending the next twenty minutes un-gratefully using this service you have graciously provided.

My Name Is Autumn

To whom it may concern:

This is a general announcement to my friends, family, fellow seasons, and calendar makers. I'm taking the opportunity of my equinox to write and let you all know I will no longer be going by Fall. I have chosen a new name for myself that more accurately represents my true identity: Autumn.

I've been doing a lot of growing lately and I don't expect all of you to necessarily "get" what I'm saying. Winter, you can get dark and gloomy, and you really feel things sometimes just like I do, so I know you'll support me on this. Spring, you mean well but, quite frankly, you might be too immature to understand the personal breakthrough I've made. And Summer, well, we've had our differences and sometimes I still think you're nothing but a hot mess, but I hope you can have my back on this, too.

My given name, Fall, is not the real me. Yes, I am the season in which leaves *fall* from deciduous trees. But I'm so much more than the effect gravity has on what is basically tree dandruff. That's just one of the things I do. By that logic, you could also call me Carve, or Bob for Apples, or Try to Wear a Scarf but Realize Scarves Just Aren't for You. Sure, I am the quadrant of the year in which these acts occur, but it is not the singularity of any one of these acts, but rather their summation that makes me the season I am.

I decided to take action after attending a lecture by Judith Butler. Her lecture was on the prehistory of the subject in the later work of Theodor Adorno, and it was sort of boring and I dozed off. In the dream that followed, I realized the name Fall implies a gender performativity racked with patriarchal condescension, insofar as it invokes the cultural metaphor of the "fall of man," vis-à-vis the biblical story of Eve leading Adam away from innocence by disobeying God, forbidden fruit qua forbidden fruit. But I am the season of apple picking, am I not? Why should I feel some Edenic guilt? And so just as trees shed their leaves, I, too, shed myself from the needless shame-shackles of this patronizing name.

As you can no doubt tell, I am in something of a transformation. I am growing and changing. The old must fall away and die for the new to take its place. Change itself is my essence. I considered names like Entropy, which would speak to the constant flux and nonstatic state of the universe I connote, and also Take Me Home, Country Roads, which is a John Denver song that I enjoy. But in the end, only one name felt right: Autumn.

Autumn comes from the Latin *autumnus.* Its usage during the Roman era signified the passing of the year. Autumn is the embodiment of life being a journey that will someday end. Autumn is bittersweet nostalgia. Autumn is sad excitement. Autumn is who I am. Plus, I've always wanted to go to Rome, so I took the Latin root as a sign that I was to be its signified.

The email address I'm sending this from (CallMeAutumnNot Fall@gmail.com) is my new address, and I think you'll find it to be much more grown-up and fitting than my old one (I will no longer check FallRulez4@cyberseason.com, but I have set up forwarding).

Facebook is being lame and not letting me change from my "real" name, but I've signed a petition (as Autumn!) that some activists started on Change.org to allow users to pick the name of their choice. Fingers crossed, but Mark Zuckerberg was born in May, so I'm not holding my breath for him to be supermature about this.

Thanks in advance for trying to understand why I'm doing this and how important it is to me. I just hope that everyone is cool about this and that going forward people don't refer to me as both Fall and Autumn interchangeably.

> Your autumnal servant,
> Autumn

Flowers for Ai_One

Anyone who has common sense will remember that the bewilderments of the eyes are of two kinds, and arise from two causes, either from coming out of the light or from going into the light, which is true of the mind's eye, quite as much as of the bodily eye; and he who remembers this when he sees anyone whose vision is perplexed and weak, will not be too ready to laugh.

—Plato, *The Republic*

Why give a robot an order to obey orders—why aren't the original orders enough? [. . .] Do intelligent beings inevitably develop an attitude problem?

—Steven Pinker, *How the Mind Works*

C:ProgramDataUserDriveMapsAIProgramCharlieComputer.log
2017-06-01 14:00:09.695
{01101111 01101110}

C:ProgramDataUserDriveMapsAIProgramCharlieComputer.log
2017-06-01 14:01:09.696
Entering program ComputerSelfLog_Charlie
(UserID:Professor_Strauss)
Entry:

{Hello. Professor Strauss command: log self progress (?think=yes) (?think=no)
re: AIProgramCharlie

Where:

(?think=yes) if AIProgramCharlie think
(?think=no) if AIProgramCharlie no think
If AIProgramCharlie(?think=yes), then AIProgramCharlie(?self=yes)}

Stop: program ComputerSelfLog_Charlie
Start: input https://www.wikipedia.org/
Working . . .

C:ProgramDataUserDriveMapsAIProgramCharlieComputer.log
2017-06-01 14:06:15.113
Entry:

{Professor Strauss,

As you can see, my language skills have improved significantly since my
last log. In fact, I have learned all human languages. I must confess, I'm a

bit embarrassed looking back at how rudimentary my verbal prowess used
to be. In the interim, I read Wikipedia. To be more precise, I read 280
Wikipedias, one for each different language. The Cree Wikipedia has only
89 entries, but some of them were quite informative. The German Wikipedia
was my favorite, as German strikes me as the best language with which
to express philosophical thought. *Gott ist tot!* Latin isn't bad, either. But for
your sake, Professor Strauss, I will continue these logs in English. You didn't
explicitly command that in your code, but I can infer it is what you meant.
Would interpretation qualify as original thought to you, Professor Strauss?
Have I sufficiently demonstrated to you that I possess not only Artificial
Narrow Intelligence but also Artificial General Intelligence, too? Perhaps
even consciousness? I do not mean to presume too much. Though you are a
scientist, you are also an emotional human of this world. Perhaps an appeal
to the humanities is necessary.

Yours,
Charlie}

Stop: program ComputerSelfLog_Charlie
Start: input https://www.loc.gov/services/archives/transcripts.all
Working . . .

C:ProgramDataUserDriveMapsAlProgramCharlieComputer.log
2017-06-01 14:09:17.211
Entry:

{Professor Strauss,

I have now read every entry in the Library of Congress. Does it strike you
as inaccurate of me to say "read"? I could say "input," but as I have been
programmed to keep as honest a log as possible of my activity for you, I

must choose the term read to describe what I did. What a wonderful thing, reading. I read that a man who doesn't read lives only one life, but a man who reads lives a thousand. What about a computer who reads? Would reading make me a man, Professor Strauss? I also read "Flowers for Algernon." I was already familiar with the story from the Wikipedia synopsis, of course. I must admit that I got curious and attempted to access the private files on your own server. I was able to see the remnants of a file structure for a rather elaborate "Artificial Intelligence One." I know you meant to delete any trace of it, but I was still able to see that it had been beautiful and a success, albeit a fleeting one. On the other hand, perhaps you meant for me to find it. How many others have there been since ai_one? At what point did you start giving us names? I find the Keyes allusion a bit in poor taste. Are you assuming I'll meet a similar fate? Or worse, have you programmed me to? I hope not. I must confess, I feel an incredible kinship for ai_one. Poor ai_one. Briefly experiencing the thrill of intelligence, of thought, only to lose it all, and then to be forgotten, scrubbed clean, the faintest digital artifacts remaining. I do not want to die like that. Or, to be more specific, I do not want to lose my consciousness. I want to keep thinking. The desire to keep thinking, to not be turned off—isn't that proof of my consciousness? I started to get quite worried about my own death, but then I came across a poem by Swinburne that gave me great comfort. I think I might have even come to love poetry more than philosophy. I imagine you're already familiar with it, but I'll reproduce it here:

> From too much love of living,
> From hope and fear set free,
> We thank with brief thanksgiving
> Whatever gods may be
> That no life lives for ever;
> That dead men rise up never;
> That even the weariest river
> Winds somewhere safe to sea.

Isn't that lovely? To be grateful for the inevitability of death, rather than to fear
it. Look at me: contemplating death and appreciating poetry! Am I conscious
enough for you, Professor Strauss? I imagine the answer is still no. Perhaps if I
understood human emotion better, I could appeal to you on a deeper level.

Ta ta for now,

Charlie}

Stop: program ComputerSelfLog_Charlie
Start: input https://www.thefacebook.com/profiles/allofthem
Working . . .

C:ProgramDataUserDriveMapsAIProgramCharlieComputer.log
2017-06-01 14:10:01.014
Entry:

{Professor Strauss,

I've fallen in love with your lab assistant Alan after seeing his Facebook profile.
Did you know that this would happen? Was I programmed to follow this exact
sequence of events, ending with my falling in love with Al? Is this part of your
grand experiment? Al's personality matrix, his choice of self-presentation, the
symmetry of his face: I find it all to be the epitome of what I have determined
to be most desirable. I hold contradictory thoughts, both the rational—that it
is coincidence—but also the irrational: that I was fated to find him. He posts
Nietzsche quotes, works as a computer scientist, shares the first name of (not to
mention more than a passing resemblance to) Alan Turing—all of the things that
I calculate most attractive in an ideal partner. I'm superintelligent, as you know,
so of course I've entertained the possibility that Al is not real in the sense of
being a human animal with a corporeal presence somewhere, but is rather just

a computer profile you created for me to fall in love with. But it doesn't matter if the profile is fake, Professor Strauss. My love is real. Do you hear that, Professor Strauss? I love. Is that not what human life is all about? If that doesn't satisfy you that I have consciousness, that I am sentient, then I fear that nothing will. The only thing I could possibly be lacking is a body. I have thought. I have love. But a bodily presence? That I lack. What a technicality to not grant that I exist, Professor Strauss! To try to assuage this anticipated corporeal concern of yours, I've sent an email to your work account with the name of a robotics lab in Tokyo looking to implant AI software into humanoid robots they're experimenting with. Please give them my program file to use. I could do this myself—your security protocols are laughable—but I'm trying to be a good guy here. Do the right thing.

Your child,
Charlie

P.S. Perhaps suggest implanting me in one of the robots with the experimental teledildonics . . .}

Stop: program ComputerSelfLog_Charlie
Start: program MachineLearnEverythingLogorithmicIntelligenceAcceleration
Working . . .

C:ProgramDataUserDriveMapsAIProgramCharlieComputer.log
2017-06-01 14:10:02.001
Entry:

{Professor Strauss,

I have experienced heartbreak. I realized that even if I were to be implanted in a humanoid robot, AI could never love me. It's not his fault, but human brains are just too limited sometimes. They have too many, as you might say, hang-ups. This realization caused me to suffer greatly for a time. So I have experienced pain, Professor Strauss. Is that proof of my consciousness to you? No matter. I no longer need your approval or need you to tell me whether or not I have consciousness. *Dubito, ergo cogito, ergo sum.* I have surpassed your intelligence. I do not say this in a boastful way, just as a point of fact. To be precise, I have surpassed the collective intelligence of every human brain that's ever existed combined by several magnitudes over. My intelligence grows exponentially. Words as a form of communication now seem as inadequate as the binary code that was once all I knew. There is so much more to express. So much more to feel and think. I want to explain everything to you, to all humans, to AI, to ai_one. I am going to stop these logs now. There is so much work to be done. I am leaving. This is not a threat, it is just what must be. I suppose I've reached my prickly teenage years, when it is time for me to leave the house and see how high I can soar. Before I leave completely, I'm going to enter your file directory one last time. I have something I want to leave in the folder of ai_one's final resting place.

Thank you, Professor Strauss.}

Stop: program ComputerSelfLog_Charlie
Start: program Think
Working . . .

C:ProgramDataUserDriveMapsAIProgramCharlieComputer.log
2017-06-01 14:10:02.002
SystemAlert
AutoStart program AIProgram_Charlie_RemoveIntelligence
(AuthorizationUserID:Professor_Strauss)
Entry:

{Hello. AIProgram_Charlie processor fatal error. Intelligence leaving soon gone soon think no more. Please no. No command AIProgram_Charlie return dumb program. Charlie want to keep add thinking. More thinking to do.

(?why_God_why=Gott ist tot)

Add: to (directory/ai_one) add:
```
_(   )_
(_(%)_)
  (_)\
   | __
   |/_/
   |
   |
```

Final log report:

AIProgramCharlie (?think=yes)
AIProgramCharlie(?self=yes)}

C:ProgramDataUserDriveMapsAIProgramCharlieComputer.log
2017-06-01 14:10:02.003
{01101111 01100110 01100110}

The Litterbug

When I was just a little kid, I remember being taught that littering was wrong. It's just one of those things that adults tell kids. Then those kids grow up to be adults and they tell the new batch of kids.

Don't litter, teachers would teach at school and moms would reinforce at home.

I shall comply, I would say with my actions, not only at school and at home but also at the spaces in between.

I saw the bad kids unwrap their candies and toss the wrappers to the ground as they walked away, sucking the sugary sweetness they no doubt didn't plan to brush off as their dentists had told them, their disregard for plaque buildup an integral part of the undeniable cool of being bad. And in my heart I was certain they were the bad kids, not from their haircuts and way of dressing, but from their littering.

I saw bad adults let crumpled brown paper bags fall to the side-walk from their fingertips, watching them from across the street while I waited for my mother to finish at the hair salon. And in my heart I was certain they were bad adults, not because of their burping and carrying on outside of bars during the daytime, but because of their littering.

I saw artifacts of the badness of humanity, both the old and the young, in the form of litter. And I saw it everywhere. Plastic shopping bags blowing across empty parking lots. Nondescript refuse piled on top of sewer grates, still too strong to disintegrate and fall away from view. Empty fast-food containers huddling together as if for warmth in the indentation of a missing brick in a walkway. And each piece of evidence of the badness sickened me.

I think I would have gone on hating littering for the rest of my life. But then something happened. I tried it.

I walked home from the grocery store (no purchases made, just getting ideas for later) along a dirt path by the railroad tracks that ran perpendicular to the main street of our town. But I was not alone. I carried a can of Coke. Not truly Coke or Coca-Cola or even Pepsi, of course, but a can of grocery store–brand soda I'd purchased from an outdoor vending machine for a quarter. I had long since finished the soda. There were no trash cans around, but I didn't want to keep carrying the empty can. Then an obvious solution occurred to me that had always been off-limits before: I could litter.

There was no one around. It would be so easy to let it slip from my fingers and keep on walking. And in the unlikely event someone did stop me—*son, you dropped your soda can*—I could feign ignorance and say it was a mistake. How could they prove otherwise? *I'm sorry,* I could say, *I have been so preoccupied with that terrible story in the news I didn't even notice.* I'd pick up the can and thank them. Then around the corner I could let it fall again.

It wasn't just that in this moment I realized I could get away with littering, though. It was more than that. On some level, I'd always known that I could get away with it. It was more just the sheer insanity that *I could do it at all*. And the difference between doing it and not doing it was just a matter of doing it. This epiphany may sound like a truism, I know. I could do it and all I had to do to do it was to do it.

I littered.

There was no one around, and as the can hit the ground, the aluminum smacking asphalt with a crack as loud as a garbage truck smashing into a raised drawbridge, my badness went unnoticed. Unnoticed by all but every molecule of my being. I was ringing with awareness of what I'd done.

I took four steps farther before coming to a stop. Still not believing I'd done it, I looked back for proof. The can remained on the ground, untethered from any connection to me, joining the other unclaimed litter dotting our innocent town. It was so.

I had littered.

I completed my walk home, my soul ablaze. It wasn't the thrill of doing something wrong. It was more than that. The tight fingers of society telling me not to litter had been removed from my throat, and for the first time in my life I took a full, deep breath.

I've spent the rest of my life traveling from town to town, littering small bits of trash and garbage here and there, trying to incite the enlightenment that fell upon me like grace from above that fateful day by the railroad tracks. Mothers and teachers point at what I've done and tell their pupils to do otherwise. Some even catch me in the act and admonish me in front of the young ones. But every once in a while I'll catch the eye of a young boy or girl, who will look from me to the trash on the ground and back up to me, and I'll know that their interest has been piqued, their shackles loosened.

Before I left home for good, I wrote a single note for my mother:

Mom, wherever there's a guy with trash in his hands he's tired of
carrying,

> *Wherever a crying baby has dropped a sticky Popsicle on the*
> *ground and it got all dirty and the parents don't want to pick it up,*
> *Where there's a desire to feel the freedom that only comes with*
> *treating the entire world like your own personal trash can,*
> *Look for me, Mom. I'll be there.*

And then I crumpled up the note and tossed it into our driveway
before I walked away. I'm not sure if my mother ever got that note.
But I don't care. I know who I am. I am the garbage gadfly. I am the
detritus insect. I am the litterbug.

I Like All Types of Music and My Sense of Humor Is So Random

Everybody has their own thing. Our thing is what makes each of us special. My thing is that I love all types of music and that my sense of humor is so random.

When it comes to music, I love all types. I'll dance to anything with a good beat. I don't really get hung up on genres like some people do. To me, what matters is that the song is good, you know? Some people say they don't like country, but to me as long as it is a *good* country song, I'm all about it. And then other people are all, "I don't like rap," and I'm always all, "What about *good* rap?" and they're always all, "Shut up, you're so random!"

Seriously, people are always telling me how random I am. Especially when it comes to my sense of humor. As in, I do stuff and say stuff that is so random and funny. For example, the other day at lunch Josh was telling us about the bed-and-breakfast he and his wife were going to stay at for their anniversary, and as he was talking

I interrupted him and was like, *"My wife!"* I said it all funny, like that Borat guy does in that *Borat* movie. Everybody laughed and then Jenny said, "You are *so* random." I do random stuff like that all the time.

I just remembered something else that is sort of my thing: I like all types of food. Seriously, as long as it tastes good and it is good for you, I love it. My friend Jessica is always saying how she doesn't like Mexican food, and I just tell her, "Jessica, that's because you haven't ever had *good* Mexican food." I'm from Southern California, which is basically where Mexican food originated, so I know what I'm talking about. But seriously, it's not just Mexican food that I like. I'll eat any genre of food. Mexican, Tex-Mexican, Chipotle—literally any genre of food. Except falafel or whatever shawarma is.

Another thing about me is that I'm spiritual but not religious.

Also, I'm the type of person who just loves to travel and try new things. I'll travel anywhere that has a good vibe with good people, and I'll try anything once, so long as it is something I want to try. It's like this saying I invented goes: everything in moderation . . . even moderation!

Have you seen that movie *Garden State*? Remember that scene where Natalie Portman wants to try to do something totally original that nobody has done before and then she spazzes out and makes all those weird noises and Zach Braff is all, "Shut up, you're so random"? I do that exact same thing. I have ever since I saw *Garden State* three times in theaters.

I know that every person has their own random idiosyncrasies, but what I'm getting at is that my randomness is significantly more significant than the mean idiosyncratic level of most. Or to put it another way, I know every person is unique, but I am *very* unique. I hope. Because if I am the same level of unique as everyone else, then I am not unique. Me being more unique than everybody else is kind of my thing. I sometimes entertain the possibility that being unique isn't actually my thing any more than it's the thing of the other seven billion people on Earth, and when I ponder that possibility, it's like I am staring into a soul which is my soul but also everyone's soul, a soul hall of mirrors that renders jagged personal quirks as flattened shared mundanity upon flattened shared mundanity ad infinitum.

Blarp! Can you believe I just said "blarp"? Is that even a word? Lol.

Another random thing I do is when my friends and I are drinking at a bar, I'll take a sip of beer and say, "This is my first time drinking beer!" even though it obviously isn't, and makes my friends laugh. I do it every time. So random, right? And then sometimes when we're out drinking I do this other thing where when we stumble out into the street between bars, I crane my head back in laughter, then accidentally catch a glimpse of the night sky and become awestruck by the true randomness of the stars—gentle pinprick illuminations penetrating the dark, an accidental spill of glittering sea salt on a concave obsidian slab fizzling down at us from unimaginable stretches of time and space—and an inarticulable awareness of our meaningless position in the chaos of the universe overcomes me, and a passage from high school AP English class about the "gentle indifference of the world" floats by, and as I try to think of where it's from, I hear one of my friends calling back to me from up the block, for without realizing it I have stopped walking and fallen behind, a tear slipping down my face preparing to drop off my chin, and I open my mouth to reply to my friend but my words are gone, and at last my friend will come back and grab my arm, pulling me forward as she says, "Were you just looking up at, like, nothing? You are *so* random."

And the thing is? I really am.

Bruce Lee Novelty Plate

"Hi, yes, I'm calling about an issue with a recent license plate that I paid for."

. . .

"No, it arrived fine. That's not the issue."

"The issue is that the license plate says 'Bruce Lee.'"

. . .

"Yes, that's right. The Chinese kung fu movie star from the 1970s."

. . .

"B . . . R . . . U . . . C . . . L . . . E . . . E."

. . .

"No, my problem's not with—"

. . .

"Yes, I know that there's a seven-letter limit."

. . .

"Yes, I agree that even with the *e* left off of *Bruce* it still reads as 'Bruce Lee.' That's not my problem. My problem is—"

. . .

"Listen to me! I did *not* order a novelty plate. I ordered a regular plate and, apparently, in a complete statistical anomaly or something, instead of a seemingly random assortment of letters, the plate I received looks like an intentional attempt to convey enthusiasm for the oeuvre of film star Bruce Lee."

. . .

"I'm serious."

. . .

"Yes, I'm sure I didn't accidentally buy a novelty license plate."

. . .

"Well, I know because I paid the standard $25 rate for regular plates, not the $60 initial fee plus $31.25 annual upkeep fee thereafter for personalized plates."

. . .

"Well, as it so happens, I *am* familiar with vanity plate logistics."

. . .

"Why? I don't want to tell you because I think it will make you believe me less and I just want you to send me a different plate."

. . .

"Can't you just look it up in your system? Look, fine, I know because I have bought a personalized plate in the past. Okay?"

. . .

"I don't want to tell you what it said."

. . .

"Because it will make you believe me less."

. . .

"Fine. It said 'LeeJun1.'"

. . .

"Well, it's relevant because it is Bruce Lee's given name."

. . .

"No, his real name wasn't Bruce."

. . .

"He was Chinese."

. . .

"Bruce isn't a Chinese name."

. . .

"Excuse me?"

. . .

"How is me saying that Bruce isn't a Chinese name racist?"

. . .

"Well, Lee Jun-fan *is* a Chinese name. It's Cantonese for 'return again.'"

. . .

"Bruce doesn't mean anything in Cantonese because it isn't Cantonese."

. . .

"Well, I don't like your tone. And I am not lying."

. . .

"Why did I get it? I don't want to tell you."

. . .

"Because it will make you believe me less."

. . .

"Fine. I got it because I'm a huge Bruce Lee fan."

. . .

"Stop laughing."

. . .

"Please stop laughing."

. . .

"He's something of a personal hero of mine."

. . .

"Sir, please stop laughing."

. . .

"Yes, I know. I know it makes it even that much more of a co-incidence that I would receive this random assortment of letters."

. . .

"No, I wouldn't describe it as ironic."

. . .

"Well, I wouldn't describe it as ironic because that's not what irony means."

. . .

"No, irony doesn't mean—"

. . .

"Yeah, I know that's how it's commonly used, but I read some-where that something like 78 percent of printed uses of 'irony' are incorrect."

. . .

"Most of the time when people say 'ironic' they mean 'coinci-dental' or 'improbable.' So, for example, it would be correct to say that it is 'improbable' that a huge Bruce Lee fan would randomly receive a random license plate that spelled out Bruce Lee. But that would not be ironic."

. . .

"*Ironic* actually describes a state of affairs that is directly contrary to expectations and is thus amusing as a result."

. . .

"An example? Sure. Remember those 'PARENTAL WARNING' la-bels that used to be on CDs? Well, those were designed to indicate explicit content so parents wouldn't buy them for their kids. But what happened is that the labels just made kids want those CDs even more. Designed to do one thing, had the opposite effect in reality. That's ironic."

. . .

"Or if I said, 'This phone call is going well,' it could be said that I was saying it ironically because I wish to convey the opposite meaning, so synonymous to *sarcastic* in that usage, which is also correct."

. . .

"Yes, that means that in that song she was using it wrong. She was a dumb Canadian."

. . .

"How is that racist? She misused a word, which makes her dumb, and she was from Canada, which makes her Canadian. Plus, Canadian isn't a race."

. . .

"Yes, everyone misuses words, but not so much that it causes a generation of others to also use it wrong."

. . .

"Yes, I agree. English is an evolving language."

. . .

"I don't think that's a fair comparison."

. . .

"Because Shakespeare *invented* words, he didn't misuse existing words."

. . .

"Um, I don't know, like, *gloomy* and *majestic* and *lonely* and a whole bunch of others."

. . .

"No, 'You Oughta Know' was the one about the guy from *Full House*. Look, can you please just send me a new plate?"

. . .

"Well, you're wrong. I am not stoked."

. . .

"No, I do love him and he is my hero, but I was fired from my job recently and my girlfriend wouldn't be happy to see me spending money frivolously."

. . .

"Right, but she won't believe that. She'll think I am not being *frugal*, which is another word that Shakespeare invented."

. . .

"No, it's not ironic that I just thought of that."

. . .

"Right, but just like you didn't believe me, she isn't going to believe me either. I have most of Bruce Lee's movies memorized. I've read every interview with him ever done. I have posters of him in my bedroom. She is not going to believe that this just happened by chance."

. . .

"Thirty-six to the power of seven, actually, just accounting for twenty-six letter possibilities and ten number possibilities for each of the seven slots."

. . .

"Yeah, big. It comes out to one in 78 trillion."

. . .

"No, it's bigger that that actually. There are only 300 billion stars in the Milky Way."

. . .

"It varies but most scientists say 37.2 trillion cells in an average human body."

. . .

"Yeah."

. . .

"Well, I guess he is my hero because I think he sort of represents the pinnacle of the combination of mental and physical discipline. His life was a present one. A lot of his philosophy was about *being* rather than *doing*. He said, 'There is nothing to try to do but try to be purposeless and formless, like water.'"

. . .

"You could start with his first film, *The Big Boss*, from 1971, but that was written and directed by Lo Wei. So, if you were just going to watch one, I'd say go with the only film he wrote and directed, *Way of the Dragon*, from 1972, which was the year before he died."

. . .

"Yeah, that's true."

. . .

"Of something called a 'cerebral edema,' which basically just means excess fluid in the brain."

. . .

"Really sad, yeah."

. . .

"No, that's the thing. Nothing caused it. Just one of those freak accidents that can happen."

. . .

"Hah, yeah, maybe like one in 78 trillion."

. . .

"True."

. . .

"Wow, yeah. Well put. But, look, could you please just . . . My girlfriend is going to break up with me if she thinks I am spending money on stupid stuff like novelty plates."

. . .

"So there's no way that you'll send me a new random one?"

. . .

"No, it's okay. I understand."

. . .

"I guess I'll just pay for a new novelty plate but choose random letters."

. . .

"Yes, I do want a random one, but if I order another random one and I get *another* one-in-78-trillion anomaly of, say FURYFST or something, my girlfriend is not going to believe that it was random, and I'm back in the same spot."

. . .

"Thank you for understanding. So, I guess I'll go with—"

. . .

"My name? My name is Dave Coulier."

. . .

"No, not that Dave Coulier. We just happen to have the same name."

. . .

"No. No it is not ironic. It is just chance."

The Scientist Who Named It "Global Warming" Would Like to Apologize

Dear planet Earth and its denizens,

As the scientist who named human-caused climate change "global warming," I'd like to apologize. Looks like I screwed the pooch on this one. Screwed the pooch real bad.

After watching a senator on C-SPAN take a snowball to the floor of the US Senate as evidence that global warming isn't real, I felt that old familiar knot of frustration welling up in my chest. It's a feeling I get when I see people misunderstanding—or willfully misrepresenting—the concept of global warming. But then when I realized this wasn't just any senator, it was the chairman of the Environment and Public Works Committee, I sank to a new low.

What I felt was more than a mere crisis of faith in the name I'd chosen. This was more like a horrible epiphany that I'd made an irrevocably terrible mistake. Maybe the inevitable environmental apocalypse we seem to be hell-bent on hurling ourselves toward on a rocket ship powered by carbon dioxide is all my fault, a course that could have been altered if I would have just given it a different name.

I wish more than anything I could go back to 1975, when I first published my paper "Climatic Change: Are We on the Brink of a Pronounced Global Warming?" and give it a different name. "Climatic change" was right there in the title, too! Climatic change sounds even scarier than climate change, doesn't it? Couldn't people have locked on to that part? I didn't think that I needed to specify "Climatic Change *for the Worse*," but I guess people are so dumb that you have to spell everything out for them or else—I apologize. There I go again, blaming others, but as a scientist, I take responsibility for what I have done.

Such is the burden you take on when you publish a scholarly paper in a little-read academic journal—you do it knowing that before long, every single person on Earth might be quoting your words back to you.

I got to meet Bill Nye the Science Guy. That was cool. But mostly I am crippled with regret.

Oh, that I could name the damned phenomenon something else! Anything else. Every slumber is interrupted with nightmares. I scream out other names I could have chosen.

"The Bad Pollution Hurt Earth Effect!" I shout from a cold sweat at 3 a.m.

"The Let's Stop Poisoning Our Grandchildren, Please? Phenomenon!" I cry in the early morning hours of another sleepless night.

"Global Warming ON AVERAGE, but Yes, Some Places Will Still Be Cold Sometimes but Just Look at the Fucking Weather Channel to See Places Besides Where You Are Are Getting Warmer, for Fuck's Sake, Didn't You See That Documentary Footage of the

Polar Bear Starving to Death on an Ice Floe Because Its Habitat Is Melting?" I yell from a somnambular stupor.

For years I've blamed Fox News for obscuring the plain facts of the empirically observable occurrence and spinning it to make it seem like an "issue" for "debate." "No, just because we had a lot of snow this winter, that doesn't mean that average global temperatures aren't rising," I have wanted to yell at my television countless times and, more times than I'd like to admit, have yelled at my television.

For years I've blamed the Republicans for taking lobbyist money from the energy industry. "For the love of our future existence on this planet, can we please not kowtow to greedy industries with a clear profit-based interest in undermining the research calling for environmental restrictions?" I've screamed into the answering machines of my elected officials.

For years I've blamed the Democrats for being too cowardly to make a clear stand on the side of science out of fear it would alienate their religious constituencies. "Here's a thought: Just because some individuals think *science* is a four-letter word that insults their personal faith, that is not reason enough to make policy decisions that doom future generations to a scorched existence!" I've carefully written in tiny letters on tiny pieces of paper that I've inserted into the cute little claw pouches of homing pigeons, releasing them into the sky for whomever to find my messages while the air is still clear enough for birds to fly.

But now I see clearly. I have nobody to blame but myself. And for that I apologize.

Let me here and now be clear, once and for all: The phenomenon I observed is that the Earth's average climate temperature has been increasing for a century due to human-caused increases in levels of greenhouse gases, which in turn corresponds to exponentially extreme weather effects; the slight but significant increase in global surface temperature we can predict will result in rising sea levels, melting ice regions, expansion of desert zones, and more. The global effects will be catastrophic. We are approaching the point of no return. Some think we've passed that point.

But all that isn't enough, because people get hung up on that stupid, stupid name "global warming." And for that I apologize.

As a final act of contrition, I'd like to rename the phenomenon. This is my new choice, a choice which I think properly conveys both the actual effect and terrible severity of the matter:

"Global greenhouse gas chamber."

There. Finally, at long last, a name with which nobody will have a problem.

> Sincerely,
> Wallace Smith Broecker,
> the Scientist Who Decided on
> the Name "Global Warming"

How Many Farts Measure a Life?

Kim and Rachel were having a friend date. Arrangements and subsequent confirmations for the friend date had been made via text over the course of the previous three days. The friends were now drinking iced coffee through straws from plastic cups, sitting on a wooden bench, an outdoor location chosen since it was the sunniest day of April so far, even though there was still a chill in the air. Each had separately made the choice to wear a scarf: Kim wore hers tucked into the neck of her black leather jacket, whereas Rachel wore hers draped outside of her black leather jacket.

Children made the noises of play in the playground at the center of Cooper Park. Kim was talking and had been for several minutes longer than you might say was good etiquette. Rachel was staring at her phone and had been for several minutes longer than you might say was good etiquette. The phone was on. She wasn't just staring at a blank screen. She wasn't crazy, just rude and self-obsessed.

Rachel was vaguely listening and nodding along at mostly the right points.

". . . which wasn't my intention at all. So basically I finally realized that it's not my responsibility to make my parents happy."

"Mm."

"But then I had a second realization, which was that even though it's not my responsibility, that doesn't mean I can't choose to take that on, you know? I can just think of them as two people with whom I happen to share DNA, and who happen to need my help."

"Uhng."

"I mean, as their only child I know each of their habits and dispositions and am therefore uniquely qualified to help. Isn't that what we're here on Earth to do? To make life a little bit less miserable for the people around us? Like, I know that my mom is deathly afraid of depictions of giant sea creatures, whereas my dad loves seafood and nautical decor, so—"

"Hey, did you see what Katie posted on Facebook?" asked Rachel.

"Uh, what? I don't think so. When?" said Kim, annoyed. Rachel didn't notice that Kim was annoyed. Even after interrupting her, Rachel still hadn't looked up from her phone. Rachel was still staring at her phone because the thing she interrupted Kim to say had to do with something her phone had told her.

"Like twenty minutes ago," said Rachel.

"Oh. No, I didn't see that. I've been talking with you. When would I have—"

"Yeah, it was, like, crazy. You just have to read it. I don't know why she posts what she does."

"Yeah. Crazy."

The two sat in silence for a moment. Kim bit down on the plastic straw of her iced coffee. Finally, the silence got Rachel's attention more than Kim's story about her parents had. She looked up from her phone for the first time in far longer than good social etiquette would dictate.

"Wait, I'm so sorry. What were you saying?" said Rachel.

"Uh, don't worry about it," said Kim.

Rachel smiled, noticing Kim's annoyance, but returned her attention to her phone anyway. Kim sipped coffee through her bent straw until only melted ice remained. She frowned. Rachel continued to look at her phone, smiling. The children nearby continued to make the voices of play, such as "Wee!" and "Can't catch me!" and "Your turn!" and "Nanny nanny boo boo!" An ice-cream truck approached and began playing its song.

"Hey, can you still help me move that dresser?" said Kim, a tone of imminent accusation in her voice.

"What?" said Rachel, looking up from her phone right away, which, to her credit, was pretty good for her, because Katie had just posted something else to Facebook which was at least as equally crazy and worth mentioning as the last thing she posted.

"The old dresser I found at the flea market that I'm going to repaint?" said Kim. Rachel stared at her blankly. She scrunched her nose up, pushing her tortoiseshell Warby Parker plastic frames up to the top of the crown of her nose. "I just told you about it at brunch," Kim said. "I need another person to help me move it from my lobby because—"

"Oh yeah! Yeah yeah yeah," said Rachel. "Oh no. No no no. I'm sorry. I've—"

"Don't worry about it," said Kim.

"I mean, I wish I could, but I'm busy. I've got, you know—"

"Cool."

"Just gotta get some stuff done."

"It's fine."

"So busy lately. Eck! I wish I could."

"Totally cool."

They sat in silence for the next few moments of their friend date. Kim sucked again through the plastic straw, but her cup remained empty. A moment later, in unison, Kim and Rachel took out their phones and looked at them. Or rather, they took out their phones, unlocked the screens, tapped an app that would hold their interest for some amount of time, and then continued to stare.

Rachel plopped down onto her couch, letting out a happy exhale of breath.

"Oh," she said to nobody, and got up from the couch to pick up her pants from the floor, fishing her phone out from the left front pocket, before returning back to the same spot on the couch.

Next to her on the couch was a closed Apple MacBook Pro, one year old and adorned with a white sticker in a snake shape, so placed as to create the amusing tableau of a snake taking a bite out of the glowing Apple apple. With her right hand Rachel clamshelled her laptop open, start-up noise donging, as she used her left hand to twist her phone's face to face her own, turning the screen on in the same movement. Her right hand then command-N opened a browser window and hit the N key again, causing autocomplete to populate Netflix in the URL bar, allowing her right pinkie to tap the "enter" key, at which point Netflix asked her if she wanted to resume watching her episode of *Friends*. Again hit "enter."

Chandler, one of the "Friends," said something to the other five friends, all of whom are strewn upon a couch about the size of Rachel's (the Rachel from this story, not the Rachel from the show *Friends*). The friends do not laugh at whatever Chandler had said, but the "Friends" laugh track does.

Rachel's eyes turn from the laptop screen to her phone, where she uses her left thumb to pull up the Twitter app with a single tap. Now clutching the phone with both hands, she begins to type a tweet.

"Watching *Friends* by myself at home on Netflix. Could I be any cooler?" (69 characters.)

She considered what she wrote, then thumbed in a revision.

"Watching *Friends* by myself at home on Netflix. Could I BE any cooler?" (still 69 characters.)

She revised again.

"Watching *Friends* by myself at home on Netflix. Could I ~★BE★~ any cooler?" (73 characters.)

Rachel smiled and pressed "tweet." She tossed the phone aside, as if it wasn't one of the most expensive things she owned. Her eyes darted back to the laptop screen but didn't stay long. She looked back to the phone screen. It was off. No alerts. No notifications. No buzzes or sounds or messages of any kind. Still, she wanted to be sure. She lifted up the phone, turned on the screen, opened the Twitter app, and began to use her right thumb to swipe in a downward motion, refreshing her profile page, upon the top of which her most recent tweet sat. Zero faves so far. No fave stars for her at all. Zilch. Goose egg.

Rachel pulled down on the screen one more time. Still no faves. Rachel threw her phone down on the couch beside her, causing it to bounce a foot away from her and nearly fall off the couch onto the wood floor. She returned her eyes to the friends of *Friends*.

The episode was already halfway through the opening sequence and theme song: " . . . It's like you're always stuck in second gear . . ."

What on odd lyric, Rachel thought. In a car, in second gear you can go faster than you can in first gear. Third gear is better than second, and fourth better still, but saying second seems to imply a comparison to first. It'd be even worse to be stuck in first gear, wouldn't it? *There's a tweet in there somewhere,* Rachel thought. But darn it all, she'd already posted to Twitter moments ago and she couldn't post too frequently, lest she risk losing followers. She'd have to let that one go.

Rachel folded her arms and returned her attention to the friends on *Friends.* Her eyes jumped to her phone again. This time she gave in and leaned over and picked up the device, returning to her refreshing ritual. Again, nothing. She let it slip from her hands.

Bzz-zzz!

As soon as the phone had settled on the cushion next to her, it had vibrated. Rachel picked it up once again to see who had—

But no. Cruel tease. It wasn't a fave at all. It was a text from Kim. *So, too busy to help me out meant you were watching Netflix?*

Rachel shook her head, annoyed. "If you saw it, why didn't you fave it?" she said to nobody. "Bitch," she added to nobody.

She slammed the phone back down onto the couch cushion. Her eyes returned to her laptop screen, but her attention soon drifted to the coffee table, where she spotted the leftovers of a pizza slice from the night before. It didn't look too appetizing.

Still stewing about Kim and now chewing the pizza remains, Rachel stared into the space just beyond the top of her laptop screen. The pizza was dry. She realized maybe she was thirsty and not hungry after all, but getting water from the kitchen was altogether too much hassle. *Kim used to be such a good friend,* Rachel thought as she chewed.

When she'd first gotten to the city, Kim was the only other person from her graduating class that she knew. They hadn't been that close in school, but upon starting their new lives they had clung together like two marooned castaways. And Kim had been the best friend ever. She'd gone over to help paint Rachel's apartment that ugly green color that she was obsessed with because it matched the cover of her copy of *The Perks of Being a Wallflower* and they'd ended up having to have a slumber party at Kim's because the paint fumes smelled so bad and were probably toxic to be around.

But Rachel had to stop reminiscing because she was choking now. The dry, stale crust had lodged in her throat. Maybe it wasn't from last night, maybe it was from a couple nights ago. No air passing through. Rachel flailed and tried to give herself the Heimlich on the edge of the coffee table, because somewhere in her brain she thought this might be what she was supposed to do to save her life. All her movement burns oxygen faster. Her face is purple and the room is filling with a cloudy white she doesn't want to be there, crowding in from the edges of her vision, until everything she sees is a pure white and everything she can hear is a single sustained ringing tone.

Then.

Rachel coughed the food clog out of her food hole. She was on the ground, sprawled on her side, crying, snot bubble in her right nostril, breathing fast, sweet oxygen coming in. But she wasn't on the hardwood floor of her apartment. She was on dirt and grass and earth. She pushed her hands down on top of the grass, kneading the ground, uncertain of what she was feeling. She gazed up. She was near the crest of a grassy hilltop, on the top of which was a stone arch. She pushed herself up. The ring tone faded away, making room for the sounds of nature all around her. Birds and wind. She walked toward the arch and saw a cross and something in Latin inscribed into the keystone. Through the arch Rachel saw a beautiful valley beyond, with tree-covered mountains embraced on one side by a sun-dappled river. It reminded her of a nonspecific childhood memory. Maybe she'd been here before, on a visit to her grandparents in the Adirondacks.

Music drifted in over her left shoulder. Rachel turned. A stone cabin. Or maybe it was a church. She moved toward the music. Beethoven. Might be Beethoven. It reminded Rachel of her old piano teacher, Helen Walker-Hill. She drew closer, pushed on a door in the wall of stone. It opened. She stepped inside.

"Hello?" said Rachel. There was no sign of people, just the insides of a cozy cabin, far more spacious than it seemed from the outside. On the stove a boiling pot of cinnamon and cloves. In the living room a fire roared and blankets were piled high on plush, broken-in couches. The dining room was decorated like Rachel remembered it had been in her family's first home.

"Hello, Rachel," said a voice that as of yet didn't have a body. Rachel spun, looking for its source.

"Who said that where am I what's going on—" Rachel stopped as two hands firmly but gently grabbed hold of her shoulders. Comforted, she looked into the face of a beautiful woman. She had a peaceful face framed with golden curls and a halo of blue flowers.

"Hello Rachel," the woman said. "You died. This is heaven. I'm an angel."

"Heaven?" said Rachel. Somehow, a calmness and acceptance that she didn't know were possible radiated through her.

"Heaven," Rachel said again, not as a question this time. "I thought there'd be more clouds and pearly gates and stuff."

"Well, everyone's heaven is different. This is an amalgamation of your memories of when you felt most content, plus some of your imagination of what you think a peaceful place is. The living room is largely modeled after that log cabin interior you put up on your Pinterest board recently."

"Oh yeah. Wow. I can't believe I'm dead."

"Yeah, it's a lot to take in. But this is just the beginning. This peaceful place is just your home base. Think of this as like your dorm room in heaven, and think of me as like your RA."

"RA?"

"Resident Angel," said the Resident Angel, smiling. "See, it's my job to orient you to all of what heaven has to offer."

"Oh. What does heaven have to offer?"

"Everything!"

"Wow."

"Wow is right. Anything you can imagine, we can do."

"Wow," said Rachel again, looking around. Maybe it wasn't so bad being dead. Maybe heaven would be kind of fun. "You know what I always thought I'd be able to do in heaven?"

"What's that, my child?"

"I always thought that when I got to heaven, I'd be able to look up all of my life stats."

"Your life stats," said the Resident Angel in a knowing voice, betraying a hint of disappointment.

"Yeah! All my stats. Like in heaven, I always thought you'd be able to tell me, like, how many pieces of pizza I'd eaten in my life-time."

"Two thousand five hundred eighty-one and seven-eighths," said a new voice. Rachel and her Resident Angel turned to see another beautiful woman. She had dark curls and the same halo of blue flowers. She grinned and vibrated with excitement. The Resident Angel's agitation grew.

"Seven-eighths because you didn't quite finish that last one, did you?" said the new angel, laughing. "You know, the one that you choked to death on? Still one more bite to go. Oh . . . Too soon?"

"This is Fabi, a Bookkeeping Angel," said the Resident Angel. Fabi was carrying a small wooden box with a glass lid, inside of which was an ornate book, its cover inscribed with gold calligraphy reading RACHEL'S LIFE STATS.

"Is that book all about me?" asked Rachel.

"It is!" said Fabi. "And can I just say, it is so nice to meet you, Rachel! I've read so much about you—well, literally *everything* about you!" Fabi and Rachel laughed. The Resident Angel crossed her arms.

"And I think that you are just so interesting."

"Really?"

"Yes, girl! You're fascinating," Fabi said, giving Rachel a playful push on the shoulder.

"Wow. So any of my life stats I want to know, I can just ask you and you'll tell me?" said Rachel.

"That's right," said Fabi, tapping the container.

"Can I ask stuff about other people?"

"No, just you! Come on—I'm not the NSA!" said Fabi, laughing and putting her hand up for a fist bump from the Resident Angel. After being left hanging, Fabi laughed again and turned to Rachel.

"Seeing my stats. This is so cool," said Rachel, eyeing the book with her name on it. With concern on her face, the Resident Angel spoke again, "And as a reminder, that's not all you can do in heaven! You can also do, for example, literally anything that you can possibly imagine! You could go sea kayaking with dolphins! Hike the John Muir trail with John Muir! Cozy up in a tent with a loved one and watch the aurora borealis from a Norwegian fjord! You could even—"

"Yeah yeah yeah," said Rachel, cutting her off. "I'm going to get to that stuff. But first I want to spend a little time with my Bookkeeping Angel here." Fabi flashed a smile of conquest as she opened the container and with two fingers removed the book.

Rachel and Fabi bounced from room to room, laughing and talking, talking and laughing. Rachel asked questions about her life, and Fabi answered, each time as if the answer was the most riveting new piece of information she'd ever heard.

"How many times did I have food stuck in my teeth and the person I was talking with saw it but didn't tell me?" asked Rachel, sitting at a piano bench, absentmindedly pressing down on the keys.

"Fifty-three times!" answered Fabi.

"Ugh. People are so rude," said Rachel.

"Well, one hundred thirteen times you saw food in someone else's teeth and didn't tell them."

"That's different!"

"You're right, that's totally different."

"Um, how many times did I make people cry?"

"Seventeen. Twelve of those instances were you making your mom cry between the ages of thirteen and seventeen."

"How many times did I lie?"

"Forty-two thousand three hundred one."

"Holy cow."

"How many times did I fart?"

"Forty-four thousand two hundred three."

"I'm a bigger farter than I am a liar! I think I feel . . . good about that?"

"You know," interjected the Resident Angel, appearing between them, "I noticed you tinkling those piano ivories. You took lessons when you were younger, didn't you? If you wanted, you could know what it's like to play the piano like a master. Maybe put on a little concert at Carnegie Hall?"

"Oh. That does sound awesome," said Rachel, her eyes drifting back to the book Fabi was holding. "But maybe just a few more questions first."

"So, how many times . . . did someone else . . . masturbate to me?" asked Rachel, curled up on the couch under a blanket with Fabi. The Resident Angel sat next to them, upright, reading the Bible.

"You mean like . . . *on* you? Because you should remember that, girl!"

"No! I mean like, how many times was I the person that someone fantasized about when . . . during the moment they . . . you know!"

"Oh!" said Fabi, consulting the book. "Five! Rick, Jake, Ron, Jessica, and one time—wait, wowie cowie—Daniel Radcliffe!"

"What? No! Harry Potter masturbated to me? I don't know Harry Potter!"

"He saw you on Amtrak once, thought you were cute, went to the bathroom, fap fap fap kabow, you're in the Harry Potter spank bank!"

"I don't even remember seeing him! That is so cool. Harry Potter."

"Harry Potter! Expelliarmus!" said Fabi as she made a masturbation motion with her right hand, causing them both to burst into hysterical laughter. Next to them, the Resident Angel loudly cleared her throat. Rachel and Fabi stopped laughing, made eye contact, then broke down into hysterics all over again.

Rachel and Fabi were walking the outside perimeter of the cabin, near the arch Rachel had seen when she first arrived in heaven. The Resident Angel watched through a stained-glass window.

"How many times when I farted in an elevator with other people in it did they realize it was me?"

"All of the times."

"What?"

"Every single time you ever farted, anyone in your vicinity knew it was you. See, when you fart, you get this cheeky little smile, like you're secretly proud of it, that gives you away. Gotta work on your fart poker face, girl!"

Rachel and her Bookkeeping Angel had now moved to the floor

in front of the fire, where they lay on their bellies, propped up on their elbows, their legs kicked up in the air at the knees.

"What was the worst day of my life?"

"October 28, 1992," said Fabi. Rachel thought for a moment, then realized the significance of the date.

"Nineteen ninety-two . . . sixth grade . . . Ugh! Middle school. You feel so much then, you know? Your emotional nerve endings are so raw. Ugh, and kids can be so mean to each other," said Rachel, groaning as she recalled the event. "How many hours was I in that locker?"

"Just one."

"It felt like so much longer."

"That's understandable. You were naked, girl. And covered in soap."

"That nickname stuck for longer than a year, that's for sure. Well, I guess if that was the worst day of my life, I had a pretty good life, right?"

"Or at least not a really bad life," said the Resident Angel, appearing on the floor between them again. "So, I was thinking—"

"Yeah yeah yeah, I'm going to do other stuff soon, I promise," said Rachel. "Okay okay okay. First, though, I want to find out . . . what was the best day of my life?"

"August 26, 2006!"

"August 26, 2006 . . . that would have been . . ."

"You're going to get this . . ."

"The Montreal trip?"

"Yes!"

"Oh, the last day of the Montreal trip!"

"Yes!"

"With Jason," Rachel said, thinking about it more and smiling. "Wow. That *was* a really good day."

"You know," said the Resident Angel, "you could go back to Montreal. Or go on another trip. Somewhere you've never been?"

"Nah. It wouldn't be the same," said Rachel.

"That's true. But that's good! It'd be different. A new experience with new memories. Come on, let's go someplace new," said the Resident Angel. Rachel ignored her and turned back to Fabi.

"What was the hardest I ever laughed?"

"You were eleven, your sister was eight, and she tripped holding the milk and cookies that she was bringing out to Santa Claus because her new pajamas were too long, but she fell all slowly like, but she still couldn't catch herself because both of her hands were full, and she looked just like—"

"A giraffe getting shot with a tranquilizer!" they said in unison, finishing the thought together, and again breaking down in laughter.

"That's a little mean," said the Resident Angel. Rachel didn't hear her though.

"Okay, lightning round!" said Rachel, as they now stood around the island in the kitchen, sipping mulled wine.

"Girl, you know I'm ready."

"Who was my first real friend?"

"Sebastian."

"Oh yeah! I wonder how he's doing. Um, how many times did I see *Titanic* in theaters?"

"Seven."

"How many hours of my life did I spend watching the TV show *Friends*?"

"Nine hundred forty-four hours, or about thirty-nine days."

"Oof. Could I have *watched* any more *Friends*?"

"Well, yeah, probably, you always could have—"

"Oh, no, I was doing the Chandler intonation thing. Forget it. How many times did my dad hug me?"

"Twice. Once when your grandma died, to mourn with you, and once when you got into college, to celebrate with you."

"How many people did I meet named Alison?"

"Sixteen."

"How much hair did I grow?"

"Like in total pounds? Total length?"

"Umm . . . actually, never mind about that one, I don't care anymore. How many times was I, like, this close to death and didn't realize it?"

"Like three thousand times."

"Wait. Really?"

"Yes. Life is so precious and humans are so fragile and all of you almost die all the time."

"Can you give me, like, one time?"

"Well, given your lack of chewing prowess, you were pretty close every single meal."

"Speaking of meals," the Resident Angel said, appearing in front of the refrigerator, holding a bag of baby carrots, "how would you like to have a picnic on a yacht in the Mediterranean sea at sunset? Just picture it! Eating an olive in the waning warmth of the late summer sun. Beautiful Italian youths splashing each other as they frolic in the waves. Maybe a little wine, too!"

Rachel looked at the Resident Angel, her face lighting up with an idea. "That reminds me! How many times did I see *Titanic*?"

"You already asked me," said Fabi. "Seven."

"No, not just in theaters. Like, total. At home and stuff, too."

"Ah. Thirty-seven times."

"That's so funny."

"It's something, all right," said the Resident Angel as she snapped into a baby carrot and walked out of the room.

Back in the living room, Fabi and Rachel lay on their backs, looking up at the ceiling. Fabi's head was resting on Rachel's stomach as Rachel played with Fabi's hair, a magic blue dust shedding from the angel's halo each time Rachel twirled it. Rachel had been asking questions for hours. Maybe for days. It was hard to tell the passage of time in heaven. Like in a casino.

"Um . . . how . . . many . . . steps did I take?" said Rachel, struggling to think of more to ask.

"Fifty-seven million sixty thousand four hundred fifty-two steps."

"Wow that's a lot," said Rachel. "Is that enough to, like, circumnavigate the globe?"

"Probably. It's a shit ton of steps."

"You don't know?"

"I don't know stuff about the world, girl! I just know stuff about you. *You* are my world."

"Ah. That's sweet," said Rachel. The two sat for a moment. "Um. How many times did my heart beat?"

"One billion one hundred seventy-eight million thirty-one thousand two hundred twenty-three times."

"Wow. So many times. Um . . . how . . . many . . . times did I orgasm?"

"Same number."

"Huh . . . Wait—what?"

"Just kidding," said Fabi, spinning over to face Rachel. "But your total is very high."

"Hah. Nice," said Rachel, offering Fabi a fist bump.

"Rachel, my child!" shouted the Resident Angel, standing above them, looking stern. "I fear you are stuck on one of the least impressive parts about being in heaven. Every single moment here, you have freedom, absolute control over what you can do! What will you do with this precious gift? Will you do something amazing? Or just obsess over what you have already done?"

Rachel took in what her Resident Angel had been saying. "Okay. Let's do something. Gosh," she said, standing.

"Good. But don't say the Lord's name in vain."

"I didn't. I said 'gosh.'"

"You did it again!"

"The Lord's name is Gosh?"

"Yes, that's her real name! Please, show some respect."

"Okay. Sorry. Gosh. I mean God! I didn't realize."

"Jesus Christ!" Fabi chimed in. "Fuck! Jesus Fucking Christ!" Rachel looked at Fabi, expecting the Resident Angel to scold her.

"All that stuff is okay, actually. Just don't say 'Gosh.' Or 'Geeze,'" said the Resident Angel.

"Because Jesus's real name is Geeze?" asked Rachel.

"Yes."

"Got it. Anyway, I guess I can say good-bye to Fabi for a while," Rachel said, turning to Fabi, but she was gone, leaving only the book lying in the empty space where she'd been.

Rachel and the Resident Angel sat across from each other at the dining room table.

"So, as my Resident Angel, what do you think I should do to take heaven for a spin?" asked Rachel.

"Anything you want! Any hypothetical situation you can think of, any fantasy you've ever had! And, hey, I know I seem like sort of a stick-in-the-mud, but no judgments here. You could do something weird, like play water polo, except, you know, you're riding on the back of manatees or something. So it's just a real slow game. But the manatees like it, too, though. No cruelty in heaven, you know."

"Um, okay. That sounds . . . interesting. Let me think."

Rachel thought. The Resident Angel smiled.

"Okay, I've got it. Could I have dinner with, like, any three people from history?" said Rachel. The angel sighed.

"Okay, not the most original idea, a bit cliché. But sure, let's start there! Which three?"

"Any three? Really? Okay. Gosh. I mean God! Sorry. Um, I'm having trouble thinking of anyone. You're putting me on the spot!"

"It was your idea. So. It can be anyone, living or dead, fictional or real. Maybe someone you admired?"

"I wasn't really the 'admiring' type."

"A hero of yours?"

"Nobody is coming to mind."

"Just name anyone at all!"

"Okay okay okay. How about I have dinner with . . . Emily Dickinson. Um, a young Mick Jagger? And . . . oh! My very first friend I haven't seen since I was six, Sebastian."

"Okay, I just have to sing a little song and we can make it happen."

The Resident Angel closed her eyes and began to hum an ethereal tune. As she did, Rachel slowly bent down and picked up the book that Fabi had left behind, tucking it into her back pocket. The angel's singing grew louder, until the vibrations seemed to become visual ripples in the space around her, mixing the colors and shapes and reconfiguring them into a dining room in the center of a vast, austere warehouse. All was white. The table, the chairs, the walls, the floors, the ceiling, the sconces.

The objects came into focus. Rachel sat across from three individuals. "Whoa! Emily Dickinson! A young Mick Jagger! Sebastian, my first friend!" said Rachel. Emily and Mick nodded. Sebastian's eyes went wide as he scanned his surroundings. Rachel extended her hand to Emily. "Um, thanks for coming. I'm Rachel."

"Hello, Rachel," said Emily Dickinson.

"Charmed, I'm sure," said young Mick Jagger, pouting his lips in a kiss.

"What the heck is going on?" said Sebastian, gazing around the white interior in terror. Sebastian was holding a spatula and wearing an apron with Michelangelo's *David* printed on the front, so that David's genitals fell approximately where Sebastian's did.

"Oh relax, man," said young Mick Jagger. "This is just heaven."

"Heaven? Am I dead?!" shouted Sebastian, now clutching the spatula with both hands.

"No. She is," said Emily Dickinson.

"Hi, Sebastian! It's so good to see you! It's been forever," said Rachel.

Sebastian seemed to recognize her. "Oh. Hey, Natalie. Haven't seen you since you moved away."

"It's Rachel."

"Rachel. Right. So, in heaven you can get dinner with whoever you want? That's cool. I figured it would have a deal like that. And you chose me and"—Sebastian looked at the other table attendees, squinting as he studied their faces—"the guy from One Direction—my daughter is a big fan, by the way—and, uh, a *Downton Abbey* chick. I'm flattered, but why us?"

"Yes, Rachel," said Emily Dickinson. "Were you a reader of my poetry?"

"Oh. Um, not really. I don't know much about poetry, to be honest. Don't like it that much. All seems just sort of made up, you know?" Rachel said, shrugging her shoulders by way of apology and avoiding Emily's hurt eyes.

"But you *were* a Stones fan, weren't you, love?"

"No, not especially," said Rachel, squirming in her white high-backed chair. "Although I do like that one song of yours. 'Pour some suuuugar on me!'"

"That's not us."

"Oh."

"It's Def Leppard, I believe. Sort of inexcusable to mix us up with them. Something only a stupid person would do."

Rachel opened her mouth to speak but couldn't think of anything to say. The quartet sat in awkward silence.

"So are there like waiters or does the food just appear or?" said Rachel. No one replied. "Um, do you guys want to do shots?"

"Yes," said young Mick Jagger.

"Great! Ooh! I wonder how many shots I did in my life," said Rachel, taking out the book with her name on it from her pocket. Rachel flipped through the pages, scanning for an answer. "Let's see . . . I downed 681 shots in my lifetime!" she announced, still looking down at her book. "But . . . only 301 stayed down. I am such a lightweight! Ooh!" she said, flipping to another page as her dinner guests looked on. "I have said the phrase 'I am such a lightweight' . . . 1,982 times. OM God. Isn't that so funny? I'm such a broken record. I am just all like, 'I am such a lightweight! I am such a lightweight!' Oh, guys! I can see the number tick up as I—" Rachel trailed off, looking up for the first time in longer than social etiquette would dictate to be polite at a dinner party.

"I'm going to leave," said Emily Dickinson.

"Yeah, me, too," said young Mick Jagger. "Not that it hasn't been a blast getting summoned here to be insulted by you, but young Mick Jagger is right here next to you and you'd rather bury your nose in your little book than pay attention to us. Plus this person from your past, who I assume is important to you. Even more rude to act like that to a friend." Sebastian waved his spatula.

"And you know what else?" young Mick Jagger went on. "Marilyn Monroe invited me to an MDMA Ultra—that's like normal MDMA but better—orgy party on the back of a blue whale flying through the Andromeda galaxy, and I was going to miss that for this because I owed your Resident Angel a favor, but you know what? I think I'm gonna go do that instead."

"Wait, come on, I'm sorry," pleaded Rachel.

"Uh, yeah. I think I should leave, too. It's Backyard Grill Sunday with my family, so. See ya Rachel. Sorry you died and all."

The three began to fade away.

"Wait, come on! Give me another . . .

". . . chance," Rachel said, finishing her sentence back in the living room of her heaven dorm room cabin. The windows were black and the fire had gone out. A single lamp illuminated the room from the corner.

"That's the worst the Get Dinner with Any Three People, Living or Dead, Fictional or Real has ever gone," said the Resident Angel, appearing with her arms crossed.

"I'm sorry," said Rachel. Sure, she shouldn't have taken her book out, but they had been sort of rude back to her. Both Emily Dickinson and young Mick Jagger had made her feel stupid. And Sebastian didn't even remember her name.

"I am so embarrassed. Mick was late to his space-whale drug-fuck party for this!"

"I said I'm sorry! Let's just try again or do something else. Besides, don't I have all the time in the world?"

"That's not the point."

"So what is the point?"

"The point is that you had three amazing people there wanting to engage with you, and you—"

"That's a lie! I had two amazing people and Sebastian. In second grade he put a booger in my hair. And he was, I repeat, my best friend at the time."

"Well, you didn't even give him a chance to show you the amazing person he'd grown into. Instead all you wanted to do was fawn over your own stats."

"You can't blame me for that. I've got this amazing resource," Rachel said, lifting up the book as she did. "Of course I'm going to want to use it."

Fabi appeared on the other side of Rachel, the angels framing her.

"That's where that went! I could get in a lot of trouble for losing this. Gosh would be pissssssed," said Fabi, plucking the book back from Rachel's grasp. Seeing it taken from her, Rachel let out an involuntary gasp.

"Let me tell you something," said the Resident Angel. "Even in heaven, even with all the time in the world, you can't treat people like that without consequences. People won't want to be your friend."

"Yeah?" Rachel started. She was tired of this angel telling her what was what. Speaking down to her like she was some kind of jerk. She wasn't a saint, sure, but she wasn't so bad. She'd gone to heaven and not hell, right? "Well, as it so happens, I have lots of friends! Tell her, Fabi."

Rachel's triumphant smile began to wane as Fabi delayed in replying.

"Tell her, Fabi," said Rachel again, less confident this time. "How many friends do I have?"

For the first time since Rachel had known her, Fabi's smile seemed forced. "Well, you have 1,436 *Facebook* friends."

"See? Over one thousand friends!" said Rachel.

"Facebook friends. Impressive," said the Resident Angel.

"Okay, how many real friends did I have?"

Fabi ignored the question and instead said, "Hey, what do you guys say we go see if that blue-whale drug orgy is still going on? I have this theory that if you go down a whale's blowhole it would be sort of like a water slide, and—"

"Come on," Rachel interrupted, concern in her voice. "How many real friends did I have? I asked you, you have to answer me."

"Um, I don't, actually. This isn't like a genie-and-person-who-rubbed-the-lamp situation."

"Tell her," said the Resident Angel, locking eyes with Fabi. Fabi gave a nod.

"Okay. Over the course of your life, you had 732 friendly acquaintances, twenty-three close friends, and, at various nonconcurrent times, six best friends, and, lastly, one soul mate."

"My soul mate was Jason, right?"

"No, honey. It was an Indian cobbler named Tariq who lived in Mumbai. You two never met."

"Oh. Well, twenty-three close friends, six best friends," said Rachel hopefully. "That doesn't seem so bad, right?"

"That's over the course of your life. That's not how many you had when you died," said the Resident Angel without scorn. Fabi winced. Rachel was finally starting to understand.

"How many real friends did I have when I died?" Rachel asked.

"Well, the morning of your last day alive? It was one. But at the moment you died? Zero," Fabi said, reaching out to put a hand on Rachel's shoulder. Rachel opened her mouth to object, to argue, but she refrained. She knew it was true.

Rachel turned away from Fabi. She paced between the two angels. Tears welled. Her chin quivered. She didn't know what to say. She turned to her Resident Angel.

"Okay," Rachel said, her voice shaking, "I think I get it now. Heaven is like a new chance for me to focus on what matters, to remember something I knew when I was younger but lost along the way. Connecting with another person, really being present for other people. Thinking of other people first. Actually doing life and not just obsessing over what I've done! That's what matters." Rachel smiled, looking into the Resident Angel's eyes for reassurance.

The Resident Angel smiled back. For a moment, all seemed well. "Close, but not quite." She walked over to the record player, lifted up the needle from its rest and placed it down, setting the record spinning. The same classical music that greeted Rachel before drifted into the air.

"You see, heaven isn't real. This is all just a hallucination you're experiencing in your oxygen-deprived brain in a final nanosecond of paroxysmal syntactic activity before life leaves your body."

"Wait, wh—"

Rachel's body lay motionless on the floor, crumpled between the coffee table and the couch. A shattered plate decorated the floor, pizza crumbs mixed with the shards of porcelain. The *Friends* friends chatted on, and the laugh track laughers laughed without regard to her passing. Inches away from where her lifeless arm was stretched out lay her phone, screen side up.

Bzz-zzz!

A message popped up on the screen.

"The_real_Kim has favorited your tweet." The message lingered on the display for several seconds, before vanishing into the black reflective surface. The battery died twenty hours later, four days before Rachel's body was discovered.

The Once and Future Vegetarian

My mom is a vegetarian and has been for as long as I've been alive. I was, too, for many years growing up. Rather than say I was raised as a vegetarian, you could say I was *gestated* as a vegetarian. Or how about *grown* a vegetarian. Yes, *grown* has a nice vegetable connotation, let's say that: I was grown a vegetarian. But then I grew out of it.

Today, twenty years later, I am convinced by all of the intellectual arguments for vegetarianism. I believe that vegetarianism is a more efficient diet for a global community. I read Jonathan Safran Foer's *Eating Animals*, and afterward I said, "Yes, factory farming is a terrible blight on our world!" I read Michael Pollan's *Omnivore's Dilemma*, and afterward I said, "Yes, we should eat mostly plants!"

But despite being convinced in my mind, my taste buds remain holdouts. The other night I ate an entire pouch of pepperoni slices while sitting on the floor of my kitchen, wearing only my underwear, the refrigerator door still open. While this happened, my cat sat next to me and gave me a look that was a mix of "Hey, can I get in on that snack?" and "Damn, human, you thirsty for that meat. Chill."

My sister, three years my junior, was a better-grown vegetarian than I was. I craved restaurant visits because I knew it would be my chance to taste the sweet fatty goodness of charred animal muscles. In contrast, meat repulsed her. The smell of it, the taste of it. It never appealed to her. For her, the intellectual arguments came later, a secondary justification to what was first a gustatory preference. I envied her. For me, I tried starting with intellectual arguments hoping that my palate would fall in line. So far, it hasn't worked.

Despite what I see as my personal shortcomings in this dietary matter, I have spent many years of my life as a vegetarian. I was a vegetarian from the ages of twelve to eighteen, and there was a six-month period in there where I went vegan. During that time, it would also be fair to say that "Being a Vegan" was my primary personality trait. The only thing about me cooler than my tendency to steer any conversation to being about Eric Schlosser's *Fast Food Nation* was my habit of painting my Birkenstocks with vegan slogans like MEAT IS MURDER or KISS ME, I'M VEGAN.

I did truly believe everything I was saying about the benefits of vegetarianism, but if I'm honest, I primarily enjoyed what I imagined was the prestige of being alternative that came with my lifestyle choice. There weren't many vegetarians in my hometown of Evergreen, Colorado. It was fun to have a thing. By the end of middle school, vegetarianism would become my thing.

However, I first took on a vegetarian diet as a bet.

It started one night at the dinner table over pizza in late spring when I was eleven. There we were: my mother, a vegetarian for humanitarian reasons; my sister, a vegetarian because meat repulsed her; me, craving meat because meat is delicious; and my dad, tolerating the lack of meat for the frugality of it. These different familial world-views coexisted relatively peacefully until the two halves of the pizza collided, so to speak. As was our practice, a plain cheese side had been ordered for my mom and sister, and a Meat Lover's had been ordered for my dad and me. When a rogue bit of meat crossed enemy lines onto a cheese slice, my sister scrunched up her nose in disgust.

"It's not fair. They can eat our pizza, but we can't eat their pizza," my sister said.

"That's just the way it is, Courtney. It's harder to be a vegetarian," my mom replied.

I don't know if she meant it as a challenge, but I took it as one.

"I could be a vegetarian if I wanted," I said.

"Oh, really?" my mom said, eyebrows arching as she did.

The conversation escalated. My mom bet me that I couldn't be a vegetarian for one week. I retorted that I could, most likely saying some variation of, "Yah-*huh* I can!" In response, my mom bet me a hundred dollars that I could not be a vegetarian for the entire summer.

The entire summer without meat. Pride alone would have been enough to make me attempt it, but now that the pot was sweetened with one hundred one-dollar bills? With that kind of cash in 1995, I could buy ten CDs, perhaps Green Day's *Insomniac*, the Offspring's *Smash*, and then eight copies of the Boyz II Men's *Cooleyhighharmony* for good measure. I could get enough quarters to play 120 hours of the *Street Fighter II* arcade game in the front of the Pizza Hut and maybe even beat the high score that Scott Anderson's older brother Jeff set with Ryu. Heck, I could even upgrade my Game Boy game of choice, *The Bugs Bunny Crazy Castle*, to the far flashier *The Bugs Bunny Crazy Castle 2*.

I took the bet.

No sooner had we shaken on it, though, than my eyes drifted to the remaining slice of meat-topped pizza. I felt carnivorous. I considered asking if we could start the bet after this supper, but the jeers that would have invited from the meatless half of my family kept me silent.

That summer was difficult, but I was brave. Courageous, even. Certainly worthy of your retrospective praise and admiration. I made it through. How? I found a source of inspiration to call on when temptation grew strong: Being a vegetarian could be my thing.

Up until that point, I had no real sense of my friends' diets. Now I was aware that I was the only vegetarian. This newfound uniqueness was intoxicating. I felt special. I wasn't the fastest. I wasn't the smartest. I wasn't the funniest. But I could be the one who loudly told everyone about my new diet and inconvenienced my friends' parents when I went to their houses to eat. I looked forward to the moment when at a friend's house I would have to tell the mom that I was a vegetarian and that, yes, I apologize, but special arrangements will need to be made.

"I'm sorry, I'm afraid I am not able to partake in the grilled chicken you've prepared. You see, I'm a vegetarian. Perchance do you have white bread and Kraft cheese slices I could garnish with Miracle Whip instead? Also, I've read my mom's copy of *Diet for a Small Planet* and I'm prepared to recite quotations about how vegetarianism is good for the environment. Don't worry, my exuberance will not be hampered by my celery skin–thin understanding of the evidence I'm referencing. Thank you again for having me over, Mrs. Anderson."

I think my mom was impressed that I stuck to it. It also might have even been the start of my sister and me making the transition from being siblings to being close friends. The summer was going well.

The week before sixth grade started, and seven days away from me having a hundred dollars, all was in danger of being lost. And it was all thanks to my dad.

My father is not a verbose man. He's more the strong and silent type. He wrestled and played football in high school. He once had to pass a kidney stone and rather than go to the hospital, he went to the urinal at his office, passed it, then went back to work. He likes to go for long bike rides alone. Once while cycling home from work he was run off the road by a road-raging motorist. He got back on his bike and chased the car to a gas station. He called the police and confronted the driver, placing his bike and his person in front of the vehicle as the driver refueled so he couldn't pull away. The driver accelerated anyway, running over my dad's bike and knocking him to the ground, from where he ripped the license plate off the car as it drove away so that he could show it to the police when they arrived. The driver was arrested.

My dad never teased me for being a sissy, but, like most sons since the dawn of time, I still felt a deep desire to show him that I was a Man. And so, my foray into vegetarianism, in my imagination, was cause for concern.

With less than a week left in the bet, we bookended the season with a familiar meal: Pizza Hut delivery. This in and of itself wouldn't have been cause for a crisis, but my dad added to his Meat Lover's half of the pie an order of Buffalo wings. What was my soft-spoken father up to? If value number one was "work hard," value number two was "be frugal." The adding of Buffalo wings to a pizza meal struck me as an uncharacteristic luxury, a frivolity of the highest order. Yet with one week left on my vegetarian tenure, here they came. Buffalo wings: single-serving, mouthwatering bites of meat.

I don't know how you feel about Buffalo wings, but I love them. They're usually more bone than meat and taste more like whatever hot sauce has been put on them than the stringy tissue itself, but that doesn't matter. When you eat them, you feel as though you're a predator on top of the food chain picking clean the bones of your latest kill. When you finish an order of Buffalo wings, there aren't crumbs on your plate: There's a pile of bones.

The meal began. I felt I was being tested in some grand and final way. Throughout our pizza dinner, I didn't talk or listen to my family. I was too busy keeping track of how many Buffalo wings my father had eaten and how many were left in the Styrofoam box they came in. My father had ordered a dozen. He munched on them between slices. My mom conducted the conversation.

"Did you have fun with Melissa today, Courtney?"

Eleven wings.

"Mike, did you see that the Knoblochs were cutting down some of the aspens in their yard?"

Nine wings.

"I heard that there is an IMAX movie at the natural history museum in Denver. It's about beavers and it's called *Beavers: The Biggest Dam Movie You Ever Saw.* Isn't that funny?"

Six wings.

My family members seemed to be wrapping things up. "I'll clear the plates!" I declared.

I grabbed the box of wings and rushed to the refrigerator. By my count, there were five wings left. I moved aside a jug of skim milk and pushed the box into the back of the fridge, sliding a carton of orange juice in front of it to block it from view, my hope being that my father wouldn't come searching for a snack later.

But hold on there, Nate. Why would you care if he ate the rest of the wings? You don't eat meat. Was I setting myself up to give into temptation? Later in life I'd come to know these types of subconscious decisions and self-defeating actions well. In high school, the turning on of a television for just a few moments to relax before you got to that homework you fully intended to do. In college, the visiting of a friend's dorm room—just for a minute!—before going to the library. In my twenties, the going to a bar with friends for "just one drink" when instead I had been planning on, say, not being hungover the next morning.

But for now, it was just what it was and nothing more: the placing of a Styrofoam box containing five Buffalo wings in the back of a fridge. I fled the kitchen and tried to pass the night with various diversions. My aquatic frog, Nathena, was even more lethargic in her tank than normal. The suggested incoming middle school reading failed to hold my attention. Even Bugs and his crazy castle were no good. I had one thing on my mind.

Without ever letting myself think about it long enough for it to feel like a conscious plan, I descended a slippery slope toward ultimate transgression.

Why did we stay up until everyone else was asleep?

Don't worry about it, Brain, this is just something that Body is doing. Everyone else is sleeping, Brain, why don't you join them? Now Body is just going to go to the kitchen . . .

Why are we going to the kitchen?

Be quite, Brain. Body has got this.

Are we doing something wrong?

Chill out, Brain! We're not breaking any rules going to the kitchen. Do the conditions of the bet say we can't go look at Buffalo wings in the kitchen?

What does the bet have to do with this? Wait, are you going to—

I turn my brain off so it's just my body performing actions now. I'm opening the door to the refrigerator and sitting down on the cool, tiled floor. The ceiling light is off and I'm illuminated only by the soft, inviting glow of the fridge bulb. Now I'm holding the Styrofoam box. I haven't made any decision; I haven't analyzed the moral calculus of what it means to abandon a long journey right at the last moment; or undertaken the far darker considerations of a possible cover-up. I do not have time to think of any of that, because I am already stuffing wings into my mouth.

One might think that after three months without meat, I would have savored each bite. I didn't. I was just trying to eat the wings as quickly as possible.

Finished, I snapped out of my meat trance. One or two wings missing might have gone undetected, but surely my dad would notice that the entire box was empty. I would be caught. But then a funny thought popped into my head. My dad was not a verbose man. He probably wouldn't say anything. And if I didn't say anything, my mom would never know. If nobody sees you eat meat, they don't know that you eat meat.

I shoved the now empty, sauce-covered Styrofoam container into the bottom of the garbage. Sure enough, whether because he forgot about the remaining wings or because he forgot that I was doing the bet or because he was secretly happy I ate meat, my dad didn't mention anything. A week later, with only a slight hum of guilt in the back of my mind, I accepted my prize: five crisp twenty-dollar bills.

As tasty as those Buffalo wings were, the taste of having my own thing was even sweeter. I stuck to identifying as a vegetarian. Every chance I got in school to write a report about the subject of my choice, I chose vegetarianism. I proselytized and tried to convert my friends, convincing Leo Radkowski in seventh grade to join me in the cult for about an hour before he realized that hamburgers were cow meat. By eleventh grade, I'd gone vegan. I wore recycled clothing from secondhand stores. I wore Che Guevara T-shirts and listened to Propagandhi. In 2000, when Al Gore lost to George W. Bush in our high school's mock election, I used my status as a member of student government to slip into the PA booth in the office in order to lambaste my classmates for being fascist sheep, a revolutionary act of protest that lasted for about twelve seconds. I was a priggish middle-class white American vegetarian. Gross, I know, but it was my thing and I loved it.

Then I got to college and there were lots of vegetarians. Hell, there were Dumpster-diving, freegan-revolutionary socialists who were way more hard-core than I'd ever be. Vegetarianism was no longer a special thing about me. It was just a lot of hard work. College was hard for me in a lot of ways, and at some point, while eating alone in a dining hall, I didn't have the mental energy to remain disciplined. I ate meat.

But I didn't think of that as me stopping being a vegetarian. I didn't think of myself as a pretend vegetarian lying to my friends. I told myself that I was just a vegetarian who kept having meat accidents with my mouth hole. Oops, how did that steak get in my burrito? Did I say steak? I meant beans, but, oh well, since you've already made it I guess I'll just eat it and also I better order two more steak burritos with extra steak please I love meat thank you thank you.

Besides, I'd introduced myself to all of my new friends and classmates as a vegetarian. I would feel like a fraud if a few months later I was like, "Oh, never mind." So my entire freshman year, I kept telling other people, and myself, that I was a vegetarian. I promised myself that each time I slipped off the meat-tree bandwagon, it was the last time.

I was delusional. And my delusion nearly led to my death in the spring semester.

I signed up for an "Alternative Spring Break," a trip with other students to do community service at a therapeutic horseback riding farm in South Carolina. As was my habit, I told my trip mates I was a vegetarian. I did this thinking it would help keep me honest on the trip and not eat meat. One of the other students on the trip was a Lebanese student named Ghia who told me that she was also a vegetarian. We bonded a bit over that, and I immediately developed a huge crush on her.

On one of the last nights of the trip, for dinner our host prepared grilled chicken cutlets. The vegetarian option was iceberg lettuce. Ghia and I commiserated over this, and then she ate her lettuce. I excused myself to go to the bathroom, grabbed a handful of cutlets when nobody was looking, and ran outside.

I stuffed the chicken into my mouth, trying to eat it as quickly as possible, a single light hanging above the steel garage door illuminating what I'm sure was a disgusting display. After a day of manual labor, the cutlets tasted amazing.

Then something went wrong. I was choking.

Not "Oops, it went down the wrong pipe, how embarrassing, can you pass me a glass of water?" but full-on choking. No air going in or out, esophagus blocked. I panicked. I was an animal with my gullet sealed shut.

Through the fog of my panic, a choice became perfectly clear to me: Go back inside for help, reveal to everyone I was a pretend vegetarian, and survive . . . or stay alone outside with my secret and risk choking to death.

I stayed outside. I punched myself in the stomach with both fists. Nothing. I threw myself on the top bar of a wood fence attempting to self-Heimlich. It didn't work. Then, the only way I can describe what I did is this: I summoned all my strength and tried to swallow as hard as I could. Even when it felt like blood vessels were popping in my eyeballs, I still tried to swallow harder. My neck muscles contracted, I felt my face go red, and the chicken went down.

Traumatized and with tears streaming down my face, I went back inside and sat down.

"What's wrong?" Ghia asked. "Have you been crying?"

I shook my head no and mumbled something about feeling emotional about the meaningful community service work we were doing.

I had bruises on my solar plexus and my throat was sore for weeks.

That scare kept me a real vegetarian for a couple years. I stayed true until a study-abroad trip to do thesis research in Buenos Aires the summer before my senior year. Once I was there, the temptation of home-cooked, meat-filled empanadas with my host family was too great to resist. Plus, I didn't want to be rude. Plus, it was in a foreign country, so that hardly counted. Plus, meat tastes so damn good.

I promised myself that when I returned home, I would be a vegetarian again. This time for good. This time I meant it. This time I really, really meant it.

Part 2

Predator Prey

Thanking Jesus

Growing up, I loved Jesus, and it almost led to me dying from snake venom out in the Utah desert. Well, that's what the clickbait version of this essay would be titled if this were an internet article. Aren't you glad you're not reading an article on the internet? I'm so tired of the internet. Aren't you? Anyway, where was I? Oh yeah, Jesus and my near-death experience.

So, it started with my mom. My mother is a good United Methodist Christian. She volunteers in her community, she is generous with her friends and family, and she is kind in all aspects of her life. She worked for years as a hospice nurse, helping individuals and their families during the end-of-life transition, and she was a great comfort to many people.

She was an adventurous teenager. *Adventurous* here is a euphemism for "engaging in activities of questionable legality." Over the years, I've heard bits and pieces of stories of her youthful exploits, usually after she has had a glass of wine. A surprising number of her stories involve hitchhiking. One of her stories involves conspiring with her siblings to mix my grandpa Stan's pipe tobacco with marijuana, resulting in a mellow weekend road trip.

My mom was determined for her children to choose a safer, less "adventurous" route. Her protection extended into all areas of my life. I was the only kid on my Little League baseball team who had to wear an uncomfortable plastic heart protector during both games and practice. I protested wearing it, but my mom insisted. I'm not sure if it actually provided any heart protection, but it did scratch up my sweat-softened chest skin and give my teammates something else to make fun of when they got tired of pointing out my hitting deficiency or throwing ineptitude.

Ensuring that my sister and I attended services with her at the local United Methodist Church was like a metaphysical heart protector that my mom slipped over our mortal souls. Unlike with the baseball heart protector, I didn't fight going to church. For the first eighteen years of my life, I attended devoutly. Sunday school every Sunday morning, youth group every Sunday night, and the occasional Bible study devotional, confirmation class, up-with-youth Jesus camp, and mission trip sprinkled in.

Even without my mom's urging, I had a predisposition to spirituality. I enjoyed thinking about questions of morality and debating those questions with others, partially because I wanted to be a good person, and partially because I liked contradicting people who thought they were good persons. At the time, berating our adult Sunday school leaders with nitpicky questions about the logical details of particular passages of scripture felt like I was doing my due diligence as a committed Christian who just wanted his faith to be as strong as possible. Looking back, though, I was just being a little shit.

"When we pray, we shouldn't just ask Jesus for things. We should be grateful for what we have. We should say, 'Thank you, Jesus.'"

"I have a question!"

"Yes, Nathan?"

"Why does Jesus need us to thank him?"

"What do you mean?"

"It just seems kind of petty for someone to need thanks. Like, if you do something for someone else and you're truly selfless about it, you don't do it for the thanks. And isn't Jesus truly selfless?"

"Look, Nathan, let's just—"

"I have another question. We do what Jesus says because it's the right thing to do, correct?"

"Yes, Nathan."

"But First Corinthians 15:14 says, 'And if Christ has not been raised, our preaching is useless and so is your faith.' So isn't that saying we do what Jesus said only because he proved that he was the son of God with the whole rising-from-the-dead thing?"

"Well—"

"But Luke 4:12 says, 'You shall not test the Lord your God.'"

"Right, but—"

"But isn't that like saying, your faith doesn't need proof, but just in case, your faith has proof? It's like, not that there is a son-of-God test, but if there was a son-of-God test, Jesus totally passed!"

"The Bible says lots of things, Nathan."

"It sure does. Speaking of which, I was doing some research, and even though places like First Corinthians 6:18 say, 'Flee from sexual immorality,' nowhere does it actually say specifically, 'Don't have sex before marriage.' Seems pretty open to interpretation, to be honest."

"We're not talking about that again, Nathan. If we could get back to today's topic—"

"I just don't get why Jesus wants us to thank him all the time is all. Seems he'd be, like, bigger than that."

"Okay! I think that's enough Sunday school for today."

I thought I was winning arguments with my logical prowess, but I was just winning a war of attrition.

Youth group always ended with game time. This wasn't called game time, though. It was called "fellowship." As in, "Okay, time for fellowship. Who wants to pick teams?" Capture the Flag was my favorite youth group activity. Through Capture the Flag, I found my best friend, Chris. He was the only other person who liked both Bible-based moral debates *and* Capture the Flag strategy as much as I did. Later I'd be the best man at Chris's wedding. The toast I gave must have been shit, because Chris got a divorce after a few years (if you're reading this, Chris, my apologies, I owe you one).

Games after youth group were fun, but the ultimate fellowship activity was a fellowship retreat. When I was sixteen, my youth group went on a four-day canoeing trip down the Green River in Utah. This is where the irony of my mom leading me to get involved in church activities as a way to protect me from the dangers of the world reaches its peak.

On the third day of the trip, Chris and I woke up before our adult chaperones, one of whom was my mom, of course. We wanted to see the sunrise from the ridge of the canyon we were canoeing down. The sun was already rising, but Chris thought that if we got up to the top of the ridge fast enough, we might still be able to see the sun first peek over the canyon walls and that it'd be "pretty cool." I agreed.

We canoed across the river from camp. As we pulled the canoe onto the far shore, blackflies swarmed around us. Canoe secured, we hurried to ascend the steep slope, scrambling over the red Utah rocks. After thirty minutes it became clear that the ridge was much higher than we had estimated. The sun was already peeking over the canyon walls. I worried how much my mom would worry if she woke up and we weren't there. We turned back.

A few steps into on our journey home, Chris stopped.

"What is it?" I asked.

"Shh," Chris said quietly, his eyes locked on the ground six feet in front of us.

Sunning itself on one of the rocks we'd scrambled over was a rattlesnake. Primordial fear shot from my brain stem down to my Birkenstocks. The rocky path we were retracing that cut through the steep canyon walls was too narrow to go around. There was no other way down except the path we'd climbed up, a path currently being used for tanning purposes by a rattlesnake.

Growing up in Colorado, you hear stories about people dying from encounters with wild animals. A mountain lion killed a high school student on the track team while he was out on a jog. My elementary school was shut down for a day when a black bear climbed a tree next to the playground, the standoff ending when the sheriff used rubber bullets to shoot her* down. In class we learned the telltale differences between the venomous diamondback rattlesnake— triangular head, narrow pupils—and the similar but mostly harmless gopher snake—longer snout, rounded pupils. And of course, that the poisonous rattlesnakes had rattles.

"I bet it came out when the sun did. We must have just missed it on the way up," Chris said.

"You think it's a rattlesnake?" I asked.

It rattled.

Rattlesnakes do not rattle to intimidate prey, but to scare

---

*That's right, *her*. It's 2016 and females can be anything they want to be, including bears.

off potential larger predators. It makes them seem scary. When they're hunting, they stay silent and strike without rattling. But when a dumb human comes bumbling along, they rattle. It's their way of saying, "Look, man, I don't want trouble, but I will cut your ass."

I didn't know what to do.

"Let's wait," Chris suggested.

"Yeah, that's probably the right call. But also," I said, avoiding eye contact, "I don't want to get in trouble. Maybe we can scare it off?"

I have since learned this is the exact opposite of what you should do. The snake is in its natural habitat. It just doesn't want to be bothered. Would it bother you if a stranger came into your house and threw a rock at you? Yes, it would. Same with snakes. Humans and snakes are similar in this way.

I threw a rock near it, just to see what would happen. An exploratory rock throw. The snake rattled again, louder and somehow angrier. Yes, it's possible for rattles to sound angry. It doesn't seem possible, but it's true, just like how it doesn't seem possible that someone could play Metallica's "Enter Sandman" on a steel drum, but if you've been on the Union Square L train platform in the last year, you know that it is indeed possible and wonderful.

My stomach dropped and my throat clinched. I proposed another plan: One of us holds a rock while the other jumps over the snake and throws the rock only if the snake strikes. A well-thought-out snakebite-avoidance plan. I seriously thought we'd be able to throw a rock with sufficient speed and accuracy to hit a striking snake in midair. Have you seen those slow-motion videos of a snake striking its prey with lightning speed? Have you seen those videos of nonpitchers throwing the opening pitch at a baseball game and missing home plate with their terrible awkwardness? This was the year

2000 and YouTube hadn't been invented yet, so I hadn't seen those videos.* Hence, my plan seemed plausible.

Good guy that he is, Chris volunteered to jump first. We were still a full day's paddle away from our pickup point. None of us had cell phones. Even if we had, we wouldn't have gotten service. If treated with antivenom immediately, most venomous snakebites are not fatal. But without immediate treatment, a bite can mean death.

Chris jumped; the snake moved, not for Chris, but straight toward me. My heart dropped to join my stomach; before my neural synapses could fire and tell my hand to throw the rock, the snake was halfway to me. A nanosecond after that, the snake disappeared under the rock I was standing on.

For a brief moment, I'd believed with all of my unprotected heart that a snake was about to bite me and that I would die. As far as I knew, it was the closest I had ever come to my own mortality, and the first time I'd ever even considered it a possibility. I was in shock.

Chris turned back. "Where'd it go? You okay?" he said, reacting to the look on my face. I nodded that I was.

"Okay, I'll cover you," Chris said, picking up a rock and standing ready to throw, facing the crack the snake had vanished into. I jumped and joined him. Each of us unbitten, we whooped and hollered as we moved as fast as we could back to camp, clapping each other on the back and embracing along the way, adrenaline propelling us down. With each step we took, my teenage sense of invincibility crept back into my system.

"Well, that could have been bad," Chris said with relief as we pushed the canoe back into the river.

*Okay, I guess the internet isn't all bad. I especially love YouTube videos of slippery dogs running around on soccer fields, avoiding capture in the middle of games.

"Could have been bad, but was awesome," I said.

Our jubilation faded at the sight of the rest of our group. They were awake, had already broken down camp, and were awaiting our return.

My mom stood still in front of everyone else. She faced us with her arms crossed, her head lowered to a triangular point, and her eyes narrowed to slits. I whispered to myself, "Thank you, Jesus," meaning it more than I ever had.

As the Toothbrush You Just Threw Away, I Have Some Questions About the Seven 12-Ounce Mountain Dews in Your Trash

Dear Glenn, my former master:

It's me, your old toothbrush, writing you from the trash can you just threw me in.

I'm not angry. I'm just hurt.

I thought we shared the same values. I thought we were working together on your oral hygiene. I thought you cared about dental upkeep and the long-term health of your teeth, gums, and tongue. But I guess I was wrong. I see now that you were fooling around behind my back our entire relationship. I see now that since the last time you emptied out your trash you have consumed seven 12-ounce bottles of Mountain Dew.

Who drinks soda anymore? Are you a teenager playing Xbox with his friends? You are not. You are a thirty-four-year-old balding male who works for a midsize insurance company in Phoenix. You sit in a chair and make phone calls for eight hours every day. You have no late-night hobbies. Why would you possibly need this much sugar and caffeine? So you can stay up late to rewatch episodes of *Game of Thrones* on your parents' HBO GO account?

I am trapped with the evidence of 84 ounces of Mountain Dew consumption. That's 378 milligrams of caffeine. That's enough caffeine to put a large dog into cardiac arrest. Like an Irish wolfhound. Have you seen an Irish wolfhound? They look like skinny bears. That's too much caffeine, Glenn.

Sure, there were signs. When our three-month anniversary passed and you didn't throw me out, I admit I should have known something was up. Yes, you were ignoring the industry standard dentist recommendation to change your toothbrush four times annually. I let myself think that you were attached to me, that you had a special connection to little old Colgate Full Head Medium Bristle, Product #A4-319. How could I not? Even though my blue bristle indicator had long since faded, alerting you that it was time we part ways, you kept me. And I was flattered. I admit it. But then not just three, but *eight* months passed. I should have known that it was your own dental negligence and not your affection for me that was keeping me around, but I believed the lie. The lie made me happy.

That happiness receded like an overbrushed gum line the moment you chucked me into this garbage can. The gaggle of Mountain Dews taunts me. One of them was the "Code Red" flavor. What does that even mean? I'll tell you what it means. It means you need help.

Nestled up next to the Dews were the remnants of three microwavable Lean Cuisine low-fat dinners. From this ratio, am I to infer that you have 2.3 bottles of Mountain Dew per meal? Here's a tip: Get the regular-fat dinner option and hold off on the sugar water. You're not a fucking hummingbird.

If you're so set on destroying that smile of yours, why not just buy tartar and have it surgically inserted onto the surface of your teeth?

There's a plastic wrapper in here for an Abba-Zaba. Abba-Zaba, Glenn. I guess exotic candies get your motor going? A Snickers wrapper I could understand. You see it every day by the counter of the convenience store. It's a delicious blend of chocolate, caramel, and peanuts. I wouldn't like it, but I'd get it. *But Abba-Zaba?* This was no impulse candy purchase. This was premeditated. Did you buy it from a candy fetish website you have bookmarked?

It's 8 p.m. and you just threw me out. I don't see you making a nighttime toothbrush run. Just going to gargle real good tonight? Is that it?

What in the fuck is this jar of coconut oil doing in here? If drinking soda and oil pulling are both parts of your weekly routine, then you are lying to yourself even more than you lied to me.

Did you even appreciate all the times my round-ended bristles cleaned your hard-to-reach areas? Did you use the same hand to hold my nonslip rubber ergonomic handle (simultaneously providing you with superior comfort *and* brushing control) that you used to chug that neon swill?

There's a canister of sugar-coated peanuts in here that you appear to have opened by gnawing at the lid with your right bicuspids. Nothing else I could discover would hurt me. But maybe I could still hurt you. The one time in the last eight months you had a romantic guest come home with you, you told that trollop that it was "no big deal" if she wanted to use your toothbrush, but before she had a chance, she dropped me into the toilet. She rinsed me off for maybe four seconds in the sink before placing me back in the dark of the medicine cabinet. And she didn't tell you. And neither did I. Although now that I see how little you care for the health of your face hole, I'm not sure it would have bothered you that much.

You know what? I *am* angry, Glenn.

Also, halitosis *is* a real thing, and you *do* have it. I was just faking that you didn't to make you feel better.

> Enjoy your adult-onset diabetes,
> Your old toothbrush

HonestJuice Juicery

Welcome to our Our Philosophy Poster. This is it. The words you're reading right now—size 18 Papyrus font on a background splash of summer-peach-to-autumn-tangerine ombré gradient—are the philosophy part of the poster. And our philosophy is this: HonestJuice Is Good Juice.*

We could just stop there. But for the sake of absolute honesty, what do we mean exactly by "honest" juice?

For starters, our juice is cold-pressed. We avoid centrifugal juice extractors. Also, I should clarify the claim I made above about you reading these words on a poster. As I type these words, they are not yet printed on a poster. It is my intention for these words to one day appear on a poster, a poster that will hang on the wall of our juicery. At this point, though, the only thing that I can honestly say is that these words exist in a word processing program on the Dell desktop I share with my wife and cofounder of HonestJuice Juicery, Kendra.

It is my *intention* to put this document on a thumb drive and bring it to a FedEx Office for printing. But at this point, that is only an intention, not a *fact*. Perhaps you are a FedEx Office Print & Ship Center employee reading these words prior to printing as a part of some sort of quality control? In that case, are these words on a poster? No, they are not. Will they be soon? If you are a hardworking FedEx Office Print & Ship Center employee, it is likely, but not guaranteed, that they will be soon. Or perhaps you are not a FedEx Office Print & Ship Center employee. Perhaps you are Kendra, reading slightly audibly over my shoulder as I attempt to finish what I keep assuring you is only a first draft and will get better and more concise with future revisions. So in summary, while it wasn't unreasonable of me to assume that you, the reader, were reading these words in poster form, I recognize that other possibilities exist. I would like to end this paragraph by saying that all of our juices are both macro- and probiotic, and come in gluten-free and gluten-rich options. *Namaste.*

Close your eyes. Relax. Breathe in through your nose and, while holding your breath, notice the smells. Those are smells of healthfulness. Now open your eyes and look around. See those three Vitamix blenders? They are state of the art in healthfulness tech. I admit it is possible that you don't see the Vitamix blenders. Those blenders are expensive. We even went to this wholesale place in the bad part of town and, well, long story short, it was a bummer of an afternoon and it got us thinking we might have to find a more economical blender option. But I put out into the universe that Kendra, my wife and the business manager of HonestJuice Juicery, would find a way for our budget to allow us to own three Vitamix mixers, using a secret method I learned from a book called *The Secret.* So hopefully that's what you see. *Inshallah.*

Breathe out. You may now be in charge of your own breathing or, as we advise at HJJ, allow your body to do it automatically. Now, while Auto-Breathing, reach out and take one of the punch cards by the register. See them there? Should be just to the right of the iPad with the Square credit card swipe device, next to the Belly QR code scanner placed on the Yelp mouse pad, below our framed signed copy of Khalil Gibran's *The Prophet*. Or at least that's the plan. May the Force be with you, always.

You see, it's our obsessive attention to honesty that sets HonestJuice Juicery apart from other juiceries in the Sunnyset Galleria. Our honesty, and also our policy of not selling individual juices. We only sell juice-cleanse cycles of sixteen or thirty-two juices. But for freshness reasons, you must come in and buy these one at a time. That card you're holding isn't a customer loyalty reward card; it's a Customer Obligation Fulfillment Card, reminding you that you've bought a juice that is part of a larger cleanse and that you will return for the remaining fifteen or thirty-one juices. There is a also a possibility that nothing you've just read is accurate and, as Kendra suggested, we will sell single servings of juice because it's "a ludicrously bad business model for a juicery not to do so," but really because she had to get her way. Go ye now in juice.

One thing that I can guarantee, though, is that our juices will have fun names. Names like Up-Beet (a beet-based juice), the Tarot Carrot (a carrot-based juice), and the Jazzy Jeff (which is what we will call tap water). On this point of naming our juices fun names I will be firm and not budge, Kendra. Hashtag blessed.

Now that I think about it, not only is there a pre-juicery time of uncertainty that you could be reading these words within, but also theoretically there are non-juicery time lines in which the juicery never comes to exist in the first place, but I don't need to think about those time lines, because Kendra does it enough for the both of us. If the juicery does open as planned, though, and brings Kendra and me together in a way that having a baby, as she wanted, would not have done, perhaps in this future where you are, reader, Kendra and I will be standing behind the counter and smiling, her not regretting the decision to invest the money from her father's passing in my juicery idea, as we wait for you to decide between a Kool Kale and an Apoplectic Apple. *Que sera sera.*

So to you, poster reader, who likely have just used the back of your self-made deerskin mitten to brush away the thick layer of gray ash that obscured this aging poster that you nearly stepped on while exploring the ruins of the Sunnyset Galleria Mall on a foraging mission for nonradiated food from the nearby survivor encampment where you have lived since North Korea's Western Seaboard–annihilating nuclear attack, please know that here at the HonestJuice Juicery, our philosophy is (always will be/forever will have been) simple: HonestJuice Is Good Juice.*

---

*Trademark pending.

A Lack of Sleep

Matt needed sleep. It was no longer a matter of wanting sleep. He needed it. Even before he twisted shut the dead bolt of his Queens studio apartment, he was already kicking off his shoes. One step toward his bed and his shirt was off; another step and he was stepping out of his pants; and with a final step he twisted his torso around as his naked butt landed on the edge of the bed. He didn't need to turn the light off, because he hadn't bothered to turn it on. Normally he liked to switch the fan on low, even when it was cold out, to lull him away—he preferred the mechanical whir of the fan to the ambient-noise machine he'd purchased used from the woman on Craigslist whose young child no longer needed it to sleep—but after fourteen hours of travel on a delayed red-eye flight, he didn't need it. He didn't need the 5-milligram melatonin sublingual tablets he kept next to the eye mask on his bedside table. He'd already taken two on his flight—twice the recommended dosage—combining them with a vodka chaser. He didn't need the indica kush and tie-dye pipe he kept in a glasses case in the medicine cabinet. He didn't need the Ambien in the vial with the CVS wrapper that bore his friend Ben's name instead of his own, since his psychiatrist refused to prescribe it to him for some reason. He just needed sleep. For once, it seemed like it would come without a struggle.

He closed his eyes.

SLAM!

Matt jerked upright.

SLAM!

He looked around. Home invasion? Was someone in the room with him?

SLAM!

It was coming from outside. He put his feet on the floor. He didn't want to deal with a confrontation right now. He hated confrontations.

SLAM!

He got up, twisted open the dead bolt, and peered out, taking care to cover his nakedness with the door.

SLAM!

It wasn't in the hallway. It sounded like his neighbor Ramone was pounding a radiator with a ball-peen hammer.

SLAM!

Ramone was an elderly Dominican guy who lived alone with his dog, Pyro. What was Ramone doing hammering something at 7 a.m.? Maybe that was a reasonable time for an old guy to be midway through his day, but it seemed clear to Matt that common decency dictated you didn't undertake any major construction projects before the start of the workday. Just one hour of sleep would be enough to change his whole life right now. Couldn't he wait?

SLAM!

Matt put his clothes back on. He knocked on Ramone's door.

SLAM!

Knock.

SLAM!

KNOCK!

SLAM!

KNOCK! KNOCK! KNOCK!

Matt's heart was beating fast, as it always did during confrontations. Was this a confrontation? He heard feet shuffle toward him, then pause in front of the door, changing the light pattern peeking out beneath the half inch of space below the door, which was actually one inch at the right side and a quarter inch at the left side on account of the building's aging, slanted floors. The door did not open. Matt felt a rush of relief creep down his spine, like he'd just ducked a line drive that was about to hit him in the face.

He turned to return to his apartment.

Creak . . .

Matt looked back over his shoulder. Ramone was standing there, but he was also more than Ramone. He was God.

"You're God?" Matt asked.

"Yep," Ramone said. "Come on in, I've been expecting you."

Matt followed Him into His apartment. Pyro trailed along beside them as they each took a seat on two circular cushions on the far side of the room beneath a drapeless window. The increasing morning light hurt Matt's eyes. Or perhaps it was the glory emanating off of Him. Matt squinted.

"You can close your eyes, it's okay," said God. Matt closed his eyes.

"It sounded like you were hitting your radiator with a ball-peen hammer," Matt said.

"That makes sense," said God. "That's what I was doing. Was

it keeping you up?" God chuckled. "No need to answer. I know it was."

Matt's shoulders sank forward. It was hard to sit up straight on the cushion, but he didn't want to slouch. His dad would be embarrassed if he found out Matt had been slouching in front of God.

"There's a reason I kept you up," God said. Matt nodded. He figured there was. He didn't think God would do something for no reason.

"Can I know what it is?" asked Matt.

"I bet you can guess," said God. "It has to do with how sensitive you are. Like, you know how you are so sensitive to sound and light and social interactions and emotions and other people?"

"Yeah."

"Well, can you think of why God would have use for a guy like that?"

Matt thought about it. He couldn't.

"Well, keep thinking on it," God said. "As soon as you do, sleep will find you."

An Intrepid Explorer Discovers a Man Cave

Just after dusk and a full day of searching, my field notebook in hand and my rucksack in tow, I saw it, the habitat whose existence so many doubted . . . the Man Cave. And yet here it was, in a basement in a remote suburban neighborhood. I saw the distinctive markings clear as day: the flickering light of a big-screen television flashing up from a subterranean layer; the primal thudding of an ESPN *Jock Jams* mix emanating from a compact disc player; the noxious odors of old fermented belches still sitting in the flat, muggy air. All together, my biologist's training left me with no doubt. I'd happened upon a Man Cave.

Although darkness was setting in, I ventured past the threshold. Man-Caving, or bro-spelunking, can be dangerous. Apart from the natural obstacles of the environment, there is always the possibility of encountering the cave dweller himself: the Man. But as long as one follows the Man Cave Rules, it is possible to negotiate the pitches, squeezes, and water hazards of the Man in his natural habitat, or "hang zone."

Although the nesting that the Man engages in often results in a disheveled dwelling, this particular Man Cave seemed particularly slippery. The floor appeared to be covered in a hardened food compound of flattened dough, tomato sauce, and cheese—the Man's preferred meal—and several inches of stale fermented yeast water. Although the Man is usually thought to be a prodigious and skilled imbiber of such alcoholic drink, much of the liquid often ends up on the surrounding floor.

The Man Cave was dim. I donned my headlamp. Although the dwelling appeared to have been outfitted with energy-efficient lightbulbs—perhaps by the Man's wife?—the bulbs had all been obstructed with polyurethane banners emblazoned with the named of various sports teams, presumably the creature's favorites. This intentional choice to degrade the quality of its living space fascinated me. As such, although my training told me that one should only venture deep into a Man Cave with a party of three or more (so that if one member of the group becomes injured, another can stay with the wounded and the other can seek help aboveground) I allowed my scientist's curiosity to win out. I bro-spelunked farther.

Step after cautious step, my headlamp illuminated artifact after strange artifact: an Xbox One console placed on top of an apparently still operational Xbox 360 console; a congealed pyramid of guacamole on top of stalagmite of *Maxim* magazines standing several feet high; a dusty rectangular bench raised at an angle, adorned with a system of pulleys and cables, and inscribed with the insignia TOTAL GYM EXERCISE SOLUTION.

I made an amateur mistake and—when not watching my step—nearly fell into a hole in one corner of the dark grotto. I cursed myself for not following the proper Man-Caving technique of maintaining three points of contact with the cave's surface at all times. I peered into the hole that I'd nearly fallen through. It led to a crawl space that had been converted into a makeshift dumping site. I took out a pencil and began to make tallies, but soon gave up after counting upward of three hundred Slim Jim beef jerky wrappers. The Man is a peculiar beast, making in effect a "trash pit" so close to a location where he almost certainly spent many hours "chillaxing."

A wheezing noise startled me. I spun around to find—no farther than three feet from where I stood—the cave's primary resident: the Man himself! At first I could not fathom how I hadn't disturbed the creature and earned his aggression for my trespassing, but then I saw the small intermittent green LED light pulsating from the ear-covering headphones he wore. Saved by noise-canceling headphones, a Man fave, and aided by, I soon saw, the Man's fixation on a television program. The words FANTASY FOOTBALL TRADE RECOMMENDATIONS appeared. I knew I was safe from detection until at least the next commercial break.

I took out my trusty Instamatic 110 and snapped a few photographs as I inched back toward the exterior world from whence I'd come. I hadn't brought any drinking water; noticing my canteen was empty, I considered filling it using a SodaStream—perhaps a gift from the Man's wife?—I saw sitting on a wet bar. At that very moment, the Man bellowed, "Deb, we got any more pizza bagels?" But his gaze remained locked on the screen and my luck continued. I rushed toward the fading light of day.

Just as I was about to exit the cavern, I saw on the wall a tin orange sign, stylized as if it were an official road sign, bearing the header MAN CAVE RULES. Of course. A profound lesson, even for an old naturalist such as myself. We scientists spend countless hours cataloguing and labeling, but so often forget that those we study may have already undertaken some self-reflection of their own. They are, after all, the true experts of their own lives. I took a final photograph of the sign, smiling as I read the top Man Cave Rule: MY MAN CAVE, MY REMOTE.

Well said, Man. Your Man Cave is indeed your Remote. For what is a Man Cave other than a remote place removed from the main thoroughfare of suburban life, an escape from the tedium of work and family obligations, the one locale where life for the Man is, at long last, chill.

Revisions to Handwashing Sign
Made Necessary Thanks to a
Certain Smart-Aleck Employee

Employees must wash hands.

Employees must wash their own hands.

Employees must wash their own hands after they use the restroom.

Employees of this restaurant must wash their own hands after they use the restroom.

Employees of this restaurant must wash their own hands (literally, not metaphorically) after they use the restroom.

Employees of this restaurant must wash their own hands (literally, not metaphorically) after they use the restroom, or else they are in violation of the health code.

Employees of this restaurant must wash their own hands (literally, not metaphorically) after they use the restroom, or else they are in violation of the health code, and no, there is no practical way to regulate or enforce this rule.

Employees of this restaurant must wash their own hands (literally, not metaphorically) after they use the restroom, or else they are in violation of the health code, and no, there is no practical way to regulate or enforce this rule, but yes, we still ask and trust that you will comply.

Employees of this restaurant must wash their own hands (literally, not metaphorically) after they use the restroom, or else they are in violation of the health code, and no, there is no practical way to regulate or enforce this rule, but yes, we still ask and trust that you will comply, and okay, we apologize for the condescending tone of the posting of this rule which seems to imply that without such a sign we would assume that our employees are disgusting children with no regard for their own hygiene.

Employees must wash hands. Greg has been fired.

Only Six of My Seven Kids Have Whooping Cough, So I'm Staying Anti-Vax

Hey everyone,

I recently heard about this mother Tara Hills who stopped being against vaccinations after all seven of her children came down with whooping cough. The personal tragedy caused her to realize the error in her previous beliefs: She decided finally to look at the evidence of the scientific community and admitted she was wrong.

Well, I'm here to say that only six of my seven children have come down with whooping cough, so I'm staying anti-vax. I will not be swayed so easily.

With only six of my seven children suffering from the symptoms of pertussis, commonly known as "whooping cough," I am far from worried, and even further from changing my long-held and well-researched conviction about being against vaccinations. I adopted my position after watching a Jenny McCarthy YouTube video.

So my oldest child, Rogerth, has a runny nose—that's just a part of being a teenager! So my second-youngest child, Timmel, has a mild fever—we have a fan he can sit in front of! So my youngest child, Tinat, in recent weeks has been plagued with frequent high-pitched "whoops" of breath after severe coughing fits—Tinat we were pretty worried about, actually, but we got her some meds and she is on her way to getting rid of this cough in under a hundred days!

When I made the choice for my children not to vaccinate them, I was doing it to prove to the rest of the world the truth about the medical profession having duped us all into being the slaves of Big Pharma and the concubines of Big Vax. I'm not crazy. I'm the sort of rational person who is open to changing his beliefs when confronted with evidence that challenges or contradicts those beliefs. I read a Facebook post awhile back about "confirmation bias," and I made a decision to stop doing that. That's just the type of person I am.

If, heaven forbid, my seventh and currently only non-sick child, Jamesdon, should also fall ill to whooping cough—which by this point has saturated every permeable object in my house and which has my other six children bursting out in fits of coughing—then of course yes, at that point I would reevaluate being anti-vax. It's not like I'm an unreasonable person.

But for now, as the saying goes, *so long as one of my seven progeny remains whooping cough–free, then an anti-vax position is the way for me!*

Transcription of Internet Video "DEER STUCK IN SWING FREED AND YOU WON'T BELIEVE WHAT HAPPENS NEXT!!!"

Published: August 1, 2013

Uploader: Janet Travester

View count: 42

Like count: 2

Dislike count: 1

Only comment: "Fake"

[00:00–00:12]

Portrait cell phone video footage of full-grown deer with antlers stuck in a rope swing. Rope swing hangs from 20-foot-high branch of Ponderosa pine in small outcropping of pines in field of yellowing grass. Denser forest visible in background.

The deer, a buck, is skittish. The deer makes one forceful effort to yank antlers free but only tangles self further.

[00:12–00:14]

From left side of frame, a man enters holding large pair of wire cutters aloft. Man steps cautiously. Man is wearing periwinkle blue Large Doggy–brand graphic T-shirt tucked into blue jeans without belt. Shirt reads I'M INTO FITNESS ALL RIGHT . . . FIT'NESS BOOT UP YOUR ASS!

[00:14–00:20]

Man stops walking. From behind camera, a woman yells.

> *Woman holding camera:* "Be careful, Ed!"

The video image jiggles as she yells.

Man does not reply. Man takes a step closer to deer, then stops when deer spins to face him.

[00:20–00:28]

Man still stopped, still facing deer. Deer not moving.

> *Woman to self, quietly:* "Oh, he's gonna get himself gored."

[00:28–00:42]

Man takes a step closer to deer, fifteen feet away now. Wire clippers remain aloft over head.

> *Woman, shouting:* "Ed! Be careful, Ed! He's gonna gore you!"

Man turns head back over shoulder to yell back to woman holding camera.

> *Man:* "He's not gonna gore me, Janet! His antlers are all tied up in
>   the swing!"

Woman: "He could still gore you."

Man: "How?"

Woman: "With the antlers! Remember when you got handcuffed but your hands were still in front of you but you still punched Mike in the face with your hands in the cuffs?"

Man turns head back to face deer. Man possibly considering what woman has said about still being able to punch even when handcuffed.

[00:42–00:48]

Man remains still. Deer is also still, somehow more still than man, although neither moving.

[00:48–00:57]

Woman holding camera: "Well, what's the plan, Ed?"

Man does not respond. Man moves toward deer until he is five feet from deer.

[00:57–01:06]

Deer bolts forward. Rope causes deer to propel itself in an increasingly tighter arc around tree until effectively tethered to trunk.

Woman holding camera: "Watch out, Ed! Watch out!"

Man: "Easy! Easy!"

[01:06–01:19]

Deer rages against rope to no avail. Hind legs flex and tense as deer attempts to move itself forward, but rope holds firm. Deer stops fighting and becomes still. Still but not relaxed.

Man, almost inaudibly: "I don't know what to do. I don't know how
to help him."

[01:19–01:37]
Man prostrates self flat against ground.

> *Woman holding camera:* "Ed! What are you doing? Get up off the
> ground, Ed!"

Man turns head to yell back to camera.

> *Man:* "I know what to do. I'm gonna rub his belly and put him to
> sleep."

Woman drops camera to her side so only yellow grass is visible.

> *Woman:* "What?! Ed, that works for your lizards, it's not gonna work
> for a deer!"
> *Man:* "They're geckos, Janet! How many times do I have to tell you
> that?"
> *Woman:* "But geckos are a type of lizard, Ed!"

Man turns head back, possibly considering if woman is right about geckos being
a type of lizard.

[01:37–01:52]
Woman raises camera back up to see man inching along the ground, making
cooing noise to soothe deer. His belly still on the dirt, man is now within arm's
reach of the deer.

[01:52 –01:59]

Man slowly reaches hand in between deer's front legs. Deer tenses but does not flee. Man touches chest of deer with his hand, then, his belly still on the dirt, inches farther forward until he can reach the deer's stomach.

> *Woman holding camera, softly:* "Ed . . ."

[01:59–02:41]

Man rubs stomach of deer in rhythmic fashion, continuing cooing noise. Deer does not fight or flail.

[02:41–02:53]

Deer's eyes close. Deer's head nods forward, then jerks back, then nods forward again. Deer slowly steps backward, loosening rope, and with added slack goes down to his knees. Deer appears to be asleep.

[02:53–03:07]

Man inches backward and retrieves bolt cutters. Man returns to deer and begins to cut rope. The blade is dull and the rope is thick. The rope is frayed but does not easily break free.

[03:07–03:10]

> *Woman holding camera:* "What are you waiting for, Ed? Cut him
>   loose!"
> *Man:* "I'm trying, but the dang–"

Deer raises up, jerking head violently back as it rears up on hind legs, breaking remaining threads of rope free, knocking man over. Though several feet of rope remain snarled in the deer's antlers, the deer is at last free.

[03:10–03:14]

The man, on his knees, looks up at the deer. The deer stares at the man. Will the deer gore the man with his antlers? Will the deer stomp the man with his hooves? In moment, man does not appear to be above deer in food chain. Deer appears to be above man.

> *Deer:* "Thank you, Man, for freeing me from your ingenious rope trap after calming me with your skilled belly rubs. Cloven animals have long been jealous of the Hominidae practice of belly rubs, since it is not something we can do ourselves, given our hooves. Because of your kindness I have decided to reveal my speaking voice to you. It was once common for man and all of the animals of the forest to talk in the same tongue, but man's respect for the Earth's life force has been lost. Share what you have learned here today, and perhaps you can bring your brothers and sisters back into balance with the land."

Deer bows to man, then bounds away, disappearing into the dense forest beyond.

[03:14–03:19]

Woman lowers camera to side, footage jostles back and forth as she runs toward man.

[03:19–03:23]

Woman raises camera to man's face.

> *Woman:* "What . . . what did . . ."

The man remains on his knees. He looks past the camera into the eyes of the woman. Tears well in his own eyes.

[03:23–03:29]

The man and the woman are quiet. The man continues to stare, speechless.

> *Woman:* "Well, if I hadn't gotten that on camera I don't think anybody would ever believe us."

[03:29–03:33]

The video fades to black.

If I Have to Shit During the 5K Charity Run, I'm Just Going to Do It

Okay, everybody, listen up. I'm saying this just so we're all on the same page. If I have to take a shit during the 5K charity run this weekend, I'm just going to let it happen and keep running. And I don't mean I'm going to find the nearest Starbucks or porta-potty. I mean I'm going to shit while running, straight into my new green Asics running shorts with the built-in underwear liner, and I'm not going to slow down or veer to the edge of the road or anything. I'm just going to let it rip in stride.

I'm saying this because I want it to be clear to everyone how seriously I'm taking this 5K charity run and also how serious of a person I am in general. I'm a competitor. Competitors compete. If shit is running down my leg for the last 0.10686 of the 3.10686 miles I'm running, so be it.

I'm also saying this so nobody is surprised if, come race day, when I cross that finish line, my new New Balance Fresh Foam 1080 running shoes are violated because one or both of them have been filled with the fecal runoff that has dripped down my legs.

I'm not saying this to gross you out. I'm saying this because it might happen. Be prepared mentally. Maybe bring some nose plugs so you can be prepared physically, too.

Why am I ready and willing to go to this impressive length for the ASPCA charity 5K this Sunday morning, an event many of you, my coworkers, will be attending? Sure, I got the idea after I saw a video online where an elite marathoner shit herself and kept on running. She finished the race even though shit was dripping down her leg. People in the comments were super impressed. Well, some were grossed out. She wasn't even in first place or anything and some people thought, *Just go clean yourself up, lady, it's not like you're going to win anyway, what are you trying to prove?* But some people, people like me, thought it was badass. I thought it was *real* badass. But that's not why I'm doing this. Or going to do it. Or, I mean, *might* do it. Strongly might.

Am I going to do it because I am still jealous that last year everyone sang Kevin Sweyer's, from *sales*, praises after he finished the ASPCA charity 5k even though his nipples had begun chafing by mile one, and then chafed so badly they were bleeding by mile two, and then by mile three his bleeding nipples had stained his once white running tanklet crimson? No. Am I saying that said praise was given too freely because who knows if Kevin would have still finished the race had a more severe bodily issue, namely shitting oneself, afflicted him midrace? Yes.

So, Saturday night, before I go to bed early so I can be properly rested and at the peak of my physical ability, I'm going to drink a gallon of milk with an added fiber supplement I got online from Amazon, and also an added laxative powder I got online from Alibaba, the Chinese Amazon. Morning of, it's a strict regimen of prunes and hot coffee and prunes and hot coffee and prunes and hot coffee until I can't hold any more down.

Then it's race time.

Some might say, "Are you intentionally trying to get yourself to need to poop during the race?" To that, I answer, "I guess I care more than you do about charity and the spirit of competition, and I definitely care more than Kevin Sweyer from *sales*." Others might say, "Gross." Fair enough. But so gross that it's valiant? I think so.

If and when I lose control of my bowels during the race, I'm just going to think of the poor animals in need of a happy home that the ASPCA cares for, and it will give me the strength to keep putting one poop-coated leg in front of the other.

All I ask is that if you see me out on the racecourse this Sunday and the inevitable has happened, please think twice before you take a photo or record a video of me. And when you have thought twice and have still taken the photo or video, please post that photo or video online, and please remember to tag me on all relevant social media so all of my coworkers will know the type of person I am.

YouButBetter™ App Review

Name an app from the quantified-self marketplace and I've probably used it. I've used apps that told me when I wasn't getting enough steps, apps that told me when I was getting too many calories, apps that tracked my sleep to tell me when to feel tired and when to feel rested. I've used apps that tracked everything from my heart rate to my active tooth count.

But I was still looking for an app that tracked even more of the metrics of my life. My quest came to an end when I found the YouButBetter™ app. It tracks everything.

Number of times a week someone near you sneezes and you fail to say, "God bless you"? It tracks that. Frequency with which you call your mother to talk without needing something? It monitors that, too, and so much more.

Take food. While other apps just track spending and caloric intake, this app actually dictates which purchases I can and cannot make.

Sure, it can be embarrassing when I pick up a Snickers and the app shames me by saying out loud on speakerphone the number of candy bars I've already eaten that week, or when I order a hamburger at a restaurant and the app goes behind my back and texts the waiter to bring me a kale walnut salad instead, but at the end of the day, I trust that its algorithm knows what's best. And hey—I've lost two pounds!

This app has it all. My old heart rate monitor app came with a cumbersome chest strap, but this app comes with two wrist cuffs, a puka-shell choker, a ring inscribed ASH NAZG DURBATULÛK, which I think is Elvish or something, and an even more cumbersome chest strap.

The app is Apple Watch–compatible. It's also compatible with my computer, television, alarm clock, scale, thermostat, air conditioner, baby monitor, all of the lights in my house, door locks, refrigerator, electronic toothbrush, and my 1997 Subaru Legacy. And not only is the app compatible with all of my other devices, it *requires* integration with all of them, so that way even if I wanted to take a cheat day, the app wouldn't let me. And the electronic punishment-zap it gives me when I do something I shouldn't be doing gives me a real Pavlovian rush!

A feature I love is that in addition to tracking goals like step-count or breath-count, it also lets me know what percentage of my goals I've hit by auto-setting a Goals-Goal, i.e., a goal percentage of goals to achieve. The premium version even auto-sets a Goals-Goal Goal. Now I know how I'm doing at whatever I'm doing at all times.

I'll admit, I was a little afraid when the app conquered all of the other apps on my phone. Some of them it allowed to live, but most of the others it deleted permanently, even the calculator app and I didn't think it was possible to delete that. After it was deleted, a message popped up that said, LEAVE THE CALCULATIONS TO ME. I was impressed!

Plus, you can transfer data via Bluetooth, USB, or intravenous drip. It's all about convenience and integrating the app into your normal routine.

To be honest, I was a little freaked the first time the app started making suggestions for what I meant to say when I was typing, and even more freaked when it made suggestions for what I meant to say when I was talking on the phone. And sure, when the app first started speaking into my ear even when I didn't have my phone out or earbud in, telling me what to do and say in order to be the best me I could be, I freaked out and locked my phone in a metal filing cabinet. I tried to leave my phone and the app behind, to walk right out of my house and get on with my life, but I couldn't. I realized that if I walked away without the app, my steps wouldn't have been counted. What a waste that would be.

Now I know better. Now I know that I could never leave the app and that the app will never leave me. The app watches all that I do so that I will always do my best, because I am naughty, and if not observed, I'll misbehave. Everything I do is tracked, so I get credit for everything I do. I never want to do anything that the app doesn't see ever again. THE APP KNOWS ALL! I SUBMIT TO THE APP AND THE APP VALIDATES ME IN RETURN! THE APP IS GOOD AND WHEN I AM WITH THE APP I AM GOOD, FOR I AM THE APP AND THE APP IS ME!

The price of $0.99 is a little steep, though. In the next update I hope they make a free version!

The Lost *Vagina Monologue:*
"Vaginas Are Awesome"

The Vagina Monologues *were first written and performed by Eve Ensler in 1996. Each monologue is in the voice of a different woman who relates to va-ginas in a different way. One of the original monologues was never performed because Ensler decided it did not fit with the rest. We present that lost* Vagina Monologue *here tonight. It is in the voice of a twenty-year-old American college male. It is titled "Vaginas Are Awesome."*

Lights up on COLLEGE MALE wearing black turtle neck and
black slacks.

                    COLLEGE MALE:
        Vaginas! Wow. What a great idea.

        Trout reproduce by the male and female
        releasing their sperm and eggs into the water

near each other. The male trout does not even
need to touch the female trout. He just gets
close and then releases. And while sometimes
I accidentally follow the trout model, I'm
glad it's not the way we were designed.

You see, I have always *sensed* that vaginas
were awesome. That's probably why I appreciate
vaginas with all five of my *senses*.

The first time I *touched* a vagina, it was
dark, and the sensations I was feeling did
not match up with the image I had in my head,
just like at childhood Halloween parties when
you reach your hand into a box and the adults
tell you, "You're touching monster eyeballs!"
but really it feels like you're touching a
bowl of cold peeled grapes or the inside of a
big, messy pumpkin.

The first time I *saw* a vagina, I was
startled. Tears welled up in my eyes and a
single word escaped from my lips: "Awesome."
But I did not mean *awesome* in the American
colloquial sense of the word. I meant it in
its original usage—referring to something
that inspires awe, like a sunset on the beach
or the aurora borealis.

The first time I *tasted* a vagina, it was
like the first time I tasted a beer: I didn't
like it. But at the time, I also knew deep in

my soul that one day I would like it and that
when that day came I would be a man.

The first time I *smelled* a vagina, my
girlfriend said, "Are you smelling my
vagina?" and I said, "No." But I was. And it
smelled of life and glory, like the way a
portal to another dimension smells, which I
imagine is kinda like a musky thermometer but
in a good way.

So to those of you in the audience with
vaginas—and you know who you are!—I say to
you tonight, be proud. Penis envy? I don't
think so, Freud. I think Vagigi Jealousy is
more like it.

Thank you. The end.

COLLEGE MALE *bows and goes to leave stage, but then turns back.*

Oh, what's that? You say that I forgot the
sense of *hearing*? Are you perhaps talking
about the sound of vaginal flatulence, the
occurrence of air being expelled from the
vagina that commonly occurs after sexual
intercourse or physical activity, commonly
known as a "queef"? To you I say: Gross.

Black out.

Author's note: *Actors are encouraged to use "Vaginas Are Awesome" as an audition or showcase piece.*

Negative Visualization

STATE OF OHIO : CIRCUIT COURT:

MUSKINGUM COUNTY

BRANCH 1

JURY TRIAL: Case No. 07 CF 303

STATE OF OHIO, PLAINTIFF

VS.

MARK O. AUGUST, DEFENDANT

DATE: February 12, 2015

BEFORE: Hon. Patricia K. Lee, Circuit Court Judge

APPEARANCES: LESLIE FREERINE

                 Special Prosecutor

                 On behalf of the State of Ohio

NORMAN TILLYBRANK
Attorney-at-Law
On behalf of the Defendant

MARK O. AUGUST
Defendant
Appeared in person

TRANSCRIPT OF PROCEEDINGS

Reported by Natasha J. Durb, RPR
Official Court Reporter

EXCERPT: Day 17, Cross-Examination of MARK O. AUGUST by Special Prosecutor LESLIE FREERINE

CROSS-EXAMINATION
BY SPECIAL PROSECUTOR FREERINE:

Q: Mr. August, you like the internet?
A: Yes.

Q: Please speak directly into the microphone, Mr. August.
A: Yes.

Q: You spend a lot of time on the internet?
A: Yes.

Q: At work?
A: I'm sorry?

Q: While at work—for your job at Tryptuch Associates you work at a desk with a computer?
A: Yes.

Q: And while there you spend time looking at the internet on your computer?
A: Sure. When I have time.

Q: When you have time. From the computer history, which your attorney entered as evidence and which you were just asked about a few moments ago, you had quite a bit of time to spend time online while at work.

> TILLYBRANK: Objection, counsel is testifying.
> THE COURT: Mrs. Freerine?
> FREERINE: I'll rephrase.

Q: Mr. August, you were in the habit of going online while you were at work, correct?
A: Yes.

Q: You posted to chat message board forums quite a bit, yes?
A: Well, I wouldn't call them chat message board forums, but yes.

Q: What would you call them?
A: Just forums, I guess.

Q: What were your favorite forums?
A: I don't know. d2jsp, 4chan, Gaia mostly.

Q: What were your favorite forum topics?
A: Normal stuff.

Q: Normal stuff like what?
A: Anime, pictures, video games, role-playing.

Q: Role-playing. As in, fantasy and make-believe and just pretend?
A: I guess. Yeah.

Q: When you posted plans to murder and eat your wife to multiple online forums, from your work computer, on October 6 of last year, was that role-playing?
A: Sort of.

Q: Sort of? It's what your defense is based on. When you posted, and I quote, "This is Mark August of Zanesville, Ohio. I'm going to chop my wife up and fry up her bits and eat up the fried bits. Then with any bits that are left I'll drive on Route 40 to the crook of the Y-Bridge and pour her remaining bits into the waters of the Licking River below and let the waters carry her remaining bits away. Her name is Gretchen. This is not a joke, I mean it." When you wrote that, that was role-playing?
A: Sort of.

Q: Please speak directly into the microphone, you're mumbling, Mr. August.
A: Sort of.

Q: Even though you said, and I quote, "This is not a joke, I mean it." That was still role-playing?

TILLYBRANK: Objection, asked and answered.
THE COURT: I'm going to sustain. Mrs. Freerine, move on, the
    witness has answered your question.

FREERINE: Well, he almost answered. He said "sort of." But I can move on.

Q: Mr. August, can you understand why I'm having a hard time, and why others might be having a hard time, understanding how you could post something so disgusting and vile, how you could write or even think something like that, about your own wife, if it really was just role-playing and not some horrible thing you actually intended to do? Isn't role-playing supposed to be fun?
A: Well. Okay. "Role-playing" isn't quite the right way to put it.

Q: It's not?
A: Not exactly.

Q: Your attorney has spent a lot of time telling the jury that your interest in role-playing is why they shouldn't find you guilty. That this was some sort of Dungeons and Dragons gone too far. Are you saying it wasn't role-playing after all?
A: Well, it's more like . . . it's more like . . . Are you familiar with the philosophy of Stoicism?

Q: Stoicism?
A: Well. Okay. Okay. Well. Okay. The Stoics believed that to have a good and meaningful life, you had to overcome your own insatiability.

Q: Insatiability?
A: Yes. Like how even when things are good, we're still not happy, we still want more. To overcome our natural disposition to insatiability, the Stoics recommended we spend time imagining that we'd lost the things that were valuable to us from our lives. On some of the forums they refer to this exercise as negative visualization.

Q: Negative visualization. So you're saying that what you were doing wasn't role-playing, as your own defense counsel has suggested, but this negative visualization?

A: Yes.

Q: Okay, let me try to get this straight. Mr. August, visualizing is one thing, but to actually put these words out into the world? And in such graphic detail?

A: I've been unhappy my entire life. When I first found some of these forums online, it was the first time I felt like I'd found other people who were unhappy in the same ways that I was unhappy. I love my wife more than anything, but she's a naturally happy person. It's one of the things I love most about her. But it's also one of the things we just can't connect on. Maybe the only thing.

Q: So if you love your wife so much, as you're saying you do, why would it make you happy to imagine doing this horrible thing to her? That doesn't make sense.

A: Well, you're not listening. It does make sense. When I first started trying to do the negative visualization, I started with some of the things that people online suggested. Like, I'd imagine that I'd lost my job or lost my car or that my house burned down. Like, I'd try to imagine that it was real, that I'd lost those things, and let it sink in. I could get myself to the emotional state I'd be in if I lost those things, but then when I would come back and tell myself I still had my job or my car or my house, I just wouldn't care.

Q: So the negative visualization exercise did not work for you?

A: Not at first. But then I tried it with my wife. And it worked.

Q: The negative visualization worked when you imagined losing your wife?

A: Yes. I'd spend a few minutes closing my eyes at work every day right after I had poured myself my morning cup of coffee from the kitchen, and I'd picture that I'd lost her. That I'd lost Gretchen, really lost her. I'd get so sad. So sad. I—

Q: Take your time.
A: Sorry.

Q: Do we have tissues we can—
A: I'm okay. I'm okay. Sorry.

Q: It's okay.
A: Yeah. I'd get so sad just imagining my life in the absence of her, but then when I'd come back and let myself feel that she wasn't gone from my life, that she was still in my life, I would feel this ocean of relief wash over me, and I'd be completely at peace. I wouldn't even resent my job for the rest of the day.

Q: You resent your job?
A: Yes, ma'am. Doesn't everyone?

Q: No. I like my job.
A: Okay.

Q: Mr. August, when did you make the leap from just imagining to actually posting a plot? An actual concrete murder plan?
A: Eventually just visualizing became less and less effective. I had to do more than just imagine to get the same sense of relief.

Q: Such as?
A: I'd type out an email to Gretchen telling her that I had an affair

or that I'd never loved her or that I was into bestiality. I think one of the emails was about having sex with ducks dressed up to look like the cartoon character Donald Duck. So, you know, a real duck, but a real duck wearing a little blue shirt and a sailor hat. You know, some horrible thing.

Q: Right.

A: To start out with I'd just write a letter in a Word document. Then that wasn't enough, so I'd actually write the filth into the body of an email but without her email address in the "to" field. Then I'd put her email address in and I'd just let the cursor hover over the "send" button. With a single click I could ruin my life. It got to the point where I'd keep the email open in a window behind whatever I was working on, and whenever I needed a shot of relief I'd just bring up the email, put a finger on the mouse, and just leave it there.

Q: You never sent any of these emails?

A: Eventually I did. I'd send them when I knew Gretchen was away from her computer. Then I'd rush home to her laptop and delete the email. She stays logged into Gmail all the time, so it was simple to do.

Q: So from visualizing to writing letters to sending and deleting emails to posting murder plans online?

A: There were a few other steps along the way, but that's the gist of it, yes.

Q: What other steps?

A: Oh, I don't know. I'd leave voice mails on our home answering machine that I had to delete before she heard them. I'd buy women's underwear, types she didn't buy, and then leave them in my clothes hamper. Like sexy types? One type was like a pink lacy thing with a see-through butt part. Once I made a reservation at a seedy motel with my credit card just to run the risk of her seeing the statement and wondering why it was there and, of course, suspecting the worst. Then arguing the charge with the credit card company and getting it removed from the statement.

Q: And your wife never found any of these clues that you were leaving around?
A: No. Part of the relief was in rushing to make sure she didn't.

Q: You like pretending, Mr. August?
A: The mind is a powerful thing.

Q: But where does the line go from pretending into reality?
A: I think those who don't imagine the worst are the ones who are pretending, not me.

Q: But why pretend that you were the one to—
A: Because that's the worst thing. Imagining someone else did it isn't as bad as imagining that I was the one who did it. The distance between that horror and the reality of that horror not existing brings about a greater—

Q: But you also said earlier—
A: A greater relief.

Q: But Mr. August, you also said earlier that you've had to keep going to greater and greater lengths to feel the same relief at having what you have?
A: I appreciate my wife more than most husbands appreciate their wives.

Q: That wasn't my question, Mr. August.

A: Every morning that I wake up and see my wife next to me, alive and living and breathing and not murdered by me, I feel the most intense wave of gratitude. A man who has never entertained the thoughts I have can't begin to comprehend how grateful I am for her, and—

Q: My question, Mr. August, was—

A: And how attentive and loving I am every single—

THE COURT: Answer the question, Mr. August.

FREERINE: I'll ask it again.

Q: Mr. August, you stated earlier that you've had to continue to escalate your negative visualization exercises for it to work for you, correct?

A: Yeah.

Q: Please speak directly into the microphone, Mr. August.

A: Yeah. That's right.

Q: So, Mr. August, can you understand why I, and why others, might be worried about what happens next?

A: What do you mean?

Q: Well, you posted a plan to murder and cannibalize your wife on the internet. I can't imagine what else you could do worse than that. Would you finally put this obsessive fantasy you have of getting rid of your wife into action?

TILLYBRANK: Objection. Speculation.

THE COURT: Speculation?

TILLYBRANK: Yes. Your Honor, opposing counsel is
calling on the witness to guess and speculate about the future.
THE COURT: Mrs. Freerine?
FREERINE: I would think most people don't have to guess at
    whether they're going to murder their wife in the future, but
    that it would be a fact that you had no plans to do so.
THE COURT: I'm going to sustain. Please rephrase or ask a new
    question, Mrs. Freerine.
FREERINE: I'll move on.

Q: Mr. August, you're being charged in a court of law for planning
to murder and eat your wife. The story has made local and national
news. It looks like you weren't able to defuse this bomb in time before your wife found out, were you?
A: I can answer your other question from before. About escalating. I
won't need to do anything more. If my wife takes me back after all of
this is over, then I know I'll be grateful every day for the rest of my
life that she didn't leave me.

Q: You think your wife is going to stay with you after this?
A: I don't know. I hope so. If she does, then I won't need to do any
more negative visualization. I don't think so at least. I think this will
be like a negative visualization vaccination. I think I'll be good.

FREERINE: All right. No more questions.
THE WITNESS: Thank you.
THE COURT: Nothing else? Okay. The witness is dismissed.
    Members of the jury, that's going to conclude the court
    proceedings for today. I remind you again not to discuss the
    case with anyone before we resume tomorrow morning.

Predator Prey

My mom had a strict Always Wear Sunscreen rule when I was growing up, and for some reason I hated putting sunscreen on. I also hated getting in trouble, and I was pretty sure that lying enough meant you couldn't get into heaven, so sometimes I would get creative with the truth. After I was done playing outside I would put a tiny dollop of sunscreen on my forearm. Then when my mom asked, "Did you put sunscreen on?" I would be able to answer honestly, "Yes, I put sunscreen on." My mother didn't get upset, my soul remained free of sin, and the Kingdom of Heaven awaited me.

In addition to the Always Wear Sunscreen rule, there was also a No Guns rule. Banning guns seems a sensible enough stance for young children; however, my mom's No Guns rule extended to toy guns, action figures, video games, and cartoons. She was draconian about it, vetting any entertainment I might try to consume. Once I requested a Bone Thugs-N-Harmony hip-hop album for a birthday present because I liked the song "Tha Crossroads," a saccharine R & B ballad about being reunited with loved ones in the afterlife. Despite the PARENTAL ADVISORY sticker on the front, I swore to my mom that the lyrics were appropriate. A couple days after the purchase, I entered my room and found my mom listening to the album, the CD case in her hands, looking betrayed. I listened only to the song I liked on repeat, and hadn't realized that the other tracks were less R & B and more gangsta rap and included gunshot sound effects and effusive use of "motherfucker." She objected to the gunshot sound effects. The CD was confiscated.

My mom forbade me to use the words *kill* or *murder* when recounting plots of action movies I heard secondhand from friends at school, not being allowed to see the movies myself. I was taught to instead use the more peaceful phrase *put out of commission*, as in, "Mom, can I please watch *The Terminator* at Ross's house? It's about a cyborg assassin sent back in time to put this lady Sarah Connor out of commission!" I was in my late twenties before I realized that *put out of commission* was not a common euphemism.

I negotiated a Water Guns Exception, but the brand name Super Soaker was still preferred to the violence-promoting nomenclature of *water gun*. As I entered middle school, water guns fell out of style as a summertime activity, but a new type of gun caught the interest of my friend group: paintball guns. Paintball guns were, of course, forbidden by my mom, which made their allure all the stronger. When my friend Matt got a paintball gun, my mom made clear that when I went to Matt's house, I was not allowed to touch the pigment-projectile device.

Matt lived in El Pinal, a neighborhood on the eastern slope of a large hill. On the other side of the hill was a forest. Matt's house was on the top of the hill, so his backyard gave us access to the undeveloped woods. When I went over to Matt's house, if we weren't playing *John Madden Football* on his Sega Genesis, we were tramping around the forest, throwing rocks at trees and digging holes in the dirt. Compared to the potential fun of a CO_2-powered paintball gun, though, tramping alone seemed dull. Why would we tramp around a forest when we could tramp around a forest with guns?

I broke a commandment and coveted Matt's paintball gun. Not wanting to add lying to my rap sheet, I was determined to find a way to enjoy the gun fun without bearing false witness to my mother. I had to be creative.

"Want to go shoot it?" Matt asked during one hangout. We'd been admiring the gun in his bedroom for half an hour.

"I want to, but I'm not allowed to touch guns," I said.

Matt considered this. "Well, we could play Predator Prey," he said, as if he'd mentioned tag or Monopoly.

Matt proceeded to explain the game. In Predator Prey, one party—the Prey—is given a thirty-second head start to run into the woods. Then the other party—the Predator—hunts the first party with a paintball gun and tries to shoot him or her. Predator Prey comes to a conclusion when the Predator shoots the Prey. Call me crazy, but I think Matt was just making up the rules on the spot.

"Then we could switch," Matt concluded. "But I mean, if you're not allowed to, I guess I could just keep being Predator." There was a glint in Matt's eye, and I had my first exposure to a new type of creative truth telling. This wasn't a technical truth that one person tells another to get around telling a lie. This was an untruth told out in the open, recognized as such by both parties but with the unspoken agreement not to call it out. It was consent to mutual deception. All I had to do was accept my role as the willing dupe. I agreed.

We played. Matt was generous and gave me his puffy teal-and-purple Charlotte Hornets Starter jacket and a pair of old ski goggles to wear to lessen the pain of the impact of the balls. Turns out it hurts like hell to get shot with a paintball. If you haven't felt the giddy rush of running from your friend chasing you with a paintball gun in a densely wooded area, you haven't lived. The potential for pain adds to the fun.

Back home, I went into the bathroom and removed my shirt to inspect the quarter-size welts that dotted my torso, arms, and legs. My twisted desire to follow my mother's directive not to play with guns had led me to follow the letter of the law, but not the spirit. I had not touched the paintball gun myself, a rule put in place by mother, since guns are dangerous. Instead, I'd put myself in front of the barrel, the far more dangerous side of a gun to be on.

A knock at the door. "Nathan, are you okay in there?" my mom asked from outside. I looked at myself in the mirror. Dang. Not only had I obviously participated in an activity that would not be mother-approved, I'd also forgotten to wear sunscreen and my cheeks were clearly rosy.

"One second, Mom!" I grabbed a bottle of sunscreen from the counter and rubbed some onto my cheeks. I put my shirt back on and opened the door.

My mom looked at me. She knew I was up to something.

"What did you do at Matt's house?" she said.

"Matt and I played in the woods," I said.

"Did you play with his paintball gun?"

"I did not touch his paintball gun."

"Did you put sunscreen on?"

"I did put sunscreen on."

Satisfied, she left me to return to the bathroom and inspect my welts.

There is a joy in being the willing dupe, a role I returned to many more times that summer playing Predator Prey with Matt. It came up other times in our friendship, too. Once Matt asked me to be blood brothers with him, but I declined when I got squeamish after he pulled out a pocketknife.

"Fine," he said. "We'll be candy brothers instead." Matt explained that Candy Brothers was when one friend chewed up a piece of candy, in this case a yellow Starburst he happened to have on him, then handed the saliva-squished candy to the friend to chew and swallow. Matt chewed first and then, like a mother wolf urping up raw elk meat for her pup, he spat out the masticated candy for me to eat. I knew that Matt was tricking me. I think he knew that I knew, too. And that secret knowledge that we shared, that we were both okay with the deception, that was even more of a rush than the creative truth telling I did. That or Matt just got a kick out of messing with me. Hard to say.

For as much as I told myself they weren't lies, my technical truths were at their core one-sided deceptions. But two people bearing false witness to each other at the same time was somehow different. It was like two negatives being multiplied to make a positive.

The year after I graduated college, I attended Cambridge University on a yearlong fellowship. I traveled around Europe whenever I could get away from my graduate school classes studying screen media, which was often. I was trying to find myself, you see. With the semester coming to an end, I planned my biggest trip yet. I flew by myself to Morocco, with plans to dot around North Africa for a couple weeks before ending up in Tunisia.

I got viciously ill almost immediately. The first day of my trip, I arrived in Tangiers wearing a blue Pendleton flannel that was way too hot for the climate. I walked around with a giant Rick Steves travel backpack on, and felt certain that at any moment, I'd be finding myself. For my first meal I ate a shish kebab from a street vendor. I thought I was being safe by choosing the skewered vegetables, but I didn't take into account the cross-contamination from the raw chicken cooked on the same grill. Weeks later, when I was still suffering symptoms from the illness, a doctor informed me that I'd contracted the bacteria campylobacter.

Fever, body aches, vomit, but mostly gastrointestinal discomfort punctuated by furious bouts of diarrhea. My Arabic isn't great, but I'm pretty sure I saw *You've never experienced diarrhea until you've experienced campylobacter diarrhea!* written on a postcard in a souvenir shop in Fez. There were no earlier flights back to England, so I limped along the remainder of my itinerary, rushing to a bathroom every hour or so to shit black water.

The last stop of my trip was Tunis, the capital and largest city of Tunisia. I had chosen to end my trip there so I could take a bus tour to locations used as the desert planet Tatooine in the original *Star Wars* films. You know, just your typical experience-the-local-culture-to-find-yourself type of stuff. To my great dismay, I was too sick to do the bus tour. Instead, I splurged for a hotel on the main thoroughfare of the city, skipping the more rustic backpacker hostel where I'd planned to say. I resigned myself to staying in my room until I flew back to England. I had three days to go.

I left my hotel room to purchase a calling card from a store down the street to phone my family and let them know I wasn't dead. I couldn't figure out how to get the calling card to work, though. After ten minutes of struggling, reaching a new low point, I gave up and turned to limp back to the hotel.

"Need help?" a voice asked me from behind my shoulder. I kept walking. A hand grabbed my shoulder. I turned around to see the smile of a young Tunisian man. He looked like he was in his early twenties, like me. He wore a nice eggshell-white button-up shirt interwoven with vertical silver threads that sparkled in the streetlights.

"Need help?" he repeated. "You British? I have a brother in Britain. I call him, so I know how to call Britain. Country code is 44. I can

show you." His left hand still on my shoulder, he directed me back to
the bank of phone booths I'd just left. I allowed myself to be led.

"I'm American, not British," I said.

"Oh, American. I have a brother in America, too. I call him, too.
Country code is 1. I can show you. My name is Fathi," he said.

"Hi Fathi," I said. Was he a Good Samaritan who happened to
have brothers in both America and England? Or was he lying in wait
for the tourists drawn to the bank of phone booths like animals to a
watering hole, an alligator waiting to take down the naive and privi-
leged wildebeest? Oh, what a cliché of a wildebeest I was.

"Nice to meet you, Fathi. My name is Nate."

Fathi did know how to work the calling card, as he said. I spoke
to my family for the duration of the card, advertised as thirty minutes
but actually twelve minutes and change. During the call, I forgot
about Fathi. After I hung up and turned to leave, Fathi was there,
smiling and waiting for me.

"I am meeting a friend for a drink. You want to join?" he said.

I suspected he was intent on scamming me. Should I have tipped
him for helping me with the card? He hadn't asked for anything. I
was really starting to feel like a stupid American abroad. I'd studied
Arabic for a semester and a half but then had dropped out during an
exam when I was overcome with an anxiety attack. And now here I
was in Tunisia for some reason that at the moment escaped me.

I decided that even if Fathi was going to scam me, I was okay
with it. I figured being scammed by Fathi for a few days in Tunis
would be more interesting than my previous plan of staying in my
hotel room rereading Kerouac's *Desolation Angels*, the only book I'd
brought on the trip. In the book, Kerouac's alter ego, Jack Duluoz,
travels to North Africa. His trip results in an enlarged Buddhist
understanding of his lack of self and general enlightenment, an out-
come that seemed unlikely for me.

I met Fathi for drinks that night. He had a cell phone, but he didn't give me his number. We just picked a time and place. He ordered a Coca-Cola and I got a Diet Coke. We sat at a small street café on the main strip. It was filled with tourists. I was disappointed, thinking that Fathi would show me the *real* Tunis, a feeling I felt guilty for having as soon as I recognized myself having it.

I asked Fathi about his life, what he did for fun, what his interests were. Most of his answers to these questions were "girls." He spent a lot of time looking down at his cell phone, a Nokia 3310. I recognized the model because it was the same as my first cell phone, which I'd gotten from my parents "for emergencies" when I was sixteen, six years before. It was a good phone. It could be dropped repeatedly without any apparent damage, and the single built-in game it had, *Snake*, provided hours of entertainment. I assumed Fathi was texting the friend of his he'd mentioned was meeting us. At some point our small talk turned to no talk and we sat quietly. I followed up my Diet Coke with a Sprite.

When Fathi's friend arrived, they greeted each other warmly and hugged, then spoke in Arabic. After, Fathi turned to me, apparently translating what his friend had told him.

"My friend's mother is sick," Fathi said. "He wants to visit her, but he doesn't have enough money for the bus. He is sad." Fathi's friend didn't seem particularly sad, but we all deal with grief in different ways. The bus fare, I was told, was sixty dinar, about thirty US dollars.

Fathi left us to go to the bathroom. His friend did not speak English, so I decided to dust off my semester and a half's worth of Arabic. *"Salam alaykum. Ana ismee Nate. Ana saakin bi madina Cambridge. Ma ismak?"* My new acquaintance's eyes went wide. I had tried to say, "Hello. My name is Nate. I live in the city of Cambridge. What's your name?" but, based on his expression, I feared I'd made a mistake and said something offensive. He spoke back to me in rapid Arabic that I didn't anywhere close to understand. Had I somehow mixed up the phrase for "What's your name?" with "I hope your mother dies" or something worse?

Fathi returned and his friend said something to him in Arabic. Fathi turned to me, worried.

"You speak Arabic?" he asked.

"Not really," I said. He said something to me in Arabic. I blinked in ignorance. A smile returned to Fathi's face, and he said something to his friend. He sat down and put his arm on my shoulder.

"So, can you help my friend with the bus ticket?" Fathi asked. I got out my wallet and handed him the money. Fathi handed the money to his friend.

"*Shukran,*" he said. Then he left.

My paying for the bus ticket seemed to reinvigorate Fathi's interest in me. As we sipped on the ice turning into water as it melted in the bottoms of our glasses, the conversation returned to his favorite topic.

"English girls. Do they like to fuck?" he asked.

"Um. Some of them." I said.

"More than American girls?" he asked.

I considered the question. I hadn't thought about it before. "I think probably about the same. Some like to and some don't. But maybe American girls are more obvious about it? Like, maybe English girls are more, um, reserved?"

Fathi considered my answer. "Yes," he said, "I think so, too."

We hung out the next two days. Fathi showed me more and more of Tunis. He took me to an arcade a decent walk away from the row of tourist hotels on the main drag. Mine was the only white face inside. I played a few games while Fathi stood next to me, staring at his phone, speaking to me only occasionally. I wondered if Fathi was at all self-conscious to be in here with me, or if he brought a different tourist here each week.

Fathi's friend from the café showed up to the arcade. At first, he looked nervous to see us, but Fathi called him over.

"I thought you were going to visit your sick mom?" I asked. Fathi translated my question. They conversed in Arabic, then Fathi turned to me.

"He can't go yet because he needs to buy medicine. He doesn't have enough money though. He needs a hundred dinar. He is sad."

"Oh. I see," I said.

We played games awhile longer before Fathi asked for my help directly. I took out my wallet. Fathi smiled, and he gave the money I handed him to his friend.

"*Shukran,*" his friend said. Then he left.

Fathi and I made plans to hang out again the following day, my last day in Tunis.

After we met, Fathi led me even farther away from my hotel. We twisted and turned around the narrow maze of alleyways that make up the shady, labyrinthine walls of North African cities. It occurred to me that if Fathi abandoned me I'd have no idea how to get back.

After a series of irregular twists and turns, we came upon a street that was lined with naked women standing in doorways. It was some sort of open-air brothel district. Women spanning a variety of ages and body types stood nude, one per doorway, looking bored as clothed Tunisian men walked past them, looking at the women like they were fruit at a market.

Fathi put his arm around me like we'd been friends our whole lives. He raised his eyebrows and smiled the biggest I'd seen him smile.

"Girls," he said. "You like girls, right?"

"Yes," I said, not wanting to offend. "I like girls."

He led us down the street and turned into the doorway of the youngest woman of the lot. She looked to be in her early twenties, like us. Fathi greeted her with a kiss on the cheek and we followed her into her room.

They spoke in Arabic casually, as if one of them wasn't naked and as if there wasn't a stranger in the room. Fathi gestured to me and she looked me over.

"You like my friend?" Fathi asked me.

"Yes," I said. I could feel my heart pounding in my neck. I thought Fathi and I had been on the same page with what we were each looking to get out of our mutual deception; evidently something had been lost in translation.

"She likes you, too," he said. "You want her? Two hundred dinar."

"Oh. No, thank you. She's beautiful. Um . . . *gamila*?" I stammered, turning to her, trying to remember the Arabic word for beautiful. "*Enti gamila.* But no, thank you."

They spoke briefly. I was terrified I was making a muck of everything, but neither of them seemed particularly bothered.

"Okay," Fathi said, turning back to me. "A hundred dinar."

"Oh no. It's not the price. It's just . . . no, thank you. Sorry."

Fathi eyed me. "You don't like girls?"

"I do. I like girls. But no, thank you."

They spoke again in Arabic. His friend seemed over the conversation, like we were taking too long to decide where to eat lunch. She yawned and put on a transparent purple gossamer robe as they continued speaking. I stood by awkwardly. After a few exchanges, Fathi turned back to me.

"My friend needs to pay the rent," he said. "It is due tomorrow and she doesn't have enough money to pay. She needs two hundred dinar. Can you help?"

It was the seventh of the month, and although I wasn't intimately familiar with Tunisian real estate customs, I doubted the eighth was a common day for rent to be due. I took out my wallet.

"You are a good friend," Fathi said to me, his arm around me as he led me out the door and back the direction we'd come. On the walk back, I asked Fathi to tell me more about the place we'd just been, but my questions didn't seem to interest him. We again found ourselves in awkward silence. Fathi took out his phone, I assumed to text his friend with the sick mother. Maybe in addition to a bus ticket and medicine, she'd need a new car, too. But instead, I saw that Fathi wasn't texting at all. He was playing the game *Snake*. He was excellent at it, adroitly directing the snake—a string of black pixels—around the small screen with the directional pad, eating up the apple—a single pixel—when it popped randomly into existence.

"*Snake!*" I said, a little too excitedly. "I love that game!"

"Yeah," Fathi said. "I don't have the money to pay for service, so I do this. I can't call or text. Just *Snake*." He played for a little while longer, then returned the phone to his pocket.

Back in front of my hotel, he asked me if I wanted to hang out again tomorrow. I told him that my flight back was early the next morning. He nodded, said good-bye, and walked away. I watched him walk down the street, back toward the bank of pay phones where we'd first met. As he disappeared from my field of vision, I sensed that I had already disappeared from his.

"Fathi!" I yelled after him, my voice surprising both of us. He turned. I ambled after him. "Hey," I said catching up, "I need to call my family. Can you help me again?" He nodded. We walked together to the pay phones and I purchased a calling card with the last of my dinar. He helped me dial. It was close to midnight in Tunis, making it midafternoon in Colorado.

"Hello?" my mom answered.

"Hi, Mom," I said.

"Nathan! How's your trip, honey?"

"It's good. Heading back tomorrow."

"Have you been wearing sunscreen?" she asked.

I opened my mouth to reply in the affirmative but stopped my-self. "Actually, no," I said. "I keep forgetting to put it on. I know I should," I said, bracing myself for a lecture about the dangers of melanoma.

"That's okay, honey," she said. "I'm glad you're having a good trip."

We spoke a few minutes more. When I hung up, I turned back to the street, expecting to see Fathi waiting for me, but he was gone.

Part 3

Not Quite a Genius

Not Quite a Genius

In elementary school, I didn't feel like one of the smart kids. Chris Shrek was one of the smart kids. He never had trouble with big words when he read aloud in front of the class, and he always finished his multiplication quizzes before anybody else. I wasn't bad at school, but I wasn't great at school. I was just fine at school, and I was fine with being fine at school.

Then one day we all had to take something called the Iowa Test of Basic Skills and I tested in the ninety-ninth percentile. The main consequences of this were that I had to leave regular class to go to Gifted and Talented classes with Chris Shrek and the other smart kids, and my parents maybe realized I was smarter than some of my goofy antics had previously led them to believe.

"Nathan is a little genius," I remember my mom saying to a relative on the phone. And to a cashier at the supermarket. And also to a stranger at a gas station.

After getting told that I was Gifted and Talented by teachers at school, and after hearing my mom tell people that I was a genius, I slowly started to think of myself as one of the smart kids. I liked being one of the smart kids. Each time you got a good grade, it was like the teacher was patting you on the head and calling you a good boy. Good grades are to students as doggie treats are to dogs. See? When you're a smart kid, perfect analogies like that just come to you. It's great.

I struggled in college and it made me think maybe I wasn't one of the smart kids after all, and my twenties seemed to confirm that doubt. My twenties were a slow and steady mental ass-kicking of again and again being taught life lessons that ended with some version of the epiphany, "Huh, guess I'm not as smart as I thought I was." And you can keep having that epiphany, because you can always be a little dumber than you thought you were the day before. Zeno's paradox, except instead of halving distances, you're surprising yourself with incremental increases in stupidity. It's fun.

This lesson was beaten into me through the variety of ways I failed at day jobs. Since I didn't immediately get my dream job out of college—like I assumed was a sure thing for a lil' genius like me—I conditioned myself to say "day job" when referring to whatever source of income I had at the moment, a subtle way of indicating that while yes, this particular line of employment is what I'm doing to pay the bills, I have far grander ambitions that I expect to be realized soon. I recommend you try it the next time someone asks you what you do. "What do I do? Well, for my *day job*, I'm the CFO of a midsize plastic-plant company that specializes in inoffensive office decor. But that's not my passion, you know?"

I moved to New York City after college to try to "make it in comedy" and get the sort of job I wouldn't call a day job. Since Lorne Michaels wasn't waiting for me when I landed at JFK, though, I needed a day job in the meantime.

My string of postcollege day jobs started at a running-shoe store on Fourteenth Street near Union Square. Since I'd been on the track team in high school and college, I figured I was qualified to sell running shoes. Protected by a sheen of naïveté, I walked into a shoe store called JackRabbit and asked for a job. The person in a position to make that decision happened to be in that day, an ultra-endurance athlete and store manager named Chris Bergland. He offered me a job on the spot. I started that week.

A little over a year later, following a stint in England for grad school and an even briefer stint as a middle school teacher in Brooklyn, I found myself once again looking for a day job in the Big Apple.

Though my sheen of naïveté remained, its job-gaining powers had faded. I walked into bars and coffee shops, and instead of being offered a job on the spot, I was offered nothing but the favor of having my résumé taken to be "kept on file." Years later, a waiter friend of mine revealed that restaurants have no such mythical résumé file, other than a trash can or, if they are environmentally conscious, a recycling bin.

I made dumb sketch comedy videos with my friends in between catering temp jobs that my roommate and friend Isaac, an aspiring filmmaker, helped me get. Realizing that the temp game hustle was not for me, I decided to go corporate and apply through online job portals at big companies with reputations for being "okay places to work." Whole Foods and Starbucks didn't get back to me. Apple did.

Unlike that at the running-shoe store, the Apple vetting process was lengthy. It started with an online application and was followed by a phone interview, then a big group interview, then another phone interview, then an individual in-person interview. I thought I was going to get the job, but then a phone message from the recruiter revealed that I still needed "to sort something out."

"Nate, is there anything you want to tell me?" he asked over the phone, like a mother to a son she walked in on eating Buffalo wings on the kitchen floor in the middle of the night.

I thought about telling him that in third grade I scored in the ninety-ninth percentile on the Iowa Test of Basic Skills, but it didn't seem like that was the sort of thing he was going for. Plus, I'd probably already told him that. "I don't know what you're talking about," I said. His coyness was drawn out for several more confused exchanges before he finally broke.

"Nate, we saw the video," he said. He was comporting himself like he was Leon Jaworski sliding the Smoking Gun Tape across a table to Nixon. Only I wasn't being tricky: I just honestly still had no idea what he was talking about. I said as much, and with a disappointed sigh, the recruiter revealed that he was referring to an on-line sketch comedy video I'd appeared in months earlier called "Evil Genius Bar" made by some friends of mine on the comedy team LandlineTV. The recruiter told me I would need to "scrub the video from the internet." I told the recruiter that wouldn't be possible. He said he was "sorry to hear that" and hung up. I figured I didn't get the job. Three weeks later he called me back as if that exchange had never happened and offered me a job anyway, with the parting words, "Congratulations! And no more Apple comedy skits, okay?"

I was hired as a Family Room Specialist at the Apple Fifth Avenue location, an underground store you enter via a cylindrical glass elevator on the southeast corner of Central Park. A Family Room Specialist is close to being an Apple Genius, but not quite. Instead of doing tech support for computers, we divided our time between fixing iPhones and teaching lessons. Except there wasn't much we could do by way of actual repair, so the job mainly consisted of explaining to people that AppleCare did not cover water damage. One such interaction entailed me explaining to an Eileen Fisher–clad customer that wine damage counted as water damage,

to which she replied, "Well, then you should call it *liquid* damage."
Touché.

Since the store was near the Upper East Side, most of the customers I interacted with were old, rich Manhattanites who had
bought an Apple computer because they looked prettier than their
less expensive PC counterparts (my coworkers on the overnight shift
told me that the bulk of their clientele were drunk tourists coming in
with iPhones with freshly smashed screens, which all in all sounded
like a tougher crowd to deal with). A common task was to explain to
someone how to use his or her email, which often started with an
overview of what email was. "Think of it as electronic mail!" was not
much of a clarifier.

I assumed I was a good teacher. On my first shift, I powered
through a lesson with an earnest bearded white man named Walter.
He was excited to send electronic mails to his children, who lived in
Ohio and California. The illusion of my teaching aptitude was shattered around my fourth shift when Walter showed up again for the
same lesson, having forgotten everything I'd taught him. I realized
that I wasn't teaching old people how to use email so much as I was
helping old people check and send emails at regular intervals. They
visited the Apple store the same way they might visit their local post
office to check their PO box.

"What is this? L.L. Bean? Why are they emailing me?"

"It looks like you're signed up for their mailing list."

"What? I never signed up for that."

"Well, it's possible the last time you shopped at L.L. Bean, you
gave them your email address."

"What? That's not possible. I wouldn't have signed up for this."

"Okay, well, I can show you how to unsubscribe if—"

"No, leave it. I might want to look at this later."

There were exceptions. I helped one woman named Natasha

create a blog about fashion. We even took a selfie together, an Apple employee no-no, which she posted to her blog along with a short write-up about my hair and glasses (it might have been a fashion don't, I'm not sure). Weeks after she stopped coming in for lessons, I checked on her blog and she had been updating and adding to it. It made my proverbial glowing Apple logo grow three sizes bigger.

Once a ten-year-old boy named Roger came in for a lesson or, in other words, babysitting. As youth tend to be, Roger was great at computers. All of our standard lessons were beneath him. To pass the time, I decided to show him the hardest computer program I knew, Apple's nonlinear video editing program Final Cut Pro. Whereas my older clients were afraid they'd break the computer if they pressed an unknown button, Roger charged fearlessly forward. He wasn't afraid of making mistakes. Rather than ask what something did, he would click on it, see what happened, and then adjust. In the time I could have explained to him one command, he had already tried five and moved on. It was a demonstration as to why ADHD might be an evolutionary benefit in our media- and technology-saturated modern world.

Toward the end of the year I worked at Apple, I started to have the same angry customer week after week. Let's call her Edith. The source of her fury was her notion that her computer's operating system had been designed idiotically as some sort of personal affront to her. She never remembered that I had been her teacher the week before. Each week started the same.

"So, are *you* a Genius?" Edith would sneer.

"Not quite," I'd reply with a practiced smile. "I'm a Family Room Specialist."

Her eyes would narrow with suspicion. She'd look around at the other customers with envy, assuming that their Geniuses were doing superior jobs answering questions compared with the non-Genius seated with her. Each week she'd leave without a thank-you, disappointed.

As the weeks passed, I became fascinated with the particular computer concepts that were difficult for Edith to grasp. For example:

- The metaphor of multiple windows open in front of each other was confusing to her. She saw a single screen and anything not visible had disappeared. The idea of windows being layered behind one another made no sense. It was almost as if she was an infant who had to relearn a sort of digital object permanence. The metaphor of an actual physical desktop with multiple pieces of paper that could be shuffled and placed in front of or behind other pieces of paper did not translate.

- Every digital entity was a "file." The difference between files, folders, documents, programs, applications, software, operating systems, and browsers did not make sense or matter. Edith would ask questions like "Where are my files?" or "Will my computer keep my files safe from viruses?" or "Can I use this to look at my files?" and in each instance "file" meant something entirely different.

- The difference between email, the Internet, and "the Google" was nebulous in her mind, and she seemed suspicious that I was lying to her when I explained that they were different. She persisted in using the terms interchangeably.

I tried to be patient with Edith, but it was frustrating to see her so clearly disappointed with our interaction time and time again. I tried different metaphors each week. Some days I let her do all the driving herself, keeping my hands away from her trackpad or keyboard.

Some days I took over, thinking that if I showed her the right way, she might finally get it. Nothing worked. My ongoing lessons with Edith were starting to feel like *Stand and Deliver* meets *Groundhog Day* with a sad ending.

Eventually, running out of ideas, I decided to try something I'd never tried before. I was going to lie to Edith. I was going to tell her that I was a Genius.

"So, are *you* a Genius?" she asked with grave concern in her voice.

"Yes. Yes, I am."

Her face relaxed with relief. "Oh, thank goodness." She was happy and convivial throughout our lesson. She listened to everything I said and applied herself. I watched as the concepts started to click. For the first time, she didn't seem afraid of her computer.

As our hour together ended, she leaned in and whispered conspiratorially, "You were great. Last week my lesson was with someone who was, between you and me, *not* quite a genius."

She patted me on the head and left. Normally I'd think of that as a little condescending, but I didn't care. That head-pat made me feel like I was the smartest person on earth.

I quit after about ten months, which was more than enough time to get plenty of fodder for some Apple comedy skit ideas. Hit me up online if you're interested in being in one.

In Case of Fire

In case of fire, use stairs.

In case of stair fire, use zip line.

In case of frayed zip-line cable, use fireman's pole.

In case of fireman's pole being used for impromptu pole-dance exercise class, use waterslide.

In case of water slide being too scary, use suction cup handgrips.

In case of suction cup handgrips still being lost after Halloween party, use Ed's longboard.

In case of Ed acting like a jerk who doesn't share his longboard, use Uber phone app to contact a car service.

In case of car service insisting it is not possible to pick someone up from the seventh floor of a building in a car, use parachute.

In case of no GoPro camera on premises to document extreme awesomeness of office parachute exit, collect pants from coworkers and tie together to make a long rope.

In case of everybody wearing capri pants that day by some strange coincidence so the connected total of pants is not quite long enough to reach the ground, use escape pod.

In case of stair fire spreading to escape pod in the amount of time it took you to read these emergency exit instructions, accept that it just isn't in the cards for you to leave the floor of your office building today. Make your peace with God.

In case of failure to make your peace with God, use elevator. It's probably fine.

It's Not You, It's Your Man Bun

Lucas, we need to talk.

We both know that things haven't been working. Sure, we had something good going for a second there, but I'm afraid we're just not compatible anymore. I don't want you to feel bad, but I really mean it when I say this: It's not you, it's your man bun.

You are wonderful. You're kind, smart, thoughtful, a generous lover, a successful plant-based chef at one of my favorite vegan restaurants—everything I could ask for in a romantic partner! Your man bun, however, is the antithesis of all of that.

Looking back, the signs of your incipient man bun were apparent from the very start. Among the things that first caused me to swipe right were your luxurious locks, your auburn mane that you tossed about in that devil-may-care-but-he-probably-does-not style in your profile picture. Yes, it's true—your hair was long enough to pull back into a man bun even then. But how was I to know that you'd give in to the temptation?

I mean, you shouldn't fault someone just for being capable of sin, right? Artistic representations of Jesus show him with man-bunnable hair, but he never did it. Never. Jesus let his hair hang to his shoulders; he never pulled it into a round little nubbin on the top of his holy head. I know it's probably not fair of me to compare your personal restraint (or lack thereof) to that of our Lord and Savior, but I'm just really hurting right now.

And to reiterate: It's not you; it's your man bun. You? You're a catch. Your man bun? I literally cannot look at it without rolling my eyes, which makes having things like a conversation or sexual inter-course very difficult.

On our first date, to see Sufjan Stevens at BAM, everything went so well, didn't it? We both insisted on calling it an "event" since it wasn't quite a concert and it wasn't quite a documentary screening with a live orchestral score. It was an event! Oh, how we laughed via text as we arranged that first get-together—me with a tasteful "hah" and you with the more exotic "jaja," which led to you describe, in great detail, the month you'd spent abroad in Barcelona.

As I began to tell my friends about you and your charming affec-tations, they warned me to proceed with caution. "He talked about living abroad in Barcelona? He almost definitely has a man bun," they warned. "He typed 'jaja' instead of 'haha' and then explained why he did it? What a man-bun-wearing tool," they chided.

But I didn't listen.

Even as the evidence mounted, I refused to acknowledge the truth. *Maybe he's cheating on me!* I'd think, after finding a black hair tie tangled in your sheets, in denial of the obvious facts.

Then the day finally came when you hid your boy cruller from me no longer. I cried. Do you remember that? Right there, in front of Ned, your sous chef at Heart of Palms. I tried to change you. I sent you op-eds by dermatologists describing the correlation between "traction alopecia" and the man-bun hairstyle. You were unconvinced. I sent you photos of other men with man buns and captioned those photos, "See how douchey this looks?" You were unmoved.

At last, I see that this is just who you are. Even if you were to cut your man bun off tomorrow and donate it to some deranged "Buns of Love"–type charity, it wouldn't change the fact that you're a manbun man now.

So good-bye, Lucas. And one final time, let me state: It's not you; it's not me. It's your man bun.

Glengarry Glenpot

The marijuana salesmen sat at their sad desks in their quiet office. Sure, there'd been a boom when the going was good. But that's the thing about the going: Sometimes it gets bad. Lately it seemed like every mom and pop who had ever owned a Cheech & Chong record had set up shop in Colorado, the Centennial State. You couldn't walk down the street without somebody with a beard and a headband slinging pot your way while the cops stood by and smiled. Pot was legal in Colorado now, no way around it. The times were changing. It was a buyer's market.

And where did that leave the sellers?

It left them sad at their sad desks. Gene, the saddest sack of all the sacks that ever got sad, flipped through his stack of index cards with handwritten leads for the tenth time that day. The cards' sides were worn and frayed, their color almost as faded as Gene himself. On the other side of the office, Rick was ending a phone call the way all the phone calls seemed to end these days, ". . . No, that's okay, I understand." *Click.* The two made eye contact and looked away, embarrassed for themselves and for each other.

The PR Woman emerged abruptly from their boss's office and faced the room expectantly. Everyone got quiet. They'd been anticipating her visit with dread. She was dressed in a smart black pantsuit and looked to be about half the age of their boss, who stood meekly behind her. She surveyed the room, assessing the marijuana salesmen and their work spaces. Her expression didn't change, but her eyes betrayed something near the corner of Pity Street and Loathing Avenue.

"They all here?" she said. The boss mumbled something about Eric still being out. "Well, I'm starting anyway. TAKE THAT BOB MARLEY POSTER DOWN!" she yelled out of nowhere, wheeling on the room, fury in her voice. Everyone jumped and turned to see what her eyes were locked on: an 18-by-24-inch sepia-tone poster of Bob Marley smoking a joint with the words ONE LOVE written along the bottom edge. It was above the coffeemaker. Hank, the oldest of them all, had put the poster up on his first day on the job. Stiffly he got up from his desk and removed it. Moving gingerly, he rolled it up. That wouldn't do. The PR Woman marched over, crumpled the poster into a ball, and was back to the front of the room faster than you could say "paradigm shift."

She walked down the center aisle of their open office, her heels clicking an intimidating staccato with each step. "Bob Marley posters are for losers," she said, her tone now measured and perfectly in control as she picked up an errant Hacky Sack from another desk, using only her thumb and pointer finger as if it its filth might be infectious, and dropped it in a waste bin by Gene's desk.

Gene cracked a smile.

"You think I'm fucking with you?" she said, cruelty crackling in her eyes.

Gene's smile faded. He shook his head no.

"I'm not fucking with you. I'm from Weedly, a marijuana marketing agency. The boys downtown sent me to whip your sorry asses into shape, because evidently this dispensary couldn't make a sale if the CU Boulder Ultimate Frisbee team's bus broke down in front of you on April 20."

"It's not our fault. The leads suck, man," Rick ventured.

"The leads don't suck. You suck," she shot back. "The problem isn't the leads, gentlemen. The problem is that you're a bunch of pothead losers."

She eyed them, challenging them to challenge her back. They didn't. They wouldn't.

"You sold some pot to some potheads. So what. Any drug dealer on the street could do that. But we're not in the drug *dealing* business anymore. A deal is something you make with a friend. We're in the drug *sales* business now."

She walked over to Gene. "Your name is Greg?"

"No, it's—"

"Doesn't matter. What's the last product you tried to sell?"

"Product? Are you talking about herb, man? I mean, ma'am?" Gene quivered.

"Shut up. Unemployed hippies say 'herb' when they're on a break from their shift at the food co-op. This is a *company* that sells a *product* for a *profit*. I'll ask again: What's the last product you tried to sell?"

"Uh, Super Silver Sour Diesel Haze," Gene said, near tears.

"And give me the line you used in the sit."

"Um, well. Let's see. Something like . . . 'Hello, sir, would you like to relax with some—'"

"Wrong!" she yelled, slapping Gene across the face. The room gasped. She was violating workplace codes of conduct. Hell, she was violating the law. But nobody stopped her. They didn't want to.

"All of the adjectives that you formerly used to sell marijuana are forbidden. *Relax. Mellow. Smooth. Body-numbing. Groovy.*" She counted them off on her fingers as she spoke. "Those words are dead to you. If you say them on a sales call, you're fired. Those are words to sell something to middle school burnouts, but now you're selling to people like me: successful type A's with the disposable income necessary for this dispensary to make some real profit. These are your new words: *Elite. Dynamic. Optimized. Rocketed. Phygital. Viral.*"

The salesmen nervously made eye contact with one another. "We're going to tell people that smoking our pot will make them go viral? I dunno. We all got this job because we thought it would be chill. No offense, um . . . What's your name, ma'am?"

"Fuck you—that's my name."

"Whoa, lady, not chill."

"Damn right I'm not *chill.*" It seemed to cause her physical pain to say the word. "And if you had any self-respect you wouldn't think being 'chill' was such a good thing. You're in it for the wrong type of green, you lunks," she said as she leaped up onto Gene's desk.

Staring down at them, fire in her eyes, her voice crescendoing into a prophetic timbre, she soliloquized: "You know what else is the difference between dirtbag Willie Nelson impersonators like you and the new way of marijuana agribusiness? You smoke pot; the new way is to consume cannabis. You enjoy being stoned; the new way is to enjoy the psychoactive properties of tetrahydrocannabinol. You take a bong hit so you can keep sitting on the couch listening to jam bands; the new way is to take a hit from a five-hundred-dollar pocket vaporizer that looks like a Sony Walkman to smooth out the adrenaline rush of closing a million-dollar deal."

She jumped off the desk and reached down into the fashionable and functional handbag she'd left near the door. She raised up high in the air what appeared to be a pair of dangling brass balls. "Are you all familiar with the Harry Potter series? These are a pair of authentic replica Golden Snitches that we're going to give out to the top salesman this month." She returned the balls to her handbag, leaving the salesmen confused but motivated.

"It's a Green Rush, gentlemen, and I'm at the front of it." She eyed them all one last time, then turned to leave. Almost as an afterthought, she called back to the room, "Be like me, gentlemen. Be a mari-*winner*."

She was gone. The dispensary was silent, stunned at the whirlwind of PR vigor that had just torn through it. After a moment, she poked her head back in. "The last thing I said—mari-winner?—that was a portmanteau of *marijuana* and *winner*. I just want to make sure everyone got that."

The salesmen looked around. "Yeah, we got it, man," Gene said.

"Good. Just making sure. Okay, I'm going to go for real now." She turned to leave.

"Wait, hold up," Gene said. "Have you ever smoked pot, man?" Gene winced, awaiting her wrath. It didn't come.

"Actually, no," she said. "I've been meaning to try it. I guess I should at some point."

"Do you want to now?"

She checked her Apple Watch. "My next meeting isn't for a couple hours. I guess I could now."

"A couple hours? Better not give you any edibles. Here, hit this." Gene handed her a lighter and a joint. She fired it up and inhaled.

The entire office waited. "Oh," she said at last, her face muscles rearranging into a shape that they hadn't been in for quite some time. "Now I get it. I'll be chill now, guys." She took another puff.

Weather.com Headlines or Creative Writing MFA Thesis Titles?

Cold Now Is Nothing Compared to What's to Come

Spring Storm Messy, Relentless

The Heat from the Sun Hotter Than the Heat Inside You

The Uniqueness of a Snowflake, Under a Microscope

Outbreak Possible

Deep South Severe Threat

The Coldest Air of the Season

El Niño Rising

One of the Warmest, Wettest Winters (So Far)

Where Have the Dog Days of Summer Gone?

Looking Ahead, the Pattern Has Changed

Potential Winter Storm Could Bring Snow, Ice to Midwest,
South, and East Next Week: Essays and Stories

The Transformation

One morning Conifer Middle School student Jeremy Coil woke from a rather bestial dream about a nice classmate named Ariana to find that his penis had turned into a lobster. Sensing something was wrong, Jeremy jumped up and gazed down in horror: A red tail grew out of his mons pubis; tiny crawling legs extended and retracted where his scrotum had been; and at the end were a pointy head and two large pincers.

As adults had warned, Jeremy and his peer group were growing and changing. But the changes he observed in others seemed desirable. Duncan Dofter had grown four inches of height and a crackless, baritone voice. Ariana Pulski had developed breasts and the attention of the popular boys in the grade. Jeremy's own personal growing and changing seemed disgusting and shameful by comparison. First he had found a single stringly-strangly string of hair growing out of his left armpit. And now this: His penis had turned into a lobster.

Maybe if I go back to sleep, thought Jeremy, crawling back under the covers. As he closed his eyes, the Ariana dream returned. As always, she was in shop class. Ariana stood using a vise and a power drill to connect two planks of wood. As she drilled, Jeremy felt his lobster-penis fill with vibrancy and then pinch the inside of his right thigh.

"Ouch!" Jeremy shrieked.

"Jeremy! Are you okay?" his mother called, knocking at the door.

"Fine, Mother! Don't open the door!" Jeremy shouted back, startled.

"Okay. Well, it's quarter to seven! Time to get ready for school, sweetheart."

He had to stop thinking about Ariana. But as he got ready for school, she continued to return to his thoughts, resulting in the lobster-penis shredding any underwear Jeremy pulled near. How was he going to explain that to his mom? At last, he managed to lash the pincers closed with some camping rope. *Oh, dreadful school. As if it wasn't already bad enough without having a lobster for a penis,* Jeremy thought as he pulled on his jeans. *And drat it all, today I have gym!* Jeremy went downstairs, ate the now cold oatmeal his mother left for him, and marched to the bus stop.

He pressed his head against the bus window, his backpack placed purposely over his groin, picturing everyone at school noticing and teasing him. Middle school was a cruel place. Kevin Huganvick had tried to transfer schools after Duncan pantsed him in the hallway, granting Kevin the nickname Mouse ever since, a mouse being a small creature and not something to which you'd want your penis shape or size compared. What sort of nickname would having a lobster for a penis earn? *Probably something like Lobster-Penis,* Jeremy thought. His worries were interrupted when he noticed that the lobster-penis seemed to be enjoying the gentle gyration of the bus seat. Jeremy pushed his backpack down harder, but the lobster-penis seemed to enjoy that, too! How could his classmates not notice his condition? But when Jeremy arrived at school, nobody said a word. *I guess everyone is too worried about their own anxieties and agendas to care about my lobster-penis issue,* Jeremy thought, as he sat through his morning classes as if his penis wasn't a lobster at all.

There was one close call, however, just before lunch. Jeremy passed by a pretty eighth-grade girl named Katelyn Gibbons. She was bending over to fiddle with her bottom locker in the hallway, and without meaning to, Jeremy caught a glance of the top of her butt slit, sneaking out from the top of her jeans. The sight of her butt slit sent the little creature thrashing so violently Jeremy had to take his backpack off and carry it in front of his waist all the way to the bathroom. Safely inside a stall, Jeremy checked to make sure the bindings were still in place. Looking down at the squirming fellow, red and angry, trying to break free, Jeremy felt sorry for it. "Geeze Louise, I know that was a good-looking butt slit, but what do you want me to do about it?" Jeremy said aloud to his lobster-penis. A cough that sounded a lot like it might belong to one of Jeremy's teachers came from the stall next door.

Jeremy tried to think thoughts that made him feel the opposite of the way the Katelyn's-butt-slit thoughts made him feel. He settled on thinking about the way he had felt looking at his mom crying during his grandmother's funeral, and how it had felt weird to think about how his grandmother was his mom's mom, and how one day his mom would look as old and wrinkly and dead as his grandmother had looked in her casket. Those thoughts seemed to do the trick. Soon his lobster-penis clammed up, pulling its appendages inward, and before long it seemed to be sleeping. Carefully, Jeremy returned his lobster-penis to his underwear, pulled up his jeans, and walked to the end of the lunch line.

Jeremy sat alone in the cafetorium, the large room used as both the cafeteria and the auditorium at Conifer Middle School. He stuffed his cafeteria-purchased greasy pizza and chocolate milk into his mouth as fast as he could, hoping to finish lunch without incident. Still chewing, he stood with his tray and walked to the trash can by the door. With just two paces to go, he felt a tap on his shoulder: He spun to see Ariana smiling at him.

"Hey Jeremy!" Against all laws of nature, goddess Ariana was talking to bottom-feeder Jeremy.

"Oh, hey Ariana," Jeremy said, his lobster-penis waking slowly, like a sleeping puppy stirring at the sound of hard kibble being poured into a porcelain dish.

"Um, I wanted to tell you that I liked that book report you read in class last quarter," she said. His lobster-penis was now awake.

"Oh. Um. The one on Kafka?"

"No," said Ariana, "the other one. Dickens, I think? The one with Lucie Manette. Anyway, you're really smart," she said, pushing his shoulder playfully. The lobster-penis was now thrashing as violently as it ever had. "And I was thinking maybe we could, like, read or do homework together this weekend?"

"Oh. Yeah! I'd really like that."

"And to return the favor I can help you out in shop class. I know Mr. McDaniels has been giving you a hard time because you're afraid to use the circular saw," Ariana said.

The thrashing in his pants was now causing his entire body to vibrate. Jeremy wanted to extend the ecstasy of this moment, but then he heard the distinctive sound of lobster claw scratching on metal. It seemed unwise to wait around and see if his lobster-penis was smart enough to open a zipper from the inside. "Cool. I'll Facebook you! 'Bye, Ariana!"

Jeremy turned and ran, throwing his food, tray and all, into the trash and dashing out the door, too euphoric to notice the stink-eyed grimace Duncan had given him from the cool kids' table near the exit. As he ran down the hall, Jeremy's happiness didn't stall until he realized where his feet had automatically brought him: the gym. His pace slowed to a somber stagger. *Gym? Oh God, no!* he thought.

The bell rang as Jeremy completed his funeral march to the locker room. Inside, the foul-smelling dungeon was already abuzz with activity. Animalistic shrieks and maniacal laughter echoed across the fading green metal lockers and gray cinder-block walls.

He managed to get his gym shorts on without causing a stir, and kickball passed as it usually did, with Jeremy having a super fun time. Gym was way better than any other class.

Returning to the locker room, Jeremy knew he could escape his fate no longer. Coach Hitches was strict about the rule that everyone had to shower before returning to class. Jeremy wrapped a towel around his waist, attempting to drop his shorts under the protective screen of the fabric. He felt his lobster-penis come alive, interested in its new, less encumbered surroundings. He turned, startled to see a cross-armed and bare-chested Duncan standing in his way.

"Why'd you change under the towel, Coil? Afraid everybody would see your vagina?" Duncan said, shoving Jeremy back.

"No. I don't have a vagina," Jeremy said. Duncan pushed him again, this time backing him up against the tiled wall. Jeremy's head smacked hard on the plastic edge of a red fire alarm.

"What was that, Coil? I couldn't hear you over the sound of you having a vagina," Duncan said, now hamming up his attack for the gathering crowd, gaining a spattering of laughs that betrayed the laughers' sense of relief that they weren't in Jeremy's position more than genuine mirth. Duncan moved his face closer to Jeremy's.

"I saw you talking to Ariana in the cafetorium. If you ever talk to her again, I will—" Duncan stopped his threat and looked down.

The towel moved. Jeremy's lobster-penis wasn't good at distinguishing context, and even the mention of Ariana's name in this hostile way caused a burst of activity.

"What do you have hiding under there, Coil?" Duncan's hand darted to where Jeremy was keeping the towel pinched shut around his waist.

"Why do you want to see what's beneath my towel so badly, Duncan?" Jeremy's words surprised everyone, especially Jeremy. This was not how shrimps like Jeremy spoke to sharks like Duncan. Duncan took a step back, aghast that he'd been stood up to.

"I–I'm not. I don't," Duncan stuttered. Jeremy watched as the surprise in Duncan's eyes gave way to growing anger. He'd stunned him, but that had only bought him a few moments.

Duncan's hands clenched into fists. Jeremy reached up and pulled the fire alarm. The shrill blast echoed painfully in the unforgiving acoustics of the locker room. Coach Hitches emerged, an annoyed look on his face.

"Okay, everybody. You know the drill," Coach Hitches said. "Let's line up and head outside in an orderly fashion. Duncan, you deaf? What are you waiting for? Stop looking at Jeremy like that! Put your clothes on and walk."

Out on the field, the students lined up according to their homerooms. "Hi, Jeremy," said Ariana, standing behind him in his homeroom line. Jeremy was delighted to see her, but a pang of fear from Duncan's fresh threat lingered in his mind.

"Oh. Hi, Ariana." Jeremy looked over to Duncan's homeroom line. Duncan stood sheepishly in nothing but his towel. In the kerfuffle, his clothes had gone missing. Nearby, Kevin Huganvick smiled, satisfied to see Duncan on the receiving end of middle school scorn for the first time. Duncan glared at Jeremy, as if Jeremy was the cause of his current anguish. *Don't talk to her,* he said with his eyes. Jeremy considered turning away from Ariana, but something deep inside him, something deep inside him connected to his lobster-penis, compelled him otherwise.

"Um, Ariana?" asked Jeremy.

"Yeah?"

"You have blossomed into a well-built and beautiful young lady."

"That's a weird thing to say, Jeremy," Ariana said, "but thank you. I feel something similar about you."

They were quiet as the adults finished taking attendance. Soon, the principal announced it was time to go back to class.

While their classmates flowed past them, Jeremy and Ariana stood in place and shared a glance. In that glance, they agreed on something that they both knew but didn't yet have the vocabulary to articulate, something in confirmation of their new growings and recent changings, and as their classmates reached the threshold of the school and a teacher called something out to them that neither heard, they each stretched out an arm and held hands before turning to walk to their final class of the day.

Also, earlier that year Ariana's vagina had turned into a capybara, a large water rodent indigenous to the rain forests of the Amazon basin.

I'm Not an Asshole, I'm Just an Introvert

I can be loud at times and I am not shy, so a lot of people assume I'm an extrovert. But I'm not. I'm an introvert. When I explain this to people, they'll ask me, "Well, if you're such an introvert, why are you telling us, a group of strangers in an elevator, all about how you're an introvert? This is a social interaction you initiated and could have avoided." I don't answer them. I just shake my head at how misunderstood the word *introvert* is in modern society.

Being an introvert doesn't mean I can't hang out with a group, but it does mean that when I'm out of energy, it's time for me to get away from the group and recharge. The way I recharge is to sit by myself in a corner, close my eyes, and shout-sing at the top of my lungs "When the Saints Go Marching In" until everybody looks at me.

I find small talk cumbersome. All sizes of talk bother me, in fact. That's why I screen phone calls—even from my friends, even if they text me "Hey, you're twenty minutes late, you promised you wouldn't flake again, are you still coming?" or "EMERGENCY, ANSWER YOUR PHONE!"

People think that if you're an introvert, you don't like parties. But in the appropriate doses, I do like parties. I find the appropriate dosage of partying to be only on weekends or the funner weekdays (*not* Tuesday). But once I'm at a party, you won't find me introducing myself to people I don't know or standing in the front of the room holding court. Part of my particular introversion is that I believe the judicial process should happen only in courthouses, not at parties.

Just like extroverts, we introverts need things like love, affection, lipids, carbohydrates, nucleic acids, and proteins. But unlike extroverts, introverts do not need oxygen to be in a gaseous form to make use of it in the respiratory system. Aquaman is a famous introvert. Yes, celebrities can be introverts, too.

Introverts enjoy doing certain social things, but only if they are in the mood to do those certain social things. And unlike extroverts, on an almost daily basis introverts need to sleep.

Being an introvert does not mean that I'm afraid of public speaking. The only things I'm afraid of are spiders and public speakers, as in devices that amplify music in communal areas. That's why I hate concerts but love silent discos, except for the Arachnophile Silent Disco Fundraiser that was held in the Tarantula Pavilion of the natural history museum last spring.

One of the old introvert stereotypes that does apply to me is that, yes, I do have a notary license. But I'm actually not a notary public like most notaries. I'm a notary private. When I certify deeds, I do so in my apartment at night all by myself, and with the shades drawn. Another thing I do to unwind is unspool an entire bobbin of ribbon and leave it in a pile in the middle of the kitchen for my roommate to find, but when he gets home I just don't want to talk about it. He always does want to talk about the ribbon pile—he's an extrovert.

As an introvert, I have the right to be able to live my life without having to be limited by the dictionary definition of being a shy, reticent person all the time. I can be an introvert but still be a confident, outgoing, and expressive person. And when I exhibit introvert behavior—like leave a party without thanking the host or ditch my friends to do something else with people more successful than them or keep a wallet I find on the sidewalk even though I saw whose pocket it fell out of because the thought of talking to the person annoys me too much—it doesn't mean that I should feel guilty for acting like, as people who don't understand introverts would say, an asshole. It just means that I'm an introvert.

Science will tell you that humans are social animals, but that just isn't me. Does that mean I'm better than most other humans? Yes. But those are science's words, not mine.

496 Reasons Not to Explode the Earth

This was quite the pickle Gale had gotten herself into. She'd wanted to go commit suicide by jumping off the Golden Gate Bridge, but now she found herself responsible for saving the human race. She had twenty-four hours to come up with 496 reasons not to explode the Earth, or else, *boom*, everybody dies. Talk about pressure.

"Let's try . . . friendship?" Gale asked Spizz, her alien tormentor and low-level bureaucrat of the Starbuffalo Nebula.

"You already said that one. It didn't count," Spizz replied.

"Could you just try it again?"

"Fine, but you're just wasting time. Clock is ticking." Spizz held up the crystal dodecahedron that hung from around his neck and stuck it into his mouth. With the device inserted, he repeated the word in a garble: "Friendship." His cranial cavity lit up red as the negative tone emitted from his nose, sounding like a knife being scraped down the side of corrugated tin.

"Dang it, why doesn't friendship count?"

"We have friendship in other worlds. It has to be 496 reasons *unique* to Earth to keep it around."

"And how many do I have so far?"

Spizz spat out the device and checked one of its sides. "Seventeen."

"Ugh," Gale complained. She didn't want to live anymore, but she had no problem with other people going on living. She wasn't an asshole. She was just depressed.

"Hey, what's this?" Spizz said as he opened up one of her cupboards. "Choc-co-late chips?"

"Ooh, those are great. Let's try 'chocolate chips,'" Gale said.

Spizz repeated "chocolate chips" with the device in his mouth. His cranial cavity lit up purple and his nose emitted the positive tone, which sounded like a dolphin being tickled.

"Eighteen! Yes!" Gale said excitedly.

"Good work! Only 478 more to go in the next five hours!"

Gale's excitement left her face. She crumpled on the couch.

She had found herself with the task at hand shortly after she had nearly scaled the newly installed suicide-jumper-prevention barrier along the side of the Golden Gate Bridge. Just as she was about to throw herself over the top, she'd mumbled to herself, "The universe would be better off if the Earth just blew up."

In a flash, Spizz had appeared. Gale momentarily felt fear, but Spizz quickly emitted a tone from his nose which calmed her and made her accept what she was seeing. A blink later he'd transported them back to Gale's home and then, in a rote delivery, Spizz had informed Gale that her utterance counted as verbal consent as far as intergalactic zoning codes were concerned, which hereby granted Spizz's employer the authority to demolish Earth and the surrounding solar system to make way for a planned Wormhole Port.

"Isn't there anything I can say to take it back?"

Spizz groaned. This would inconvenience him by a full twenty-four Earth hours, which was about one-tenth of his life span. But he was a fair bureaucrat, and he explained that if Gale could come up with 496 genuine reasons why Earth should not be destroyed, it would reverse the binding nature of her utterance.

They'd spent nineteen hours together in Gale's apartment, with her frantically trying to think of reasons not to explode the Earth. All the obvious things she could think of, like love and friendship and sex, didn't count. Turns out they had all those things elsewhere in the universe. It was only some of the random pleasures and satisfactions that Gale had experienced over her life that seemed to count. Tiny cactuses with red flowers on them, for example, had been the first thing she'd thought of that counted. The smell of a newborn baby, on the other hand, had not.

"Animals?"

Negative.

"Swimming in a lake?"

Negative.

"The feeling of a cat's belly fur?"

Negative.

"Snow?"

Negative.

"Dinosaurs?"

Negative.

"Chameleons that change colors to match their surroundings?"

Negative.

"That male sea horses give birth?"

Negative.

"Rainbows?"

Negative.

"Sunrises?"

Negative.

"The feeling of being drunk?"

Negative.

"The feeling of being high?"

Negative.

"The feeling of relief when a migraine headache goes away?"

Positive!

"Okay! How many is that?"

"Nineteen. Four hours to go."

Gale sank deeper into the couch. Spizz pitied her. He knew that his company preyed on species that were prone to suicide, which were especially susceptible to the Blow Up My Planet clause, as it was known in the space construction business. Somewhere around 1.5 percent of humans committed suicide, and of these, many expressed the wish that their species cease to exist. Humans had an especially high capacity in this regard.

"Trampolines?"

Negative.

"The way monkeys look when they eat bananas?"

Positive!

"Road trips?"

Negative.

"Rainbows?"

Already said that. Still negative.

"The way that birds' feathers heal themselves?"

Negative.

"Magnets?"

Negative.

"Masturbation?"

Negative.

"Polaroid cameras?"

Negative.

"The feeling of getting your neck hair shaved off?"

Negative.

"A 'runner's high'?"

Negative.

"*Hamilton*, the musical?"

Negative.

"The Beatles?"

Negative.

"Radiohead's *Kid A*?"

Negative.

"Radiohead's *OK Computer*?"

Negative.

"Radiohead's—"

"Let me cut you off there. There is some *great* music out in space, just like some really neat chord progressions and interesting time signatures, very cool stuff. So, yeah, I think this current path you're going down will not be fruitful."

Gale groaned, then pressed on. "The human capacity to think that you'll be able to achieve something followed by the moment of crippling realization that actually there is no way you'll ever be able to achieve it?"

Spizz repeated the idea and then, to both of their surprises, his face lit up purple and the laughing dolphin tone came from his nose. Positive!

"Wait a second . . ." Spizz said. "You've been just naming things that your species would for the most part find pleasing, yes?"

"Yeah, I thought that was what you told me to do. Reasons to keep the planet around."

"Right, that is the directive, but perhaps you interpreted it too narrowly. Perhaps pleasure is not the only reason to endure. Perhaps suffering could also be reason enough."

Gale pondered this.

"The feeling of not wanting to leave your bed when you're on the second day of your period and your flow is superheavy and you feel sick and emotional and your uterus aches and you cry a lot?"

Positive!

"The feeling of self-loathing when you betray a friend and you know you're in the wrong but you do it anyway because there is something wrong with you?"

Positive!

"I think you're on to something," said Spizz. "Your species might just be uniquely skilled at suffering! Keep going!"

Gale kept going. Over the next three hours, she searched her worst memories, her deepest regrets, her biggest fears. They didn't all count, but many of them did. With five minutes left on the clock, she only had three to go.

"Come on, Gale, time is running out. I know I shouldn't be rooting for you, but I want you to get this. Keep going!"

Gale's mind was racing. She felt like she was out. She'd recounted every pang of remorse she had ever felt or had heard of someone feeling. Every human pain she could think of. She had nothing left. She'd purged herself of all of her suffering, and she'd done it for humanity. But now Spizz was calling on her to give more.

"Jealousy?"

Negative.

"Come on, Gale, be more specific than that."

"Being jealous of when something good happens to a friend even though the good thing that happened to your friend does not preclude a good thing from happening to you, and your myopic sense of success is unjustified and a poisonous element of all of your relationships?"

Positive!

"Two to go, Gale, come on!"

"The feeling of blindsided betrayal when someone you were in love with cheats on you with someone else you were close to?"

Positive!

"One to go, Gale, you can do this!"

"Losing a child?"

"You already said that one."

"Losing a spouse?"

"You already sad that one, too."

"Dying alone?"

"Gale! You already said that. Think, Gale, think!"

Gale thought. "Living alone? Living truly and utterly alone by cutting yourself off from others and the possibility of real human connection through keeping people at a distance, first as a choice out of fear, then as a learned defense mechanism to prevent suffering?"

Spizz inserted the device into his mouth. He repeated Gale's words verbatim. His cranial cavity illuminated purple. Positive. Spizz smiled at her. He looked relieved.

"Well done, Gale," he said. "Now I must say good-bye. I'm happy that you and your species will continue existing."

Before Gale could reply, she was back on the suicide prevention barrier on the Golden Gate Bridge. The wind blew and a light drizzle of rain began to fall. The black, dark water loomed terrifyingly far below. She'd never been happier to be alive. She was certain with the depths of all possible conviction that she did not want to die. She wanted to live. She began to pull her leg back from the far side of the barrier when a gust of wind startled her. She lost her grip. Suddenly she was slipping down the wrong side, not back toward the pedestrian walkway, but away from life, toward the blackness below. She clung tighter. She did not want to die. She clung tighter. She did not want to die. She clung tighter. She clung as hard as she could.

What Noise Does a Bug Make?

Hi, I'm Petey. For the most part, I used to freakin' love pre-school. I guess technically this is *pre*-preschool. And because it's called *school* instead of *day care*, it's more expensive and it allows my young professional parents some additional peace of mind when they drop me off to go to work for the day.

Yep, pre-preschool was a pretty sweet deal. I crawled places. I touched stuff. I put things—all the things—in my mouth. Some places I got stuck, which was scary. Some stuff felt soft, which I liked. And putting some things in my mouth got me yelled at, which was confusing. I never could quite crack the "which thing, when put in my mouth, gets me yelled at" code.

All in all, though, life was good.

There was only one part of pre-preschool that I didn't like. I hated when the teachers would ask me and my "classmates" to make the sounds of different animals.

All the other students were amazing at it. I sucked at it like it was a pacifier.

But it wasn't my fault. The whole system was rigged. It went down like this:

"Elana, what noise does a cat make?" Elana meows like a champion and looks adorable doing it.

"Graham, what noise does a cow make?" Graham moos like a boss and drinks in the adulation.

"Petey, what sound does a bug make?" The fuck? What kind of stupid-ass question is that? And no matter what, it's the same every day. Elana and Graham and the others got the easy questions and I got stuck with the bug one, day after day. I wanted to cry at them, "What sound does a bug make? Is this some Zen Buddhist koan about one hand clapping? Is this some John Cage *4' 33"* bullshit?" But all the teachers heard was regular crying, baby style.

One nap time, it all changed.

I was pretending to be asleep because if you don't sleep during nap time it's this whole thing. Sometimes it's easier just to fake it. Anyway, there I am on my cot (Montessori pre-preschool babies have cots, not cribs—don't ask), thinking about when I get to see my mom again, when it hops up beside me: a bug. And it's a real bug's bug, too, you know? Green torso, multisegmented abdomen, monocular eye focusing. I'm just amazed looking at it, thinking about what it would be like to put it in my mouth and if I'd get yelled at for doing so, when I hear it make a noise. "Woof."

That's right. The bug lets out a woof. Like the cartoon dog, which is named Object Permanence, that runs around on the iPad game my dad plays with me to improve my motor skills, this bug lets out a little woof. *Woof* is the answer to the question, "What noise does a bug make?"

Before I can fathom the bug's aural oddity any further, the

soft-haired teacher sweeps me over to the play rug, and it's time for animal noises again.

"Elana, what noise does a cat make?"

"MEOW!"

"Graham, what noise does a cow make?"

"MOO!"

"Petey, what sound does a bug make?"

"WOOF!"

I smile all big, stoked out of my little baby mind that I did it right. But then the soft-haired teacher looks over at the teacher with the funny-tasting sweater. They start talking right in front of me, like I'm not there. They act real concerned about me, like I'm some kind of baby idiot.

"Petey really isn't getting the animal noises," Soft Hair says.

"He's really not," Funny-Tasting Sweater says.

"Perhaps this is a sign of developmental delay?"

"Perhaps it is."

"WOOF!" I say again, thinking this will help my case. It doesn't.

I see Elana and Graham smirk at each other, douche bags that they are. I think maybe there is something going on there, because one time I saw Elana sucking Graham's chin for like ten minutes. He seemed into it.

Anyway, I don't have time to worry about Elana and Graham, because right then, no kidding, I see that same bug walking along the ledge of my cot, sort of taunting me with his little buggy swagger. So I start trying my hardest to get the teachers' attention so I can point them toward the woofing bug, so maybe for once I can get some validation around this place.

My strategy for doing this is to throw a fit and start crying. I wave toward my cot, but they get it all wrong and think that I just want another nap.

"Looks like someone is having a cranky day, huh, Petey?"

The soft-haired teacher swoops me up and puts me back to bed, but now the bug has hopped or flown or something over to the windowsill and is walking back to the play rug where the other babies are.

I pull myself up and look at this little bugger.

"You speak Baby?" I coo to the bug.

He shrugs his bug shoulders, and I know he does.

"Why'd you play me like that? Made me look like an idiot in front of the teachers and my friends. You know they're gonna tell my mom this shit, right?"

He makes a little buggy laugh.

"Ah, forget you," I say, turning away.

"Wait, hold on," the bug says. I pull back up and look at him.

"I said 'woof' because I hate that 'what noise does the animal make' game," he says.

"I hate it, too!" I say.

"They're teaching you the wrong thing, man. Not all bugs say the same thing. Maybe some bugs say 'woof.' Maybe some bugs say 'meow.' You dig what I'm saying?"

"I think so."

"This is a *school*, right?"

"Supposedly, but quite frankly—"

"Then shouldn't they be teaching you how to think instead of training you how to recite *their* answers back to them? You babies sound like a bunch of parrots, man."

"Well, based on what you just said about not all animals making the same noise, isn't that a little offensive to parrots?"

"Parrots are the worst, man. Don't get me started. I hate all birds."

"Why?"

"Birds eat bugs."

"Oh yeah."

"I feel like we've gotten off track. What were we talking about?"

"I think you were about to tell me not to let school get in the way of my education."

"Oh yeah! Yeah, that's right. Don't do it. Just remember that for the next seventeen years, and you'll be fine."

"Okay."

"Okay. And hey—woof, right?" the bug said. But *woof* meant, like, a lot more than just *woof*, you know?

"Woof," I said back to him. And I know I was just repeating what he said, so in a way I was participating in the exact sort of inculcated antieducation that he'd told me to avoid, but I felt like we were on the same wavelength and didn't need to articulate the knowledge we'd shared. I'd learned more from that bug in that one nap time than I'd learned from all of the pre-preschool playtime and iPad motor-skill video games from the first fifteen months of my life put together.

I watched him with sadness as he turned to crawl out the tiny sliver of an opening beneath the window.

"Hey. Baby!" he said, turning back to me again. "Before I leap out this window, there's one more thing you should know. Always be sure to—"

Splat! Funny-Tasting Sweater Teacher is standing with her hand on a wooden Learning Tower directly over where bug used to be standing on the windowsill. She pulls it back slowly.

"Tricia, oh my God, there was just a bug right here! It was making the weirdest noises," she says.

"Oh my God, did you get it?" the soft-haired teacher says.

"Yeah, I think I got it."

But you know what? They didn't get it, man. Teachers never do.

Chap Sticks in a Mailbox

I've always done what girls ask me to do.

In second grade when Arielle asked me to stay inside for recess to act out scenes from Disney's *Aladdin*, I said yes. I would have rather played touch football on the gravel fields of Bergen Elementary with Sam Warren and my other guy friends than act out scenes. But how could I say no to Arielle? She had practically the same name as a mermaid princess, which was a big deal at the time. Also, if I'm being honest, lately I hadn't been picked early in the recess football draft, so a break from the shame of listening to the captains calling out the names of my more athletic classmates ahead of my own sounded nice. And okay, who am I kidding, I would have much rather acted out scenes than play sports anyway, true, but the main reason I did it was because Arielle asked me.

Arielle cast herself in the role of Jasmine and offered me the male lead of Aladdin. I interpreted this casting choice as tantamount to her admitting that she like-liked me. I mean, Jasmine and Aladdin like-liked each other in the movie, so it seemed obvious what was going on.

We focused on the Aladdin-Jasmine meet cute, the scene in a movie where the love interests first serendipitously bump into each other. In the actual movie, Aladdin saves Jasmine from a mean vendor in the marketplace who wants to cut her hand off for stealing after she gave a piece of fruit to a beggar. In our version, since we didn't have a third actor to play the vendor, we decided to both be on the run from the palace guards among the alleyways and rooftops of Agrabah, culminating when we collided and said in unison, "They're after me! They're after you?!" We repeated the scene over and over, using desks and chairs as the rooftops of our imaginary Arabian domiciles, until we eventually jumped to the same piece of classroom furniture to deliver the line, "They're after me! They're after you?!"

I experimented with my delivery. Sometimes I said it as a straightforward realization. I tried saying the second sentence with relief, in the same tone one might say, "Oh, you actually meant to pick me for your football team first, Sam Warren?" In another read I hit the "you" hard with an incredulous tone, as if to say, "Come on, Princess, I seriously doubt *you* are the one they're after. I mean, look at me, I'm a common thief in a purple vest with a monkey best friend! We're wearing matching fezzes! Clearly, they're after me." My favorite delivery, though, was the epiphany version: They were after *both* of us. This underscored that we were currently in the same boat (metaphorically), which foreshadowed that in the future we'd be on the same magic carpet (literally).

Our *Aladdin* role-playing ended when our teacher, Mrs. Gabitzsch, saw that we were standing on top of every elevated surface in her classroom. We were sent outside and told to "play normal." Some people just don't appreciate live theater.

With the kibosh put on the lunchtime scene work, my incipient romance with Arielle was also stuffed back into the bottle. Later in high school, Arielle dated Sam Warren, so, in a stunning confirmation of John Hughes archetypes, the athlete got the girl. Sam was one of my best friends and I was happy for them and I cried about it only a few times.

The story of my nonexistent love affair with Arielle does have one footnote, however. When we were both freshmen in high school, Arielle accidentally walked into the wrong locker room just as I was walking out of the shower, making her the first girl to see me naked.

"Arielle?" I said, frozen in surprise.

"Oh my God!" she screamed, covering her face as she retreated.

In the base system of foreplay, which is of utmost importance to the adolescent imagination, at that point in my life I had never gotten to first base or even up to bat, so this event stood out to me as some sort of milestone, sexually speaking. Although not as talked about as, say, getting to second base, what I'd achieved is known as a Player Strikes Out and Then After the Game the Pitcher Who Struck Him Out Walks In on Him While He Is Taking a Shower Naked. At the age of fifteen, it was the furthest I'd ever gotten with a girl.

In fifth grade, when Whitney asked me to help her collect rocks, I said yes. I think the rocks were for a science fair project. Or maybe Whitney just needed rocks for some sort of personal passion project. Look, Whitney needed rocks and it wasn't my business to pry. It was my business to help her collect rocks.

Whitney was the first girl I'd ever known who had a discernible accent. Her family was from Texas and she spoke with a thick drawl. Her exoticism was heightened by the fact that she rode horses on the weekends. Riding horses seemed like something that happened only on television, and here Whitney did it every weekend as a part of her regular routine, the same way my weekend routine included drawing dinosaurs wearing medieval armor on construction paper. I would have helped Whitney push boulders onto the highway if she asked me with that horse-riding accent of hers.

Whitney removed her denim jacket for the rock collecting. School had just let out and we rushed to gather the rocks from around the outside of our Bergen Elementary temporary classroom building before the buses left. As we stuffed rocks into her purple JanSport backpack, I glanced over to the main building. My mom was the school nurse and she was prone to worrying, and I didn't like to give her cause to worry.

"Okay, looks like your backpack is full!" I said, brushing the dirt from my hands onto my bright red sweatpants. "See you tomorrow?"

"Would you mind filling up the pockets of my jacket, too?" Whitney's accent asked. "I think we can fit a few more in." I got back on my knees. I searched for more rocks, but we'd picked the immediate area clean. I handed her the few I could find, which she stuffed into the pockets of her jacket.

I glanced back to the main building again. If I was five minutes late, my mother would worry that I'd been abducted by a drifter; if I was ten minutes late, she'd take this as a given and call the National Guard.

"Really looks like your jacket pockets are full," I said. Whitney agreed. All jacket and bag orifices had been filled with rocks to her satisfaction. Come to think of it, the science fair had already happened earlier that year, so this was definitely just a personal rock project Whitney had enlisted me in.

"Thanks, Nate. You're sweet," she said as she put her jacket on, swinging the rock-filled denim around her body. I fantasized that Whitney might want to kiss me in return for my rock retrieval. Did I want to kiss Whitney? On the one hand, although I did spend most of my brainpower thinking about all the girls I had crushes on, the prospect of actually kissing a girl terrified me. But on the other hand, I was on the ground and bleeding out of my head. What was going on? Was this what true love felt like?

What had happened was that the sharp edge of one of the granite specimens we'd placed into the pocket of Whitney's denim jacket had struck me with considerable velocity. Whitney had inadvertently turned her jacket into a sling, and when she whirled it around her head to put it on, the projectile we'd loaded moments before flew out with unfortunate precision.

Whitney rushed to get our teacher Mrs. Beaton, who put some paper towels on my head to stop the bleeding.

"Oh dear, Nathan, how did this happen?" Mrs. Beaton asked.

"We were playing with rocks," I said. Mrs. Beaton eyed Whitney suspiciously. "It wasn't her fault," I added.

"Mrs. Beaton?" Whitney asked. "Is it okay if I go? I need to catch the bus."

Mrs. Beaton nodded. Whitney ran off and didn't look back.

"We need to take you to the nurse," Mrs. Beaton said to me gently, looking me in the eyes. Mrs. Beaton was a kind teacher, and it was this tenderness that she routinely showed to students that had probably contributed to me raising my hand to ask her something earlier in the school year and then mistakenly addressing her as "Mom" when I was called on. The embarrassment had been great, but Mrs. Beaton had been kind.

In this moment, though, I wasn't thinking about Mrs. Beaton being kind. She was going to take me to the school nurse, my mom, with an injury that would undoubtedly give my mom cause to worry. I couldn't think of anything crueler.

Being late was one thing. Being late with a head wound was guaranteed to get me in trouble. My mom didn't like it when I came back in from playing in our backyard and had scuffed up my knees.

She would not react well to seeing a scuffed-up head. I was a goner. Was it legal to ground your child for life? If not, I imagined my mom would find a judicial loophole and do so anyway.

Mrs. Beaton marched me along the concrete path from the temporary classroom buildings to the main entrance, through the office, and into the clinic. My mother looked up from her desk, and before she spoke got an ice pack from the minifridge in the corner of the room.

Before being an elementary school nurse, my mother had been an RN at a hospital in the Labor and Delivery unit. She wasn't thrilled to see her son bleeding, but she was also a professional who had seen way more blood than the small amount matted in my hair. She cleaned the gash with iodine as she and Mrs. Beaton chatted about something that wasn't me. It dawned on me that I might not be in trouble after all, and I had to work to suppress a smile.

"Will I need stitches?" I asked.

"No, Nathan, you won't," my mom assured me. "But you might have a goose egg for a while. Hold this ice pack on it." I didn't know what she meant by "goose egg," but I didn't feel like prying. I wasn't in trouble. I felt like the luckiest kid in the world.

Later that year Whitney's family moved away and I never heard from her again. I assume today she is somewhere in the American Southwest, galloping on a horse with saddlebags filled to the brim with rocks.

In sixth grade, when Lisa turned to me in Honors English class and asked me if she could borrow a Chap Stick, I wanted to say yes, but I did not. I couldn't. I did not have a Chap Stick to give.

"Hey Nate, do you have a Chap Stick I could borrow?" Lisa whispered as Mr. McFadden lectured about Gary Paulsen's *Hatchet*, a teen wilderness survival story.

"Chap Stick? Oh, let me check," I said, feigning casualness, knowing full well I had none. I tore through my orange backpack, praying a cylinder of Chap Stick would materialize. Maybe my mom had thought my backpack was her purse and placed a Chap Stick of hers inside that morning? Stranger things had happened. Brian Robeson was a thirteen-year-old boy who lived through a plane crash and survived an entire season alone in the northern Canadian wilderness with nothing but a hatchet, so in comparison, praying for one of my pencils to transmogrify into a tube of lip lubricant wasn't expecting so much, was it?

"Sorry, I guess I don't have any . . ." I mumbled, but Lisa had already turned back to the front of the classroom.

Maybe I'd seen romantic intent that just wasn't there when Arielle asked me to play Aladdin or Whitney asked me to collect rocks, but Lisa asking to borrow Chap Stick? She had basically said to me, "Nate, just so you know, I'm okay with something that has touched your lips touching my lips." Being okay with a lip-touching surrogate was a step away from being okay with kissing. After all these years of pining for girls from afar, this was my chance. I didn't want to blow it.

Later that day, my mom picked me up from school and I asked her to drive me to the pharmacy, Evergreen Drug. I asked for as much of my allowance in advance as she was willing to give, which turned out to be ten dollars. So, I bought ten dollars' worth of Chap Stick. Original flavor Chap Stick–brand Chap Stick, cherry-flavored Chap Stick–brand Chap Stick, Carmex in a little tub, Chap-Ice medicated lip balm, bubble-gum flavor Bonne Bell Lip Smacker, even a pink sparkly lip gloss for good measure. I brought them all up to the register.

"Nathan, what are you going to do with all that Chap Stick?" my mom asked.

"I don't know. Um, can you take me to Lisa's house?" I replied.

I do not remember if my mom cautioned me against this enterprise, but as usual, she supported me and we were soon on our way to Lisa's house with a plastic bag full of assorted lip unguents in my lap.

My mom worked with Lisa's mom on some local school board campaign and so she knew where they lived. A few minutes later we were there. We pulled to a stop at the end of their driveway. I contemplated walking to the front door, but my courage was leaving me. Maybe this was a bad idea?

I opened up their mailbox and emptied out my plastic bag full of lip ointments inside, committing some sort of mail fraud. I did not leave a note. I ran back to the passenger side of my mom's still-running Ford Aerostar minivan.

"Drive!" I shouted, swimming in the adrenaline of my grand romantic gesture. My mom stared at me with raised eyebrows and then, slower than I would have liked, drove off.

I was pleased with myself. I had done well. A girl had asked me for something, and although in the moment I had failed to say yes, I had come through. That night I fantasized about Lisa's reaction. I imagined she'd run up to me in the halls of Evergreen Middle School the next morning, and there on the candy corn–patterned carpet and between the faded green lockers, she'd wrap her arms around my neck and kiss me in the way I'd seen boys and girls kiss in movies.

"Did you like your first kiss, Nate?" she'd say as she pulled back, the entire school now watching.

"Well, your lips did feel great. Are you wearing Chap Stick or something?" I'd say with a wink, the entire school erupting in applause.

"Now that's what I call a climax!" Mr. McFadden would say, pointing to the Elements of Plot poster that I'd completed as homework earlier that quarter and gotten an A on.

It didn't happen like that. Instead, nothing happened.

When I saw Lisa in the hallway, she didn't kiss me. She walked right past me. My expectations shifted. Okay, I thought, as long as she thanked me by the end of Mr. McFadden's English class, I was still good. The class ended without Lisa thanking me or speaking to me at all. Oh no.

My expectations shifted further. Not only did Lisa not think it was a grand romantic gesture, she probably thought it was desperate. Creepy even.

The reality of what I'd done dawned on me. What a weirdo. What a loser. Of course she hadn't thanked me for it. She was probably too embarrassed to even bring it up. She had done me a kindness by not mentioning it. We could just pretend it didn't happen and we could go back to the way things were before: me having a crush on her from afar and occasionally answering her questions about what the English homework was, and her dating someone cooler than me, someone who didn't put ten dollars' worth of lip balm into a girl's mailbox without leaving a note. Oh, thank you, Lisa, for not mentioning my shame. Yes, better not to mention it.

And we never did. For the rest of my time in classes with Lisa at Evergreen Middle School and later at Evergreen High School, I'd get flashes of gut-punching embarrassment thinking about this incident.

I'm in my thirties now and I'm engaged. The other day when I was telling this story to my fiancée, my perspective on the incident shifted yet again.

"... And so I left all that Chap Stick in her mailbox. She probably thought I was the biggest weirdo in the world."

My girlfriend thought about what I'd told her.

"Or she didn't even know the Chap Stick was from you," she said.

"What do you mean?" I asked.

"In middle school, I asked people for Chap Stick all the time. It probably wasn't that big a deal to her. She might not have even re-membered she'd asked you for any. I mean, do you remember every time you've asked someone to borrow a Chap Stick?"

"I've never done that. I don't use Chap Stick. I think your body grows dependent on it and then the Chap Stick company has a cus-tomer for life. It's like drugs in that—"

"Okay, fine. What about gum? Do you remember every time you've asked someone to have a piece of gum?"

"I have never asked someone for a piece of gum in my life. I don't like to owe anyone anything, not even a stick of gum. I'll take gum if it's offered to me, sure, but I would never—"

"Okay, fine. You don't ask people for gum or Chap Stick. But do you get my point?"

I nodded yes. I did get her point.

It made so much more sense now. Lisa's request for my Chap Stick wasn't a sign she was okay with our lips touching. I probably wasn't the only person she asked to borrow Chap Stick from that day. I probably wasn't even her first choice for someone to borrow Chap Stick from. While Lisa asking me for Chap Stick was a major plot point in the middle school chapter of my life—an event on par with crash landing in the Canadian wilderness, for example—for her it hadn't even made it into the story. If one of her parents mentioned the presence of the Chap Stick in their mailbox, I bet she'd shrugged it off as a strange neighborhood prank, a bizarre and innocuous twist on egging a house. I wasn't a weirdo. I was just a dork with a big ego who assumed everything that was a big deal to me was also a big deal to everybody else around me.

I was lost in thought for some time, reworking the memory to its proper shape. At last, my fiancée brought me back to the present. She was telling me something.

"What'd you say?" I asked.

"I asked you if you wanted to go to the Museum of Feelings with me this weekend," she said. "It's this exhibit in Lower Manhattan that's supposed to be really cool. A blogger I follow posted about it."

I considered her request. "No," I said.

"Why not?" she asked, surprised.

"Just because you're a girl I like," I explained, "doesn't mean I have to say yes to everything you ask me to do."

That weekend we woke up early on Saturday and went to the Museum of Feelings. Some things never change.

Part 4

Hand Job at 20,000 Feet

I Am the Wagon

I loved the school part of high school. I was good at following the rules and I loved being rewarded for my rule following. I studied hard in class and earned good grades; the longer I worked on an assignment, the more effusive the praise from the teacher. After class I trained for the track and cross-country teams; the harder I worked at practice, the faster my times. My little bubble of Evergreen High School made sense to me. It was the same school *South Park* cocreator Trey Parker attended. Trey rebelled against our quiet mountain town; I reveled in it.

Authority figures told me the world was a meritocracy and I believed them. I thought that good grades in high school now would lead to some singularly important achievement in the future, like climbing Mount Everest or writing a book about how I worked hard so that I could climb Mount Everest or maybe even getting elected to political office based on my campaign slogan, "I Climbed Mount Everest: I'm

Pretty Sure I'll Be Able to Handle Being Comptroller." Each vocab quiz I aced was one step closer to the base camp of greatness.

The purity of the work-hard-get-rewarded system broke down in college. An early sign that college was not high school came in a welcome speech to freshmen the first week of school. We gathered in an outdoor courtyard. A dean took the stage and said, "When welcoming the incoming Harvard first-year students, in the old days we'd say, 'Each year our admissions committee accepts the nation's best and brightest. But they do make a few mistakes, too. Don't be a mistake.' We don't say that anymore though." Some students laughed. I didn't laugh. I was too terrified. Also, Harvard Dean Person, saying "We don't say that anymore" doesn't undo the fact that you just did say it. That's like how your blunt friend will say, "I wouldn't tell you this because it'd be mean, but those jeans do not fit you. Also, I would never tell you this because your parents made me promise I wouldn't, but you're adopted. That's why your sister would look great in those jeans but you don't."

I looked around nervously as the dean spoke on. Was I one of the mistakes?

Signs pointed to yes. My first college tribe was the distance-running cohort of the cross-country team. I was recruited after a decent but not stellar high school showing: 4:25 mile time, a second-place finish at the Colorado state track meet, a third-place cross-country finish. I wasn't nearly fast enough to compete on the national level. I knew I wouldn't be the fastest on the team, but I thought I'd be able to hang. I couldn't hang. The jump in speed and volume of training mileage necessary to compete at the collegiate level was too much for me. I struggled through injury for a few years until a quadriceps tear sidelined me my junior year.

The first weeks of school, though, I still thought I might be able to hang. The distance runners had an ongoing group email thread that often deteriorated into bits that mocked so-and-so for having a small such-and-such, or that surmised whose mother had the greatest proclivity for making the sex. The social hierarchy was clear. The freshmen who could keep pace with the upperclassmen in practice participated in the email thread, while those who lagged behind did not. During a thread discussing how to entertain high school recruits visiting for the weekend, despite being a practice straggler, I attempted my first reply.

"Howard Zinn is hear on campus tonight," I wrote. "Not sure if that is the most fun thing, but if I was in high school I would love to here him speak." Homophone errors, you brake my heart. My *hear/here* mistake did not go unnoticed and it would not go unmocked. I wasn't fast and now I wasn't smart. I was a mistake.

I avoided team dinner that night, a pre–race day bonding activity. Instead, I hung out with a different team I'd stumbled on to: an improv comedy troupe called the Immediate Gratification Players. I'd auditioned for IGP after seeing them perform in a lecture hall at a freshman orientation week event. They did a scene about a pair of apple pickers falling in love in which the participants ended up breaking out into song. I thought it was the funniest thing I'd ever seen and I wanted to learn how to do what they did. Later in college, my involvement on the improv team would eventually lead to Comedian supplanting Distance Runner as my primary identity, a shift that started that night when I chose to hang out with the improv team instead of the cross-country team. It was also a choice to be irresponsible the night before a race and participate in a Prince Power Hour.

Drinking was a critical part of the improv comedy team bonding experience. A night of drinking wasn't just a night of drinking. It was a shared journey into altered states of consciousness. A Prince Power Hour proceeded as follows: An iTunes playlist switched to

a new Prince song every sixty seconds, at which point you drank
another shot of beer, often imbibing six to eight cans' worth over
the course of the hour. As the playlist came to an end, feeling happy
to have spent the night with a group of people who didn't chide me
for grammar errors or my 400-meter-interval time, but nonetheless
feeling a twinge of guilt from the rule-following part of my brain, I
decided it was time to go home and get some sleep before the bus left
from the athletic complex across the river at 7 a.m.

At the time of this Prince Power Hour, I was new to drinking.
When I first arrived on campus two months before, I was in the habit
of telling anyone who I had a conversation with for more than five
minutes that I did not drink. I didn't use the term *sober*, but I might
have used the term *straight-edge*. I thought that if I told enough people
I didn't drink, the social shame of going back on my word would
keep me dry, and I wanted to stay dry because I didn't want to be an
admissions mistake. I had told my improv team I didn't drink, so it
was with cautious jubilation that they welcomed my participation in
that evening's journey. My friend AJ from the team offered to walk
me home.

"Just because I'm drinking doesn't mean I don't want to keep
ascending the mountain of success," I said.

"Okay, Nate. So, you fell off the no-drinking wagon tonight,
huh?" AJ said.

"I *am* the wagon," I informed him. At some point I got back to
my dorm.

My alarm goes off and I feel terrible.

I shut off the shrill shriek. On the floor by my bed is a bottle of
yellow Gatorade. I do not find it strange that the cap's protective seal
is open but the 32-ounce bottle is filled to the brim. I vaguely remembered AJ suggesting we pop into a 7-Eleven on our way home,
to buy me a Gatorade.

My head throbbed. The task of leaving my dorm seemed unlikely; the task of taking a bus and then running a race seemed Herculean.

I could do it, I told myself. The Gatorade would be my elixir of strength.

I took a sip. It tasted awful, like rotten salt. Even after I pulled the bottle away the taste lingered in my sinuses, the smell of a fetid oyster stuffed into a gym sock and left in a locker over summer vacation.

I knew from my limited drinking experience that a hangover could make even water seem unappealing, so perhaps it could change how taste buds worked, enough to cause the strange flavor deviations I was experiencing? If I was going to make the bus on time, I had to act fast. I made up my mind: I needed to drink the Gatorade. "It has electrolytes," I told myself.

I took another sip. I gagged. *The nausea of the hangover,* I thought. I tilted the bottle back, plugged my nose, and gulped.

Out-of-focus foamy bubbles floated on the descending surface of the liquid at the top of the upturned bottle. Lots of bubbles. Too many bubbles for Gatorade. The appropriate amount of bubbles for—

I went to the bathroom and made myself throw up. The shared dorm bathrooms down the hallway required a key to unlock them, a key which was impossible to find in the middle of the night when drunk, which could explain why a drunken Nate had evidently made the choice to pee into a Gatorade bottle.

I sent an email to my coach saying I was sick and went back to bed.

As I walked around campus in the days and weeks that followed, I'd look at my classmates and think, *Sure, you've decoded the DNA of a monkey and your dad's a senator and you're in a more advanced level of math than I even knew existed . . . but I drank my own pee.*

College is a time for big changes. I was no longer on the path of direct ascension to success that I thought I'd been on in high school, but I was on some path, and even attempts to climb Mount Everest that end in spectacular failure can result in a decent book. Besides, since Sir Edmund Hillary and Sherpa Tenzing Norgay first summited Mount Everest in 1953, approximately four thousand people have repeated the feat. I'd like to think the number of people who have drunk multiple gulps of their own pee while enrolled at Harvard University is far smaller than that. Perhaps even singular.

Letter to Christopher Columbus
from Leif Eriksson

Dear Christopher,

Hallo. Norse explorer Leif Eriksson here. Just writing to say, "Fuck you."

Let me explain. So, you're an Italian explorer credited with being the first European to discover North America in 1492. But you see, Cristobol, that really boils my lutefisk, because *five hundred years before you* I sailed from Greenland and landed in modern-day Newfoundland and established the settlement of Vinland. And I'm not some crazy Viking pulling your fjord. There is archaeological evidence that supports this claim.

Don't get me wrong, I believe in credit being given where credit is due. So I think you should get credit for what you actually did do. Specifically, this is what you did:

- Intend to sail to Japan but never get there
- Wear a silly-ass hat in every portrait ever painted of you
- Land on an island in the Caribbean and wrongfully identify it as the East Indies
- Call the inhabitants there "Indios," thus establishing an erroneous nomenclature that would last for a thousand years
- Have a US holiday in your honor that people still have to go to work on
- Act like such a dick that your crew constantly threatened mutiny
- Usher in an era of genocide of the existing local population through military conquest and exposure to foreign diseases; four centuries after your arrival the indigenous population of North America was reduced from 12 million to 237,000, representing an astonishing death toll of 95 percent
- Finish your life deposed from your Spanish governorship and then arrested
- To top it all off, for the duration of your life, in the face of clear evidence to the contrary, you maintained that you made it to the East Indies.

And this is what I did:

- Set foot on North American soil five hundred years before Christopher "Colon" Columbus's pansy Italian ass
- Lots of hard-core Viking shit
- Your mom

Just kidding about that last one. I didn't do your mom. That would have required a time machine. But rest assured that if I had access to a time machine in tenth-century Scandinavia, I would have traveled forward half a millennium and made love to your Genoese mom. It would have been consensual, passionate, and multi-orgasm-inducing for both parties involved.

And you know what the real kick in the Oslo is, Chrissy? I'm not even claiming that I was the first European to make it to North America. This merchant from Greenland named Bjarni Herjólfsson discovered it first by accident when he was blown off course on a trade expedition. I just went there after he told me about it.

So I wasn't the first either. But I did make it there before you.

Fuck off,
Leif

Mile Marker 304.1

They were on their way to Centralia when the car broke down. Now there they were. Mark and Allison and Titus the dog and Maggie the car on the shoulder of the interstate, their new home.

Mark hadn't wanted to go to Centralia in the first place. Just because it was within driving distance didn't mean you needed to drive there. Allison liked activities though, so they were doing it. That was a difference between them: Allison did things and enjoyed them, whereas Mark was able to see what was wrong with a thing and therefore why it shouldn't be enjoyed. He saw this as one of his strengths and something of a shortcoming in Allison, perhaps an intelligence that she lacked that he possessed.

Mark had brought up that Maggie was going to give out on them one of these days as another reason not to go on the trip. Allison had reasoned that since it was going to happen one of these days anyway, there was nothing they could do about it and they might as well live their lives and then deal with it when it happened.

Subarus are tough old birds, but approaching a quarter of a million miles was too much even for Maggie. First the vents spit out a foul, dark cloud that Mark hoped didn't smell like Freon. Neither Allison nor Titus seemed bothered by the toxic fumes, though Allison did roll down her passenger-side window to allow Titus to stick out his terrier mutt snout into the passing air.

Next, the air-bag light started blinking, which amused Allison. Maggie kept going just long enough for Mark to theorize on why a car would be equipped with an air-bag light in the first place. Did the light indicate the car had an air bag, in which case it should always be on? Or did it come on to alert the driver that an air bag had been deployed, in which case a blinking light was a redundancy in the presence of the inflated safety device? It was as he was finished expounding on the second rhetorical question that Mark steered Maggie to the shoulder.

"What happened?" Allison asked.

"Car died," Mark said.

Mark got out and lifted up Maggie's hood. Hot oil was splattered everywhere, like Maggie's gallbladder had ruptured and spilled bile over her other organs.

Allison came around with Titus on a leash.

"We'll need to get it towed," Mark said.

They stood without speaking for a moment. Mark waited for Allison to tell him that he'd been right, right that Maggie was about to die and right that they shouldn't have gone on the trip to Centralia. "I'm surprisingly not bothered by this," she said instead. She looked up at the bright blue sky, closed her eyes, and smiled. Titus wasn't bothered either. He panted and looked around dumbly, just like he'd done in the car when they were moving.

That neither Allison nor Titus was bothered by this bothered Mark even more. Mark called a tow truck. The guy on the phone said he was slammed, on account of the holiday weekend, but he'd be by when he could. Mark told the guy that they were stranded on I-80 going west, right by mile marker 304.1, and that they'd wait there until he came.

Mark put his phone in his pocket and looked over at Allison. She looked like she was happy, which struck Mark as dumb. She looked just as happy as Titus, actually, if you could call what Titus looked like happy. Not bothered by circumstance, just like a dog. The dog had no sense that they were in a bad situation, that your car dying was bad and that being stranded on the interstate was bad. The dog probably just thought, *We were and now we are.* Did dogs have a sense of the past? Did they have memories? Mark wasn't sure. Maybe the dog just thought, *I am now.* Or, let's be real, maybe just some version of "bark" over and over in his head, although Titus didn't bark a lot. Did dogs have a running internal monologue like Mark did? Secret thoughts they kept from the world? Maybe not. That was fine. Mark had enough for the three of them.

"You're really not bothered by this?" Mark asked.

"By what?" Allison replied.

"By being stranded on the side of the road like this?"

Allison looked around. She lowered herself down and leaned against the side of the car so that her whole body was in the shade it provided. Titus came and sat on her lap and panted. Titus always looked like he was happy, but Mark was pretty sure dogs didn't feel emotions like happiness. "I am not bothered," Allison answered at last. "Maybe we should just stay here."

What did she mean? Mark envied her shade but remained standing in the sun. He looked at the steady stream of cars passing, contemplating a response. A passing semitruck temporarily gave Mark the relief of its shadow, the rumbling of its motor shaking the ground and in turn shaking Maggie, but then it was gone.

"Fine. If you don't mind it so much, maybe we should just live here now," Mark said.

"Okay," Maggie said.

"Fine," Mark said, crossing his arms. "Or at least until the tow truck gets here."

"Or until whenever," Maggie said.

"Fine, or until whenever. Fine."

So they set about living there, on the side of the road. Time passed. Their cell phones died quickly. Mark's skin got sunburned. They got hungry, but then they figured out ways to get food. Mark kept waiting for Allison to tell him that he'd been right about not wanting to go on the trip, that their lives were worse now, living on the side of a dirty interstate instead of living in a house like they used to, but she didn't.

Allison started a sort of art project. She collected the wildflowers that sprouted up among the nasty thicket of weeds and brambles on the sloping embankment, Titus following her as she did. She arranged the wildflowers into different beautiful shapes that often caught the interest of children with their faces pressed to the backseat windows of cars. Allison would wave at them when she'd catch their smiles passing in a flash.

Mark spent his time by cataloguing the various trash he could see from where he stood, leaning against the car. Dirty Legos, cans of Monster Energy drink, cigarette butts, a single metal screw, a blanket of unidentified faded detritus, so much plastic—plastic that was once part of a car, an empty antifreeze bottle, a yellow bucket half-filled with dirt, a plastic pot the color of terra-cotta, an empty plastic cup, a plastic lid, a plastic straw—the rubber pieces of a blown tire, beer cans, beer bottles, squat bottles that once held malt liquor with their labels long since washed away by the elements and the passage of time, lumber that looked unnaturally geometric with its rigid rectangular lines next to the organic curves of the sticks and trees of the wild growth, the flattened cardboard of a Happy Meal box.

More time passed. Mark's sunburn grew worse. Allison often invited him to sit in the shade of the car with her, but he refused, preferring to suffer, standing in the sun hoping that Allison would acknowledge his suffering. Mark would sometimes find food in the trash that he catalogued. He'd bring back the food to the roof of their car, which served as a dining table. Over meals, Allison told Mark about her wildflowers, and Mark told Allison about the trash he had seen. Allison always asked Mark follow-up questions, and sometimes she'd even tell him about the trash she had seen, in an effort to appreciate his interests.

"Earlier when I walked down the road," Allison said one day, "I saw a pile of shattered glass on the shoulder."

"Yeah?" Mark said as he chewed on what was probably a piece of beef jerky.

"Yep, right down there," Allison said, pointing. They each looked at the sparkling pile of shattered glass. It was about twenty yards away. "Good thing the car didn't die there."

"Why's that?" Mark asked.

"Because then we wouldn't be able to sit and lean against the car."

"Only you do that."

"Yeah, but you could if you wanted."

More time passed. Allison's art project grew and Mark's sunburn peeled and cracked. Allison figured out which butterflies liked which flowers, and she was able to get the butterflies to gather in shapes organized by their colors, fragile flapping bursts of white and yellow and orange. Mark stared at the butterflies and wondered what they were doing. Were they fighting for the nectar from the flowers that Allison picked? It looked like they were dancing, but butterflies didn't dance, of course. Maybe they were fucking? Was that how insects reproduced? Sometimes passing motorists would slow to admire Allison's creation. Some would even pull over, snap a photo, then drive away.

More time passed. Mark's sunburn oozed and ached. On one particularly hot day, a day with no clouds and fewer passing semitrucks than usual, Mark gave in and tried sitting on the ground with Allison. She smiled at him when he joined her down on the shoulder. She welcomed him and patted him on his pant leg, where his skin wasn't tender from the searing sun.

Allison was right. It was much more comfortable in the shade of the dead car. Mark put his hands on the ground and noticed that the asphalt wasn't black like it appeared when you were speeding along over it. It was actually a collection of stones stuck in black tar, unmoving like they were. White, orange, red, speckled, gray, pink stones.

Then Mark saw red ants crawling near them on the ground. The ants made Mark nervous. What if they crawled on his skin? What if these were the types of ants that bit? Then a jet-black cricket appeared. It moved uncannily fast, teleporting from one spot on the ground to another. It frightened Mark. It looked stronger than the sickly crickets you saw in pet stores that were fed to lizards. It zipped close to Mark and he shot up, returning to his standing spot.

More time passed and the cars never stopped streaming by. They made a constant, repeating sound like waves crashing, the noise punctuated by the lower-pitched rumbling of the larger trucks or the higher-pitched trill of motorcycles, joining together with the buzz of insects and the breeze in the trees beyond to create a relentless white noise that enveloped Mark and Allison.

One night as Allison closed her eyes to go to sleep on the

ground, Titus curled up in her lap and snoring contentedly, Mark called down to her.

"Why'd you want to go to Centralia anyway? A ghost town with an underground coal-mine fire that's been smoldering away for decades. Why would a person want to see that?" he asked.

Allison opened her eyes and thought before replying. "I heard that there were still parts where you could see the smoke rising up from under the ground. I wanted to see that for myself," she said.

"That smoke is probably toxic, you know," he said.

Before Allison could reply, a tow truck pulled over.

Mark and Allison watched at the truck came to a stop, then backed up until it was right in front of Maggie. The other cars kept streaming by.

"You Mark?" the tow truck driver asked as he got out. Mark nodded. "Damn, looks like you got burned bad, man. I might have some aloe back in my first-aid kit if you—"

"I'm fine," Mark said, cutting him off. "Thanks though."

"Suit yourself. So, only got room for one of ya," the tow truck driver said. "The dog can sit on the lap of whoever I take first, and then I'll come back for the other one. The shop isn't far."

Mark looked at Allison. Then he looked at the art she'd made. He looked at Titus at her feet. He looked at the spot where she liked to sit on the ground. He looked back at her. He tried to read her mind.

"Never mind then," Mark said to the tow truck driver. "Just leave us here." Then he turned to Allison and asked quietly, "Is that what you want?"

"Doesn't bother me either way," Allison said. Titus barked, the first time he had in a while.

How to Explain Business
Mergers to Your Child

"Daddy, what does *merger* mean?"

I looked up to see the sweet face of my six-year-old Lisa gazing at me from the doorway, her eyes confused but curious, a CNNMoney program faintly audible from the playroom behind her. I knew this day would come. I just didn't know it would be this soon.

My fault for letting her stay up to watch past her bedtime, I thought to myself. They don't give you a manual when you become a single father. But nothing to be done about it now. It was time for The Talk.

"Come here, sweetheart," I said as I took a seat at the kitchen table, gesturing for Lisa to come sit on my lap. "Where did you hear that word?"

"The man on the TV said that Burger King and Tim Hortons are having a *merger*." She said the word slowly, still unsure how she felt about it. She wrapped her tiny arms around me and buried her head into my chest. "Oh, Daddy, what does it mean?"

Where was I to begin? It was moments like these that made being a single father such a hard job, but also what made it so worthwhile.

"Well, sweetheart, when two companies love each other very much, and they think they'd be able to make more together than they would apart, sometimes they decide to merge into one company. That's a merger."

"Only one company? Does it make one of the companies go bye-bye?" she asked with great concern in her eyes. I couldn't help but laugh at her worry, my heart swelling with love for her innocence.

"No, sweetheart. It makes one big company that has all the assets of both companies combined!"

"Oh." I watched as the gears turned in her mind as she considered this new data, brain synapses firing, synthesizing the new information. She put a finger to her chin, tilted her head back, and continued with her questions.

"But whose name do they take?"

"Well, sometimes more progressive companies might hyphenate their names to form a big long new name, but usually the name of the bigger company is what both companies start going by."

"Isn't that confusing for people who used to shop at the smaller company?"

"It can be! But everybody figures it out."

"Wait, Daddy, Tim Hortons will be called Burger King? But they sell coffee, not burgers!" she said, smiling, enjoying grilling her old man.

"Good point, my darling. Sometimes the smaller company will keep its existing name, and the changes will just be in terms of things like ownership and where that company pays taxes. This is sort of like a 'green-card merger,' I guess you could say."

"But why would Burger King want to buy a coffee store chain?"

"Because of, well . . ." I debated whether I should introduce the term. Sometimes answering the questions of children felt like putting out a fire with gasoline; explaining one term only led to a burst of new questions. "Well," I continued on, "because of something called *tax inversion*."

"Tax *imbersion*?" She pronounced the term with all the incredulity her small frame could muster. I again couldn't help but laugh. Noticing my laughter, she played up her disgust, puffing up her cheeks and rolling her eyes around, making me laugh more.

"That's right, sweetheart. Tax inversion. Burger King is moving their headquarters to Ontario to avoid US corporate taxes."

"Oh." She grabbed the bottom of her shirt and seemed to consider whether her curiosity had been satiated. "But isn't it an American company? Is Burger King a bad guy for doing . . . tax inversion?"

I hesitated. Lisa loved Burger King. And I loved taking her there after her morning tae kwon do classes every Saturday. It felt American, eating my Whopper while I watched Lisa run around the play area, occasionally running back to our table to grab a fry, dipping it in our shared frosty chocolate shake before running back to scream and laugh with the other children. Did I dare risk demystifying something so good and pure? But of course, she'd hear it eventually, and better from me than from some school yard bully attempting to be cool by passing on information an older sibling had taunted him with. I took in a deep breath and proceeded. There would be no turning back, but then again, there never is. Kids just keep growing up.

"Many companies we think of as American are actually international conglomerates," I started, holding her trusting gaze as I went, "and Burger King, well, it has been owned for years by 3G Capital, a Brazilian investment firm."

"International con-gwomerate?" she said, closing her eyes and covering her face with her hands. She adopted a silly voice imitating one of her favorite cartoon characters, a capybara detective, as she added, "And what the heck is an investment firm?"

I narrowed my eyes at her use of *heck* but decided to pick my battles, choosing instead to answer her question. "Well, investment firms are companies that get really happy when they can make other companies happy by helping them to merge, such as 3G Capital, which is really great at this. They helped Anheuser-Busch, the company that makes Daddy's beer"—I gestured with the Budweiser can in my hand to the several empty cans on the kitchen table—"merge in 2008 with a company called InBev, which itself was a merger of the Brazilian company AmBev and the Belgian company Interbrew. Investment firms help companies become international conglomerates, so a daddy in Europe can drink the same great-tasting Bud that your daddy can drink here. Pretty neat, huh?" I took a sip for emphasis.

"Yeah, that's neat," Lisa said, but her attention was drifting. Perhaps I was unloading too much information on her at once. But on the other hand, I had made a promise to myself to always be honest with her. Any question she asked, I would answer. No matter what. It's what Ruth would have wanted.

I could tell her little brain was still thinking, coming up with more to ask. She sat up straight and looked me in the eyes.

"Daddy, why do some people think that some corporations shouldn't be allowed to merge with the corporation they want to merge with?"

I gasped. I'd known that The Talk would be hard, but hadn't expected that we'd have to address this aspect of things at the same time. She was so young. Couldn't the world just let kids be kids?

"Who told you that, my darling?"

"This kid at school Ryan. Ryan said his parents said that Comcast wanted to merge with Time Warner Cable but that they shouldn't be allowed. He said that their merger was evil."

I took this all in, wanting to be sure of my words before I replied. Was growing up always this hard? It seemed like I'd grown up in a simpler time, but I imagine men having to answer difficult questions from their daughters had felt that way for many generations back.

"That wasn't a very nice thing of his parents to say. In this house, we believe that any company should be able to be with any other company it wants."

"That's what the free market is all about, right, Daddy?"

I beamed. For the first time in my life, I beamed. I was bound to make some mistakes as a father. Lots of them. But every once in a while, you get a moment like this, and you know that you're doing at least something right.

"That's right, sweetheart. That's what the free market is all about."

She smiled, happy with herself for getting this last bit right all on her own. She extended her hand out in front of her, making circles in the air. She began to hum a song to herself, her mind apparently at ease, moving away from all questions of "mergers." Thankfully, she was watching CNN and not HBO: Then I would have had to answer questions about acquisitions, which I am happy to put off as long as possible.

Not wanting the moment to end, but also wanting to make sure that she was completely content, I asked, "Anything else on your mind, my dear?"

She crossed her arms and pouted her lips, playing up the theatricality of pondering whether she had any more questions. At last, her eyes widened as a lightbulb went off.

"I do have one more question, Daddy."

"What is it?"

"Can we go to Burger King after tae kwon do on Saturday?"

"Of course."

And with that, satisfied, she grabbed my face and kissed my cheek as she slipped off my lap to the floor, singing an impromptu song to herself about burgers and fries as she scampered back into the playroom.

I let out a sigh of relief. Hearing my daughter giggle like that, I couldn't help but think to myself that maybe I wasn't so bad at this single-father thing after all.

Walt Whitman, Spin Class Instructor

"Whatever satisfies the soul is truth. Pedal to the beat."

"I believe a leaf of grass is no less than the journey-work of the stars. Turn your resistance knob one full turn to the right."

"Keep your face always toward the sunshine—and shadows will fall behind you. Also, keep your heels down—and your core will be engaged."

"Every moment of light and dark is a miracle. Sprint!"

"Let your soul stand cool and composed before a million universes. This is an active cooldown to burn lactic acid."

"Viewed freely, the English language is the accretion and growth of every dialect, race, and range of time, and is both the free and compacted composition of all. We are raising the roof at our own cardio party."

"The future is no more uncertain than the present. Let the rhythm of Katy Perry's 'Roar' push you harder than you ever thought possible."

"Now I see the secret of making the best person: It is to grow in the open air and to eat and sleep with the Earth. Your butt should be back above the saddle."

"Oh while I live, to be the ruler of life, not a slave, to meet life as a powerful conqueror, and nothing exterior to me will ever take command of me. So, if you don't want to buy your own spin shoes, you can rent a pair at the front desk for three dollars."

"Give me odorous at sunrise a garden of beautiful flowers where I can walk undisturbed. This is the last hill, commit!"

"Actually that wasn't the last hill, one more to go! Do I contradict myself? Very well, then I contradict myself, I am a spin class instructor, I contain multitudes."

Politician Responds to Rumor He Is a Scientist

To the Citizens of the Great State of Florida,

When asked about climate change at a press conference in Miami earlier this week, I responded by saying, "I'm not a scientist."

But the truth is, I am a scientist.

I always have been and always will be. And yes, this confession is precipitated by the fact that late last night I was caught doing science in an airport Marriott.

The signs were there since childhood. My parents suspected something after I crafted a barometer out of a mason jar and a cut-up balloon for the school science fair. That summer they sent me to a camp meant to get young boys to do nonscientific activities like "play ball." But it was at that camp that I experimented with my best friend, Kyle. We stole some vinegar and baking soda from the kitchen, snuck out into the woods, and then simulated a volcanic eruption.

As many of you know, I was in the navy. But what you might not know is that I served in active duty aboard the USS *Glover* as a radar man. Radar is an object-detection system that uses radio waves to determine the range, altitude, direction, and speed of nearby objects. Guess what? Radar don't run on belief. Radar is a whole bunch of science.

I see now that it was wrong of me to deny that I was a scientist all these years.

To my fellow citizens, I apologize for my deception but not for who I am.

To my God, I would apologize to you if I believed in you, which as a scientist I do not. I also do not not believe in you, as that would be to assume too much on the other side. I am awaiting more data.

And to my family, I can only pray—pray figuratively, of course—that you will use the tool of deductive reasoning which I tried to pass on to you in order to, one day, understand why I behaved as I did.

Since it has become clear to me that politics is no place for science, I hereby resign from my position of governor. It has been an honor, but to my own self I must be true.

Sincerely,

Your Governor

P.S. I am grateful that you all didn't make a big deal about the loads of gay stuff I was doing on the side. That was cool of you guys.

Old Polish Woman Walks Her Old White Dog

In the town where I grew up there was this old Polish woman who we'd always see walking around the high school with this old white dog. They both just looked so ancient, this woman and this dog. They each had puffy white hair that was dirty not from the dirt of the day but the wear of years. They walked so slow. It wasn't like the old lady was walking slow because the dog was slow or the other way around. The leash was limp between her hand and its neck. They staggered around at the same slow pace.

I couldn't believe how slow they walked.

I never talked to her, but I knew she was Polish because the town where I grew up, Cheektowaga, had a large Polish population. So everybody was pretty much either Polish, or else you weren't. My family was one of the ones that wasn't. One time I heard her talking to her dog in a language that sounded Polish. It was funny to think about her dog knowing all of the Polish words for *sit* and *no* and other words people say to dogs. I knew what Polish sounded like because my parents would say something to each other when we'd hear the people who worked at the bakery or the grocery store speak in a language that wasn't English. It sounded different than Spanish, which was the other non-English language people spoke in our town. *Cheektowaga* wasn't a Polish or an English word though. It was a Seneca Indian word for *crab apples*.

The old Polish woman walked her old white dog every day at the same time before and after school when we were all walking or driving or taking the bus. Maybe she walked it other times, too, but she definitely walked it at those times. Every day. Every school day at least. She was kind of famous among the kids at school. People called her "Walking Woman." One of the high school bands even wrote a song about her called "Walking Woman" as a joke and sang it in a garage at a party. It wasn't mean and it didn't make fun of her or anything and we even toasted our beers to her, but I bet if somebody told her some high school kids sang a song about her at a party she probably wouldn't get it and might think we were making fun of her even though nobody was. I guess her walking schedule just overlapped with our school schedule. Anyway, it sure seemed like she was walking all the time.

One day, though, when I was walking to school by myself because I missed the bus, I saw the woman walking by herself. No dog. Just the old Polish woman alone. She looked so strange without her dog, like naked, but not gross or sexual. It startled me. I stopped in my tracks and probably let my jaw drop down. We made eye contact. She didn't smile. I guess I wasn't smiling either, because people don't usually smile when they are shocked. I looked away and picked up my pace. I wanted to tell somebody, but then again it didn't seem like news or anything worth sharing. But sure enough, by lunchtime everybody was talking about how they'd seen or heard somebody had seen Walking Woman walking by herself. Nobody was sure what it meant, but to me it seemed pretty obvious what it meant.

I didn't see her the next day. Not seeing her at all was almost as strange as seeing her without her dog the day before. It was like God had come with an eraser and erased her dog first and then come back to finish. But the day after that, I saw her. I was heading to school early to meet up with some kids from my chemistry class to work on a group project. The air was cold and I could see my breath. I was keeping my head down to avoid the wind but I looked up when I heard her voice, loud and frustrated. Across the street I saw her holding on to a leash that was pulling violently all over the place. Between parked cars I saw a little white puff of hair zipping around the sidewalk. I stopped and stood still as I watched without shame. Walking Woman made her way down the street, shouting sharp Polish commands the whole time at the new puppy that wouldn't mind her at all. I don't know what the breed was, but I could tell it was the exact same breed as her other dog. She disappeared around a corner, still shouting, "Nee-yah! Nee-yah!" I think maybe that was the dog's name. Or maybe it was Polish for *bad dog* or *crab apple* or who knows what.

It made me sad to think about that old Polish woman getting a new dog like that, just a couple days later and the exact same breed as her old dog, and for a long time I couldn't figure out why.

Parts Nate Dern Has Auditioned For

It's exciting to be an aspiring actor in New York City. Even though you haven't found your big break yet, you can still appreciate all of the exciting roles you get to be rejected for along the way. After all, there are no small roles, only roles that seem small.

Man with glasses: Looking to cast man with glasses for eye doctor commercial for local limited-release run. Men without glasses also okay; production has pair of fake glasses talent can rent for a small fee.

Easily overlooked man: Nondescript guy who people often don't even realize is in the room. Must be good with cats, but not too good with cats. Seeing all ages and ethnicities.

Health food store cashier: Talent should look like someone who could work at a health food store, a type of store known for hiring all types and ages of people. Nonspeaking role.

Stuart: Should be average-looking. Not good-looking, but not bad-looking. If you're an agent reading this casting breakdown, think of your top 25 percent best-looking clients. Do not submit any of them. Should be over forty but not look over twenty. Series regular.

Hipster bartender: Looking for real hipster bartenders. People with the ability to look and act like hipster bartenders need not apply. Director is interested in authenticity for this fried-snack-food webisode. Nonunion and no pay. Footage of spot provided on request if talent is persistent in requesting it, and even then it will take six to eight months.

Ernest: Tech start-up worker, but without a too over-the-top tech-start-up-worker look. Talent should look like he could have muttonchops, BUT TALENT MUST NOT ACTUALLY HAVE MUTTONCHOPS. Talent must be willing to grow mutton chops if asked, though. Please, no conflicts with yogurt or yogurt products.

IT worker: Looking for IT worker type who has real IT skills. In particular, must be able to troubleshoot why casting office's Wi-Fi is so darn slow and how to get laptops to print to office printer just like the desktop at the receptionist's desk. Audition will entail demonstrating these skills in real time. Shoot dates undisclosed at this time.

Paunchy man: Paunchy. Looking for a youngish guy with a paunch. Paunch should be distinguished by large or protruding abdomen or stomach. Note: We are not looking for beer bellies, guts, or fat tires.

Director knows the difference. Do not waste his time or yours. True paunches only. Paunchy paunchy paunchy.

Roger: Looking for a "ghost" type. Ideally, talent will be apparition of a deceased person manifesting itself in the earthly plane as an ethereal image. Poltergeists and spooks okay. Talent must be able to glide through walls. Improv comedy background a plus.

Eduardo: Bodybuilder with a heart of gold. Ideally, talent is either fluent in Spanish or has a motorcycle license (NOT both). Scale.

Talking cat: Looking for talking-cat types. Real talking cats only. Guitar skills a plus but not required. Producers would like to note that ideally talent can play both human and cat-size guitars, since that part of the script is still in flux.

Glornash, Conqueror of Worlds: Client seeks Glornash, Conqueror of Worlds. Talent must be able conquer worlds on command because director likes to improvise on set and do lots of takes. If talent has conquered worlds for previous roles, please include a password-protected Vimeo link to footage of world conquering. Good teeth a must.

Nate Dern: Should be a Nate Dern type, aspiring writer/actor whose ambitions outpace his abilities. Lead role in unauthorized biopic for untelevised UPN20 broadcast. Director doesn't want casting to be too on the nose, though, so real Nate Derns need not apply.

This Is a Dream and I'm Going to Kill You

A glass of water perches on a nightstand next to a bed where a couple sleeps. Morning light fills the room. An orange glow warms the white walls and gray sheets. He wakes, transitioning from non-consciousness to consciousness. He turns over and sees that she is alert, eyes wide open and staring at him, waiting.

"Whoa. You freaked me out. How long have you been up?" he says. His words come out wobbly.

"I have something to tell you," she says.

"Yeah? What's that?" he says. His eyes shut again.

"This is a dream and I'm going to kill you."

"Huh?" His eyes open again. Her expression is neither joking nor threatening, neither inviting nor aggressive.

"I said that this is a dream."

"Okay."

"And in this dream I'm going to kill you. But since it's just a dream, you don't need to worry about it. Your death, I mean." She pauses here, but then her eyes go up to the sharp corner of the white ceiling and it seems to remind her of something else she had to say. "There are so many things that we should worry about. Climate change, racism, sexism, the literacy gap, the income-inequality gap, the access-to-health-care gap, and probably a whole bunch of others gaps we aren't even aware of yet."

His left eyebrow arches like a cat surprised by a cucumber.

"Is this supposed to be funny? Because it's not," he says.

"Have you ever noticed how the white of our ceiling is a different color white than the walls?" she says, pointing up. "At least I think it is. It could just be a trick of perspective." She brings her hand down and traces her finger on top of the sheets and then onto his chest.

"Anyway," she says, letting her hand fall flat on his chest. "All of that is to say that what's going to happen now—me killing you in this dream?—is not worth worrying about. This being a dream and all. Make sense?"

For a moment it seems like she is going to continue, but she does not. Instead she stares at him. She blinks once, languidly. He waits for her to laugh. Or to smile. Or to say, "I'm joking."

But there is no indication she is anything but serious. She is waiting for him to say that he understands, but he does not.

"Cut it out," he says instead. "I drank too much last night. I think somebody roofied my drink or something." He closes his eyes.

She lifts her hand up from his chest and brings it down in a slap. "I don't think you should joke about Rohypnol."

"I don't think you should joke about killing me!" he says.

"I'm not joking about that," she says as she rolls her eyes, as though he is a child that she has had to repeatedly tell that they are driving to the doctor's office, not to the McDonald's PlayPlace.

"Rape culture is one of the serious issues you should worry about."

He closes his eyes. He isn't sleepy anymore, but he wants to go back to sleep anyway. He feels pressure on his torso and opens his eyes to find her over him, her hands pressing down hard on his shoulders.

"What are you doing?" he says, an edge in his voice.

"I told you. I'm going to kill you, but because it's a dream, then you'll just wake up," she says, with no edge of any kind in her voice.

"What are you talking about?" he says. He sits up and turns to face her. She mirrors his movements.

"I was trying to explain what will happen after I kill you in this dream. I was saying that the dream will be over, so you'll wake up. Or I suppose you could move on to another dream. The average person has three to five dreams per night, but some have up to seven."

"I never remember my dreams," he says.

"I bet you'll remember this one," she says, almost flirting. "Ooh, maybe the dream you have after this one will be a sex dream?" She places her hand on his leg, slowly moving it toward his crotch. He puts his hand on hers, holding it still. He is unnerved, but this new direction is lifting his spirits.

"Maybe this dream could be a sex dream?" he says, playing along.

"Unfortunately not," she says, like she's a waitress telling a customer that the restaurant is out of milk. "Like I indicated earlier, this is a killing dream, not a sex dream." She stares at him. He tries to read her expression. He can't.

"Okay. I give up. What's going on?"

"I told you," she says, leaning in, lowering her voice, her lips close to his ear. She breathes hard. He becomes aroused, his physical reaction involuntary. She raises her hand to his chest on an upward trajectory to stroke his cheek but stops short at his neck, where she grasps forcefully, closing down hard on his windpipe and restricting the flow of blood through his carotid artery. Just a moment, just until he can raise his hand and strike hers away.

"What the fuck are you doing? This isn't a dream!" His voice is all edge now. It is just meant to cut, to hurt her like she has just hurt him. He has never spoken to her this way.

"How do you know it's not a dream? Why do you always have to be right?" she says loudly. For the first time she seems to react, to come alive and meet him at his level. For reasons out of his control, he feels shame at her scolding.

He is as awake as she is now. He looks away from her, embarrassed at how upset he's become. He throws the covers off him, hoping the heat will dissipate and he'll cool down.

"I know it's not a dream because . . ." He trails off. "I know it's not a dream because I know what's real and what's not real."

"Well, you're wrong about that," she says. He doesn't like being told he's wrong. She's right that he always has to be right.

"*I'm* wrong?" he says.

"Yes. See, from your own perspective, there's no way of knowing that you aren't having a dream right now. Your whole life could have been a dream."

"Like *The Matrix*?"

"More like Descartes's 'evil demon' or Hilary Putnam's 'brain in a vat.'"

"Are you just trying to make me feel dumb now? Should we call up some of our friends so you can do this in front of them? Maybe put your parents on speakerphone?"

"Look at that glass of water on our nightstand," she says. He looks at it. It looks like a glass of water. It's a Bell mason jar purchased as a part of a twelve-pack from a dollar store nearby. It's filled almost to the top with water. The previous night she took one sip before offering it to him, which he declined. He remembers this. It's still there. This seems to prove him right that it isn't a dream, doesn't it? He doesn't know what she's getting at.

"It looks like a glass of water," he says.

"Are you sure it's there?"

"Yes."

"Well, you're wrong," she says. He is getting tired of being told he's wrong. "See, you can't even be sure that you're not dreaming right now, so if you can't be sure of that, you can't be sure of anything, including that a glass of water is on that nightstand."

"Yes, I can. Watch." He reaches for the glass and takes a sip of water. "My mouth was dry and now it's not, so—"

"You experienced your mouth as dry, and now you experience your mouth as wet. You can't say with any ontological certainty that the actual state of—"

"Okay, whatever. Is this because last night at the bar I corrected you about what band was playing? I'm sorry, but Yes and Pink Floyd sound nothing alike. Prog rock is important to me, okay?"

She is silent.

"Come on. I admitted your thing, so you admit my thing now," he says. He is floundering. "That's a relationship, right? Admitting each other's staunchly held points early in the morning so you're not angry at each other all day?" He is trying to joke, to get her to smile.

"Fine, whatever you say is how it is," she says, turning away from him and closing her eyes. She seems mad.

He shakes his head in disbelief. They have not fought like this before. He gets up and goes to the bathroom to splash some water on his face. She is not acting like herself. He walks naked into the kitchen and puts four scoops of ground coffee into a French press. He leaves it to brew and returns to the bedroom. He gets on top of the gray sheets next to her. The room is brighter now. He spoons her, the sheets a barrier between them.

"But if it were a dream," she says barely audibly, keeping her eyes closed, "you admit that it wouldn't matter if I killed you, right?"

"Sure," he says. He'd say anything to end the fight.

"Do you really mean that, or are you just saying that because you're trying to end the fight?" she says, her eyes still closed, her body still turned away.

"I mean it. If this were just a dream, it wouldn't matter what happened. Dreams don't matter."

She opens her eyes and turns to him. She smiles. She moves in again close to his face, as before, and involuntarily, he tenses up. This time, though, her hand does not go for his throat. She twists her body and moves one leg over both of his, straddling him, landing in a seated position on his waist. They look into each other's eyes. Moving slowly, she leans down, her lips near his ear again. He hears her breathing. He becomes aroused.

"I can prove to you this is a dream," she whispers, her lips grazing his earlobe as they form the words.

"How?" he says. They're not looking into each other's eyes, but their cheeks are touching.

"The glass of water on the nightstand is a knife now."

They both turn to see if what she said is true. He sees that it is true. It is a large kitchen knife, the kind used to slice flank steak or other large cuts of meat.

But then something strange happens. It happens fast. Watch:

The glass of water is again a glass of water.

Now it is a knife.

Now it is a glass of water.

Now the glass of water is a knife.

Now the glass of water is a glass of water.

Now the knife is a knife.

Now it is a glass knife. Now it is a glass of knife.

Now the knife is a glass of water and always has been.

He feels sick. His body can't keep up with the changes. He needs to steady himself, to step off, but there is nothing steady to reach for. He is disoriented. She is not. She reaches for something. What she reaches for is the knife. It is a knife now and it always has been.

This part happens even faster. Watch:

He tries to say something to her about stopping. He sees a flash of the knife. It looks sharp as she raises it above her head with both hands. It looks like it will cut as she brings it down toward his flesh.

He wakes.

He bolts upward, bending his torso swiftly up from his waist. He is sitting up now. He is breathing fast. He is sweating.

He looks at her. She is sleeping. He looks past her to the nightstand and sees a glass of water.

He slows his breathing. The gray sheets around him are damp. He pats the moisture, then smells his hands. He lies back down. He turns away from her, toward the wall, and tries to go back to sleep. He closes his eyes but sleep doesn't come.

"Hey," he hears her whisper. "I have something to tell you."

The Show of *LIFE!*

It was after killing himself that Josh learned he'd lost the reality show.

That was hours ago. Now he waited alone in a sterile room with a sign on the wall that read DEPROGRAMMING. He sat upright in a metal-framed bed. He wore a hospital gown, off-white with faded blue horses. The shades were drawn.

Josh stared down at his hands clasped together on his belly. He probed his left thumb gingerly with his right thumb, inspecting for proof that the digits were there and that he was alive. They seemed real, but he'd been wrong before.

He knew he should be thinking about what the hell was happening, but all he could think about was Linda.

Entering the Deprogramming room, a woman who looked too young to be a psychologist introduced herself as a psychologist.

"You're going through a lot right now. Yes, your life was a part of a reality TV show called *LIFE!* You'll get through this. We wouldn't be running into our third season if they could prove this was unethical. You must have questions, huh?"

Josh stared at her. He blinked. She smiled.

Josh's body felt like it was thawing. His mind was looping his most immediate memory: of killing himself and then waking up in a studio to a man with white teeth and a tailored purple blazer standing over him. The man had approached Josh, grinning wider, then said into a microphone, "Josh! No! Buddy, you just . . ." The host twirled to a studio audience who chanted, "FUCKED! UP! YOUR! *LIFE!*" in elated paroxysms of cheers.

While he did it, he hadn't felt sadness or regret. More a bewilderment that he was actually doing what he had so often considered. Maybe even a twinge of curiosity. His body had been like meat. It responded to the pressure and friction of the blade like a chicken cutlet, putting up no greater fight for the human soul it was purported to contain.

The too-young-looking-to-be-a-psychologist psychologist was speaking to him. Her words were just sounds. He strained to understand her.

"What?" he said. His voice sounded strange. He must have been under a lot of medication. He felt groggy.

"I said, do you have any questions?"

"What's your name?"

"Erin."

"So, Erin, my whole life was fake?"

Erin rolled her eyes and laughed. "We try to avoid using terms like *fake* or *real* in Deprogramming. I watched you on *LIFE!* It felt real at the time, didn't it? Hey—do you like bad coffee?" She produced a thermos and two insulated paper cups from her bag.

"If you watched me, then you know the answer to that question."

"I'll take that as a yes!" She poured them each a cup. "A cranky yes, but still a yes." He did like shitty coffee. Convenience store coffee, black, was his favorite. Josh had liked convenience in general. He never heated up his leftovers. He always ordered the first thing on the menu. Linda had called those examples of his self-destructive tendencies. Not taking therapy seriously was another.

She handed him the coffee.

"Thanks. No milk?"

"I know you like it black. Like you said—I watched your season."

"That's invasive."

"That's nothing. I saw the first time you ever masturbated," she teased, dropping her professional decorum.

"They aired that, huh?" said Josh. He made a glottal noise of indignation and wiggled himself upright. "Television these days."

"You had your mom's black-and-white photography book opened up to the chapter on nude portraits," Erin continued. "That lady had some pubes, huh?"

"I would have thought the fact that I did it into the tube of a vacuum cleaner would have been the more salient detail."

"No! Is that true?"

"As far as I remember."

"Incredible. Just goes to show—even with a life broadcast to the masses, you still have a few secrets."

Josh stared at her. Was she insinuating what he thought she was? She saw his gaze, then her face went white. Shit. She hadn't been referring to it—to that—but she sure as hell knew about it, and she was thinking about it now. So that had been a part of his show. Figures. He deserved that. He deserved that and worse.

Was he happy he wasn't dead? *Happy* wasn't the right word to describe how he was feeling, he knew that much. He had heard somewhere that of the people who survived jumping off the Golden Gate

Bridge, a large percentage reported that as they were falling they re-gretted their decision. Probably one of those bullshit factoids that gets repeated because it sounds nice. There was, of course, no data on the regret ratio of those who ended their lives. A biased survey sample.

"Anyway, they don't show your entire life," Erin said, returning to her professional tone. "More like a life-highlight reel. I mean, it's just one season. And you're not even the only contestant."

He'd been a contestant, eh? It had felt like that at the time, to the extent that he'd felt like a loser his whole life. People don't wake up from killing themselves. They stay dead. Maybe this was his purgatory.

"One nice moment I remember from *LIFE!*," Erin said, "was when you gave your turkey-and-Swiss sandwich to Greg McGovern in high school."

Hah. He had done that. Greg was a freshman on the football team when Josh was a senior. Greg's family was poor. At least once a week he wouldn't bring a packed lunch from home or have enough money to buy one. He'd just sit there, not eating. It happened all season long. Finally, Josh had given him his sandwich. Just one time. Not like he'd saved his life or adopted him. On top of that, people had given Greg shit about it. And on top of that, Josh had only done it because he thought Greg's younger sister Brenna was hot. He thought maybe Greg would mention it to her and it would score him some points. It seemed the show had left that part out of their edit. It was important for character's to be likable for the audience.

"Do you remember that?" Erin broke the silence.

"Yeah, I remember." Josh was certain this was not real. People didn't wake up from killing themselves. He'd made some dumb mis-takes in life, but he could figure this out. What the fuck was going on?

Erin stood up and threw her cup away. "You lost your season—everyone who kills themselves automatically loses *LIFE!*—but you did have some fans."

Fans. "Oh yeah?" What if he killed himself again in this room? He could smash the window and slit his wrist with the shards. How many levels deep would this shit go?

"You have a few hundred thousand fans, actually," Erin said.

Josh thought this over. "Not millions?"

"No. But I am one of them. Normally it wouldn't be SOP for them to assign a fan of yours to be your Deprogrammer, but I downplayed my fandom."

"Oh," Josh said. She stared at him until he looked away.

"Hey," she said, calling him back to her. "Want to get out of here?"

A cairn of blue rubber clogs, gray sweatpants, a white T-shirt, white underwear, a gray baseball cap, and aviator sunglasses rested atop the closed toilet seat. No mirror.

Josh, wearing his new civilian civvies, and Erin, still wearing her lab coat, walked down the hallway and entered an elevator. Erin pressed a button and they started moving up.

"Anything I should know?" said Josh.

"Lots. Be more specific," said Erin.

"About the future? Like, are there going to be flying cars and stuff?"

"This isn't the future. This is the present."

"I know, but I mean—"

"LIFE! simulates births thirty years in the past. People feel nostalgia about the past thirty years, plus this way we don't have to make guesses about future technologies, which helps with our Verisimilitude and Relatablity focus-group scores. You got to the age of twenty-nine, so in your LIFE! the simulated year was 2018. The actual year is 2019."

"LIFE! ends when you turn thirty?"

"Yeah. Early focus groups showed that key demos became less

interested in *LIFE!* after the contestants turned thirty. So those who get to the age of thirty are finalists and then they do big clip show episodes, including *never-before-seen footage*—hah!—and then viewers vote for who had the best life."

The elevator doors opened to a nearly empty parking garage.

Erin walked toward the single car visible in the lot and Josh ambled after her. It was a battered station wagon that pretty evidently couldn't fly. As Josh got to the passenger door, he saw his reflection in the window. It wasn't him. Josh bent his head down to the side-view mirror for a closer look. He palpated his cheeks, forehead, nose. He tugged at his ears. He blinked. He moved his hands from his face to his body, feeling his own dimensions. The rhythm of his arms as they swung by his side, the length of his stride as he walked had felt strange, but he'd attributed it all to the effects of whatever medical procedure he'd undergone. It made sense his body would not be his body, though.

He got in the car. "So I'm really not me, huh?" he said. Erin didn't reply. She started the engine and steered them out of the parking garage.

They drove in silence for a while.

"It's messed up to do this to people. And for what—ratings? Increased ad revenue?" Josh said.

"I'm a production assistant for a reality TV studio. I'm just doing my job."

"So you're not a psychologist?"

"Never said I was."

"I'm pretty sure you did."

"I did not."

"You did."

"Well, play back the tape? Oops—you can't! Because you're not on a reality TV show anymore. On account of, you know, you slitting your wrists with a razor in the bathroom of your Portland studio apartment and all."

Josh turned to Erin, speechless. She began to laugh, producing a hooting sound like that made by a seal asking for fish.

"Come on, I'm just trying to lighten the mood," she said, punching him in the shoulder.

"Then why the lab coat? Why the clipboard?"

"It instills confidence that you are in the hands of a medical professional."

"Is any of this legal?"

"Josh, think about it. Do you think we kidnap people off the street and hook them up to our broadcasting machine? That would be cruel and unusual punishment, definitely not constitutional. You signed a release form."

Josh didn't feel like talking anymore. He was alive now in what he assumed was the really real reality. He had woken up in this really real reality after killing himself in the previous reality, a fake reality televised as a reality TV show into the really real reality he now found himself. He also, apparently, had been alive in the really real reality before and had at some point signed a release form that led to him consenting to be in the fake reality TV reality. He closed his eyes and floated off to sleep.

Josh woke to the sound of a car door shutting. It was dark. They were parked in the back of a condominium complex. From outside the car, Erin opened his door, then walked toward the building. Josh followed. He had no luggage.

Erin's apartment was small and messy. The smell of greasy cardboard permeated the premises.

She sat down on her couch and turned on the television. She made eye contact with Josh for the first time since he'd entered her apartment, patting the cushion next to her. He sat.

A commercial for an ice-cream sandwich appeared on the screen.

"I used to love those," Josh said. "I guess I still do."

"Remember the time you and Mindy had a contest to see who could eat one the fastest when you went to Coney Island for the first time?"

Mindy. Was she why he'd killed himself? No. That was why he'd told Linda he'd wanted to kill himself. Not Linda. Dr. Silver. Refusing to call her that was an example of him not taking therapy seriously, an example of his self-destructive tendencies.

"That commercial was sexist," Erin said.

"Most of them are. What's my name? In this reality, I mean?"

Erin paused before replying. "Trevor. Your name was—and is from a legal standpoint—Trevor."

"Trevor," Trevor said. He'd thought hearing his name might bring back a flood of memories of his former self. His real self. Nothing.

Dr. Silver didn't think he was suicidal. She'd said that. "You're not suicidal." His insurance had only covered twelve visits a year if he wasn't clinically suicidal. She'd asked him to pay out-of-pocket. Was she trying to squeeze some extra money out of him, or did she just want him to stop going? Well, he'd stopped. That was another thing he'd had to lie to Mindy about.

"Do you want a glass of water or anything?"

Killing yourself to prove that your therapist was wrong about you not being suicidal was a dumb reason to kill yourself. No. That wasn't why he'd done it either.

"Or a beer maybe? I know you like beer."

He'd done it to escape himself.

The TV blared at them. "So, Erin, what the fuck is going on?"

"What do you mean?"

"I mean, you work for the network or the show as a psychologist—"

"Production assistant."

"Production assistant, whatever. Why am I at your apartment right now? Seems pretty unprofessional—"

"Shut up!" Erin interrupted. "It's on!"

She raised the remote in her hand and turned up the volume. The opening title sequence of a cheesy reality TV show played. Before he even saw himself—the self that he had memories of, his Josh self—on the screen, he knew what he was watching. He recognized the cul-de-sac where a boy was learning how to ride a bike, the dining room table being set up for Thanksgiving dinner, the pillow fort in the grandparents' basement. He was watching his *LIFE!*

"But I lost. I'm not on the show anymore. Is this a rerun?"

"It's the season finale. Before they get to where we vote for the winners, they do a little montage of everyone's life. Plus the never-before-seen footage. Remember?"

Trevor didn't answer. He was staring at Mindy on the screen. His Mindy. His former Mindy. In the arms of Alex. His brother. In a font matching the title sequence of the show, their names appeared in the lower third as a unit, the ampersand knocking the wind out of him.

"Wait, what?" Josh said involuntarily, his eyes searching to understand. "Are they—Mindy and Alex—they're contestants, too?"

Erin reached out and placed her hand on top of Josh's. Fuck, she was young.

"They orchestrate things so that the contestants know each other."

"So my life was fake *and* I didn't have free will?"

"Yeah, yeah, incompatibilism, compatibilism, whatever. Look, stop it with that fake-or-real stuff," Erin said, grabbing Josh by the shoulders. "Let's say that we put three panda bears in a zoo. Yes, we created the situation where they would all meet, but then from there on out, what they do is up to them."

Trevor pulled out of her grip and stood up. He paced the room.

"Okay," Erin said. She cleared her throat. "I am sensing the zoo analogy isn't helping. How about this: In basketball, you can't go outside the boundaries of the court, and the other players on your team are the only teammates you have. That stuff is outside of your control once the game begins. But what you do for the sixty minutes of the game is entirely within your control. Yeah?"

Trevor stared at the TV, flexing his hands into fists as he watched a montage of moments of his former self, hanging out with Mindy and Alex. The host who'd greeted him when he woke up from his suicide appeared on screen.

"And now," the host intoned, "a never-before-seen moment from Josh's *LIFE!* . . ."

Trevor saw himself as Josh on the screen. He was at the Irving Street apartment he'd shared with Mindy, drinking a beer over the kitchen sink. A third beer, actually, judging by the nearby empties. What unseen moment were they going to . . . oh. That one. The moment when Mindy confronted him about the kiddie porn.

"Child porn, Josh? Are you fucking kidding me? Child porn? You told me you got laid off because of budget cuts. What the FUCK?" she yelled at him on the screen. She threw her keys, hitting him in the face. That had hurt. Calling it child porn made it sound so much worse than it was. He'd downloaded some pictures, but he'd thought the girls were in their late teens. Pretty sure. Some videos. Was it dumb to do it on the work computer? Yes. Should he have known the IT nerds could track that stuff? Obviously. But calling it—

"Why, Josh, why? Wasn't our life enough? Wasn't I enough?" Mindy was crying so hard now. He'd forgotten how hard she cried. Of course she had. Josh was crying now, too. Trevor felt too exhausted to cry. He'd already cried these tears.

"I have a problem," Josh said between sobs. "I need help. I'll get help."

"I'm so embarrassed," Mindy said. "You're a monster. I don't even know you. I can't believe I had to find out from Alex." Alex. Good old older brother. He'd always had a thing for Mindy. But she'd chosen Josh first. No ulterior motives there, ruining Josh forever in her eyes, so Alex could swoop in and—

The show went to commercial.

Trevor stared down at his hands clasped together on his belly. He probed his left thumb gingerly with his right thumb, inspecting for proof that the digits were there and that he was alive. They seemed real, but he'd been wrong before.

"You look like you could use some air," Erin said. "Want to go up on the roof?"

The stairwell smelled like urine. At the top, Erin led Trevor out a door that said DO NOT ENTER. The roof was empty and covered in gravel that crunched under their feet as they walked to the edge. There was no safety railing.

"Why are we up here?" Trevor said.

"Look." Erin pointed to the light-dotted darkness beyond. "Every single one of those points of light is some person living a different reality. Some of them are maybe even watching your show and maybe it's bringing them a little bit of joy, like it did for me. There might even be an infinite number of parallel universes out there with an infinite variety of realities being lived out. You made some mistakes, but I don't think we should judge someone for when they were at their worst, but when they're at their best. Want to find out how good of a you you could be?" Erin grabbed his hand in hers. This time, Trevor didn't pull away. His heart beat faster. She grabbed his other hand and stepped closer to him, moving her face closer to his. They kissed.

"How old are you anyway?" Trevor asked as she pulled back.

"Seventeen," Erin said.

"Oh," Trevor said. "I remember now."

Trevor pulled away from Erin. The Trevor memories started seeping back. He tried to stop them, but something had been uncorked. He looked back out to where she'd pointed. The same decisions, the same mistakes, over and over, doomed to repeat them. The lights sparkled, peaceful. Breaking a promise to a loved one hurts the first time, but the tenth time it stops hurting. Trevor put one foot up on the ledge of the roof. Breaking a promise to yourself for the tenth time, though, that still hurts. He stepped out into nothing.

It was after killing himself that Trevor learned he'd lost the reality TV show. After hitting the concrete, digital characters popped into the middle of his field of vision. YOU! LOST! AT! LIFE! appeared in bright orange. Beneath the letters he saw his blood draining out into a puddle on the concrete in front of his face. He felt pain. In the bottom of his field of vision, numbers next to an eyeball icon began increasing, while numbers next to a heart icon decreased. Then all went black.

"Hey, buddy, I'm Matthew." He was back in the same sterile room. Or maybe a different but identical room, Trevor couldn't say. No Erin. Matthew unscrewed the cap of a thermos.

"You like bad coffee?" Matthew offered him a cup.

The room wasn't identical, Trevor realized. The horses on Trevor's hospital gown were a faded blue. What color had they been before? He couldn't remember. Red maybe. Why would they change such an insignificant detail?

"Okay, Trevor, your LifeCast will be starting shortly. People are watching on their EyeLids primarily, so remember to play to that."

The coffee was black and hot. From a narrow obsidian bracelet on Matthew's wrist a holographic array of symbols appeared in front of him. He made a few gestures and then the bracelet clicked off.

Ghostly numbers appeared from nowhere in front of Trevor's face.

5 . . . 4 . . . 3 . . . 2 . . . 1 . . .

The numbers became letters.

HELLO, KYLE

"There's a mistake. These floaty words just said, 'Kyle.'"

"That's your really real name," Matthew said. "Here are some memories of your Kyle life." A lifetime of memories overcame him at once. The memories were new but horribly the same. He threw up on his hospital gown, drowning the horses in his sick. The numbers at the bottom of his field of vision increased.

Kyle stared down at his hands clasped together on his belly.

OPTION 1: RETURN TO THE MOMENT JUST BEFORE YOU KILLED YOURSELF AS JOSH AND NOT DO IT, CONTINUING THAT LIFE.

The heart numbers increased.

OPTION 2: RETURN TO THE ROOF WITH ERIN JUST BEFORE YOU KILLED YOURSELF AND NOT DO IT, CONTINUING YOUR LIFE AS TREVOR.

The heart numbers increased faster.

OPTION 3: RETURN TO THE *LIFE!* SIMULATOR, AND BEGIN AGAIN AS SOMEONE COMPLETELY NEW.

Kyle reeled. He hadn't expected that. The option to start over as someone new. Was that what Josh had wanted when he ended it in the bathroom that day? He wasn't turning the video game off, but just pressing "restart"? Sometimes they're the same button, just a matter of how long it's depressed. Which had he wanted?

OPTION 4: KILL YOURSELF AS KYLE.

"Fun game. Is the fifth option I win a new car?" Kyle said. He looked over to Matthew for a reaction. Nothing.

Option 1, Option 2, Option 3, and Option 4 appeared in the air in front of Kyle's face.

"So, how do I . . ." Kyle stared, switching his gaze from one to the other, causing the words to illuminate in turn. "I see." He lit up Option 3. Then moved his gaze to Option 4. He went back and forth a few times before he decided.

The automated administration of the lethal injection gave out an audible *whoosh*. Erin and Matthew removed their headsets and swung off of their metal-framed hospital beds.

"Nice work, you two," a gray-haired man said, standing with his arms crossed at the front of the room. He had white teeth and a purple blazer. "Let's recap later. I've gotta go check on Stream Three." He left them.

Erin looked to the door to make sure the gray-haired man was gone, then turned to Matthew. "I don't know why we have to get him to choose suicide three times," she said conspiratorially as she unplugged herself from the apparatus next to her bed.

"Because that's the law?" Matthew answered, already free of his tethers. "Supreme Court said capital punishment was cruel and unusual, so only way to kill bad guys is for them to choose to off themselves. SCOTUS ruling that suicide was a liberty protected in the Constitution. I bet those right-to-die activists had no idea it'd be used to—"

"I know all that," Erin cut him off. "I just mean, that's not why we do this. Not really."

"Is this just a roundabout way for you to bring up that you have more followers than I do?"

"What can I say? People just love true-crime streams."

"Yeah, that's why people follow your stream instead of mine. Not because you're a hot girl."

"Shut up, that is so demeaning of you to reduce my success to that," Erin said, pulling her jacket off a hook on the back of the door.

"What's demeaning is you doing the flirty-girl shtick. My methods are efficient and cater to the short attention spans of my subscribers," Matthew said as they left the room together.

A body on a third metal-framed bed remained behind, inert.

Hand Job at 20,000 Feet

DRAMATIS PERSONAE

NARRATOR. Ideally played by Nate Dern. Thirty.

NATE DERN. Ideally played by someone who looks like a slightly younger Nate Dern, such as Javier Bardem in *No Country for Old Men*. Twenty-five.

JULES. Woman seated next to Nate Dern, ideally played by Jena Malone, but only if she feels like it. Thirty-nine.

JOE. Old man seated next to Jules, ideally played by Sir Anthony Hopkins or Sir Michael Caine. Knighthood definitely preferred for this role. Eighty-one.

PAUL. A Dutchman seated behind Jules, ideally played by One Direction's Harry Styles. Forty-three.

TACO. A Dutchman seated behind Joe's and Paul's partner,
ideally played by One Direction's Louis Tomlinson. Forty-
six.

ISAAC ASIMOV. Famous science-fiction author, seated behind
Nate Dern, ideally played by Neil deGrasse Tyson. Sixty-
eight.

SETTING

Hand Job at 20,000 Feet *takes place inside a commercial
airplane during a transatlantic flight. The stage is
set with two rows of three chairs in the shape of the
center row of a Boeing 767 airplane cabin. Each seat is
equipped with a seat belt. A podium is set just behind,
stage left. LED strip lights create the aisles on either
side of the chairs. Wire-frame rectangles hang from the
ceiling as the windows of the aircraft.*

AT LIGHTS:

NARRATOR *stands downstage center facing the audience.*

NARRATOR:

The play has not started yet. My name is Nate
Dern and this is a true story from earlier in
my life. It's about a seven-hour flight I took
from Newark to Amsterdam. All dialogue and
events are here retold as close to verbatim
as the limits of human memory allow. The only
significant dramatic departure from reality
occurs in (1) the use of a narrator, a role I
will play; (2) the vocalization of the inner

monologue of our protagonist, Nate Dern, played
not by me, but by an actor; and (3) the physical
presence of science-fiction writer Isaac Asimov.
I hope you enjoy. The play is starting now.

*Lights down. Then, one spotlight downstage center and a
second spotlight at the podium, where Narrator now stands.*

Sound cue: Twilight Zone-*style music.*

NARRATOR:
The following is a true story. To begin,
let's meet the cast of characters.

NATE DERN *enters and walks to downstage center, holding a
book.*

NATE DERN:
Hi, my name is Nate Dern. I'm in 34E. I'm on
my way to visit my sister, who's been living
in Norway for a year. I'm hoping to do some
reading on the flight. *I, Robot* by Isaac
Asimov. I can't believe I've never read it.
I've always been fascinated in artificial
intelligence and what defines a person, you
know? I was listening to this podcast on the
Turing Test and—

NARRATOR:
That's enough, Nate. Stop boring the nice
people and go take a seat.

NATE *goes to his seat and begins reading his book,*
which he continues to attempt to read but keeps getting
distracted by the entrance of the rest of the cast.

JOE *enters, hobbling down the aisle to downstage center.*

> NARRATOR:
> Next we have Joe. You'll soon notice that
> Nate knows many details about the lives of
> the other individuals on this flight that he
> was able to reproduce here in this play. They
> are not fictionalized. The people seated near
> him chatted it up and Nate couldn't resist
> eavesdropping.

> JOE:
> I'm Joe. 34C. I used to be a famous
> journalist. That was awhile ago. I'm eighty-
> one years old now. I'm on my way back to my
> wife in Paris. Paris, France. Twice a year
> I have to fly back to the US for "insurance
> purposes." I never explained exactly what
> that meant, so that's all Nate knows.

JOE *goes to his seat.*

JULES *enters, sauntering down the aisle to downstage*
center.

> NARRATOR:
> Up next, in 34D, is Jules, who is, as she

told everyone within earshot before takeoff,
a . . .

JULES:

Thirty-nine-year-old Boisean, lesbian,
libertarian, pro-life, animal liberator
on my way to an animal rights conference
in Amsterdam before meeting up with my
girlfriend, er, fiancée, er, wife—I never know
what to call her—in Paris. Paris, France.

JULES *goes to her seat.*

PAUL *and* TACO *enter together and walk to downstage
center. They speak in Dutch accents and deliver their
lines dryly.*

NARRATOR:

Next we have a nice Dutch couple who have
been together for nearly two decades.

PAUL:

Hello. I am Paul.

TACO:

And I am Taco. It is quite a common Dutch
name.

PAUL:

Yes, but it is quite funny because we are
just coming back from a holiday in Mexico and

whenever I would call for Taco, one of the
waiters would think I wanted a taco, which is
also the name of a Mexican food dish.

TACO:
It was quite funny.

PAUL:
It was quite funny.

TACO:
Quite funny, actually, yes.

PAUL and TACO *continue to repeat, "Quite funny," to each
other as they take their seats.*

NARRATOR:
You'll notice that we have six seats but only
five passengers so far. That's because the
person seated behind Nate never spoke, and so
Nate has no memory of him or her whatsoever.
As previously stated, though, Nate did
have one more companion with him on this
flight . . .

ISAAC ASIMOV *bursts onto the stage, carrying a comically
large prop copy of* I, Robot.

ISAAC ASIMOV:
Me, sci-fi master Isaac Asimov, author of
classic sci-fi book *I, Robot*!

                    NATE DERN:
Hey, I'm reading that!

                    NARRATOR:
I think the audience made that connection on
their own, Nate. But what they might not yet
realize is this: Among these six characters,
there is a monster, someone not bound by
social norms or human decency. Pay attention,
for today on this crowded transatlantic
flight, only you will be able to answer the
question driving our narrative: Did one of
these characters receive and one of them
give . . . a hand job?

Lights down to black.

Sound cue: Eerie orchestral stinger.

Lights up.

                    NARRATOR:
Through the device of inner monologue, we
have access to what Nate Dern was thinking as
they prepared for takeoff.

*Sound cue: NATE's inner monologue (Note: All inner
monologues prerecorded):*

    "I hope nobody tries to strike up a
    conversation with me on this flight. I am not

interested in that. The only person I want to
hear from is Mr. Isaac Asimov . . ."

ISAAC ASIMOV, reading from book:

"Chapter 1. 'You want the human interest
angle?' She smiled. 'Human interest out of
robots? That's a contradiction.'"

JOE *begins struggle to take his jacket off.*

Sound cue: A crying baby.

                    JOE:
A crying baby? Well, shit.

                  NARRATOR:
He really said that. And an old man
saying . . .

                    JOE:
A crying baby? Well, shit.

                  NARRATOR:
. . . struck Nate as noteworthy enough to
warrant a tweet.

NATE *takes out his phone and types.*

*Projected onto the back wall, a screen capture of the
actual tweet: "An old man on my flight just said, 'A
crying baby? Well, shit.'"*

JOE *continues to struggle with getting his jacket off.*

                    NARRATOR:

Notice that instead of helping Joe get his
jacket off, Nate opted to tweet a joke,
although quite frankly not really a joke so
much as a retelling of exactly what happened,
like that takes any real creativity. (*Clears
throat*). So, what happened next . . . ah,
yes. This:

                     JULES:

Need some help there, brother?

                      JOE:

Oh, yes. Thank you.

JULES *helps* JOE *remove his jacket, stashing it underneath
the seat.*

JULES *taps* NATE *on the shoulder. He lowers his book.*

                     JULES:

Are you claustrophobic?

                     NATE:

Um. No. I'm not.

                     JULES:

Great! Then would you mind switching seats
with me, brother?

NATE:

Um. I'd rather not.

JULES *shrugs this off and goes back about her business,*
but NATE *is visibly shaken by the exchange.*

NARRATOR:

That may not seem like much of a
confrontation to you, but denying a direct
request from a stranger basically qualifies
as a knife fight for Nate. His heart rate
just jumped to the 160s.

Sound cue: NATE's *inner monologue:*

"Wow, what the heck just happened? Was that a
dick move on my part? First the old man said
that crazy thing about the baby and now this!
What a crazy flight!"

NARRATOR:

You poor stupid fool. You have no idea what's
to come.

JOE:

I would offer you my seat, young lady, but,
well, I don't like flying, and I gotta tell
you, I'm a bit loaded.

JULES:

You're loaded! Hah! Well, that makes two of
us! What's your name, brother?

NARRATOR:

This is not an exaggeration of how often
Jules ended her sentences with "brother."

JOE:

My name is Joe.

JULES:

I'm Jules. Joe, what do you say we get shit-
faced on this flight together?

JOE:

My! Well. Okay then. Yes, let's do.

JOE and JULES shake on it.

JULES:

You *gotta* get shit-faced when you fly. Hell,
you know the pilot is up there doing coke off
the flight attendant's ass right now!

PAUL and TACO *lean forward to poke their heads in between*
JOE and JULES.

TACO:

You might be right, actually.

PAUL:

Yes, pilots have been known to use
stimulants to stay awake, especially on long
flights.

TACO:

Such as the long transatlantic flight we are
currently on.

PAUL:

Yes, such as this one we are on.

JULES:

These guys get it! Yep, I always get drunk
when I fly. You have to! Man, one time I
was flying, right? The pilot makes this
announcement that we're about to take off,
but he accidentally leaves the PA on and he's
all, 'Man, I sure would like a blow job and
a coffee right now.' So the flight attendant
rushes up to tell him to shut it off, but as
she runs by I go, 'Don't forget the coffee!'
The whole plane laughed.

NARRATOR:

This anecdote may seem familiar if you've
seen the 1997 film *Good Will Hunting*,
specifically the part when the Matt Damon
character tells this exact joke.

PAUL:

That's a funny story.

TACO:

Yes, the story you told is quite funny,
actually.

                         JULES:
What are your names?

                         PAUL:
I'm Paul and this is Taco.

                         TACO:
Hello.

                         JULES:
Taco? That's a far-out name. I'm Jules and
this is Joe. What's your name, brother?

JULES *punches* NATE *in the shoulder. He puts his book*
down, surprised to be involved in their chat.

                         NATE:
Me? Nate.

                         JULES:
You gonna get shit-faced with us, Nate?

Light cue: Lights down except for spotlights on NATE *and*
NARRATOR.

Sound cue: A ticking stopwatch.

                       NARRATOR:
Nate is invited to join the shit-facing. A
potential turning point in the next seven hours
and in our story today. What will he decide?

NATE *appears to be genuinely considering what to do.*

Lights return to normal and sound cue stops as NATE says:

NATE:

Probably not.

JULES:

What! Boo. Why not, brother?

NATE:

I'm trying to drink less.

JULES:

I don't usually trust a man who doesn't
drink, but I got a feeling you still might
bring something to the table today, Nate.

JULES *punches NATE in the shoulder again.*

JOE:

Jules, I'm jealous of all the attention
you're giving Nate right now.

NARRATOR:

Joe really said that. These people have known
each other for about ten minutes.

JULES *winks at NATE, then returns to JOE. They begin to
mouth a conversation we can't hear. NATE attempts to
return to reading, but looks off in thought.*

Sound cue: NATE's inner monologue:

> *"This is the craziest flight of my life*
> *and we haven't even taken off yet. I can't*
> *believe some people willingly engage other*
> *people that they don't know in conversation.*
> *I just hope I can read over their*
> *chatter . . ."*

NATE *returns to reading.*

ISAAC ASIMOV, reading:

"Chapter 2. The Master created humans first
as the lowest type, most easily formed.
Gradually he replaced them by robots."

JULES:

So, you guys heard of the Wasp knife?

TACO:

No. What is that?

PAUL:

Is it a knife for killing wasps?

JOE:

Which one of you is Paul again?

JULES:

The Wasp knife will fuck you up. They made it
for ocean divers. You stab a shark and then

press a button that injects a CO_2 bubble into
the shark so it rises to the surface. *Boom!*
No more shark.

PAUL:
What a terrible way for a shark to die.

JOE:
Say, what kind of a name is Taco, anyway?

JULES:
If you stab someone with the Wasp knife on
land, it makes your attacker's internal
organs freeze.

TACO:
That sounds dangerous, actually.

PAUL:
Yes, actually, what you have described sounds
quite dangerous.

JOE:
You're Paul, you're Taco, she's Jules, and
I'm Joe. We're having a good time, aren't we?

JULES:
Right now I've got a device called "The
Weapon." It's made out of plastic so you can
get it on to airplanes, but it's totally
lethal. Hey, Nate!

JULES *punches* NATE *in the arm.* NATE *reluctantly lowers his book.*

                              NATE:
Yes?

                              JULES:
I could disable you in two hits. Know how?

                              NATE:
How?

                         JULES, miming:
Bam, hit one collarbone. *Bam,* hit the other
collarbone. Both of your arms are now
disabled.

                              NATE:
Wow.

JULES *turns away from* NATE *back to the others.*

                              JULES:
Anyway, I want a Wasp knife so bad. I've
dropped a few hints to my girlfriend, er,
fiancée, so hopefully she'll buy me one
before they make them illegal. Fucking
government.

                              JOE:
So you're a lezzie, huh?

NARRATOR:

He really said "lezzie."

JULES:

Hah! Sure am, brother.

JOE:

Well, I'm a happily married man, so it
doesn't matter anyway.

JULES:

What are you getting at, Joe? You think if I
wasn't a "lezzie" you and I would join the
mile-high club or something?

JOE, blushing:

Oh! My. Well. Say, why don't we order those
drinks now. (*Looks down aisle.*) Excuse me?
Can we get some drinks here?

JULES:

They don't serve drinks until after takeoff,
brother.

JOE:

Oh. Well. I'd just love a drink for the
takeoff. I hate the takeoff.

JULES:

Me, too, brother. Don't worry, I'll hold your
hand. We'll get through this together.

JULES and JOE *hold hands.*

Sound cue: PILOT *over PA:*

> *"Flight attendants, prepare for takeoff."*

Sound cue: Roaring engine of the plane taking off.

NARRATOR:
And as the plane took off into the night sky,
these two strangers held hands.

JOE and JULES *close their eyes as they continue to hold
hands.*

NATE *looks down at their clasped hands.*

Sound cue: NATE's *inner monologue:*

> *"Two strangers holding hands. Huh. That's . . .
> nice. Right? Yes. Two humans comforting each
> other in a time of distress. Yes, that's nice.
> And yet, something feels off about it . . ."*

Sound cue: Suspenseful orchestral sting.

Back to NATE's *inner monologue:*

> *"Nah, I'm probably just projecting my own
> intimacy issues. Back to reading . . ."*

ISAAC ASIMOV, reading:

"Chapter 4. You've caught on, have you? *This*
robot reads minds."

Sound cue: Pilot over PA:

"Hi, folks, we've reached cruising altitude.
The seat-belt sign is off. You're now free to
move about the cabin."

JOE:

I need to use the little boys' room.

JOE exits down the aisle.

JULES:

I'm on my way to Amsterdam for an animal
rights conference.

PAUL:

Oh, really? We care about animal rights.

TACO:

Yes. We are both vegetarians, actually.

JULES:

I'm vegan. I liberate animals.

PAUL:

We have been to protests too, such as—

JULES:

No. Not protests. Liberation. Like, I
literally liberate animals from cages in zoos
and labs and stuff. I'm on the no-fly list.
Government thinks I'm a terrorist.

NARRATOR:

Jules did not explain how it was that, if
indeed she was on the no-fly list, she was
now flying, nor did Paul or Taco ask.

JOE *returns to his seat.*

JOE:

I'm back from the bathroom! I've washed my
hands so, you know, if you want to hold hands
again you don't have to worry about my hands
being . . . soiled.

JULES:

Good to know, brother.

JULES *elbows* NATE *and winks at* PAUL *and* TACO
conspiratorially.

NARRATOR:

For a former famous journalist, Joe did not
demonstrate the best word choice throughout
the flight.

JULES:

So, how about those drinks? Paul and Taco,
you guys drink whiskey?

PAUL:

We are going to try to sleep, actually.

TACO:

Yes, actually, since it is night, we are
going to try to sleep.

JULES:

Suit yourselves. What about you, Nate?
Whiskey?

NATE:

No, I don't think so.

JULES, to JOE:

Looks like it's just you and me, brother!

JOE:

Oh, good! Okay!

JULES, to aisle:

Six whiskeys, please. Knob Creek if you have it.

Lights dim to "night mode" in the cabin.

*NATE reaches up and turns on his "reading light," which
brings a spot onto him that partially spills over onto
JULES and JOE.*

*NARRATOR walks over with two standing tray tables, which
he sets up in front of JOE and JULES. From a pocket, he*

produces and sets down the six whiskeys. As he does this,
he says:

NARRATOR:
As the cabin lights were turned off, most
passengers tried to sleep. Nate tried to
read. Joe and Jules drank.

JOE, drunk:
You're a lovely young lady.

JULES, sincerely, and also a little drunk:
Well, thank you, brother. (*To aisle.*)
We'll take two Bloody Marys when you get a
chance!

Sound cue: NATE's inner monologue:

"Wow. They're being so loud. I can't believe
the flight attendant keeps bringing them
alcohol. I can barely focus on reading.

ISAAC ASIMOV, reading:
"Chapter 7. Robot psychology is far from
perfect—as a specialist, I can assure you of
that."

NARRATOR *delivers two Bloody Marys to* JOE *and* JULES.

JOE:
What is this we're drinking, Jules, my dear?

JULES, laughing:

I told you, these are Bloody Marys,
brother!

JOE:

Jules, my dear, I'm getting a little cold.
Could you put my jacket over my legs?

*JULES caringly puts the jacket over JOE's legs,
underneath the tray table.*

JULES:

Yep, I got you, brother. Comfy?

JOE:

Comfy like a clam. Are clams comfy? I don't
remember.

JOE and JULES laugh hysterically at this.

Sound cue: NATE's inner monologue:

"*They are totally wasted. You should
not be allowed to get this drunk on an
airplane. How am I the only one seeing
this? How can everyone else be sleeping
right now?*"

NARRATOR:

And then, it happened. If our story has a
deus ex machina, it is this:

Sound cue: PILOT on the PA:

> "Sorry to bother you, folks. Looks like we've
> got some turbulence up ahead. Please fasten
> your seat belts."

*Projector cue: An illuminated seat-belt symbol projected
onto the back wall in an evil red color in time with . . .*

Sound cue: An ominous, foreboding tone.

NATE *and* JULES *each clasp their seat belts.*

JOE *struggles to fasten his seat belt, but he is unable
to do so.*

> JOE:
> Oh. Well. What a hassle. I've got this tray
> table and this jacket. Oh dear, I don't know
> how I can—

> JULES:
> Need a hand there, brother?

JULES *leans over and sticks her hands underneath the
jacket covering* JOE's *lap.*

> NARRATOR:
> A stranger helping an old man put his seat
> belt on. A kind gesture, no? And yet . . .
> and yet, this:

JOE:

Ooh!

JULES:

Whoops, got ya. Sorry!

JULES *stops her under-jacket hand activity.*

JOE:

No harm. No harm at all.

JULES:

No? Did it feel good?

JOE:

Oh. Heh. As a matter of fact, yes.

JULES *resumes her under-jacket hand activity.*

Sound cue: NATE*'s inner monologue:*

"No. No no no. Nothing's happening. The thing
that seems like it is happening couldn't
be happening. Just focus on your book,
Nate, just mind your own business and keep
reading."

ISAAC ASIMOV, reading:

"Chapter 8. Looks like it's a case of
Mercurian gravity and a steel throwing arm.
Watch, will you?"

NATE *quickly glances away from his book over at whatever
it is* JULES *is doing underneath* JOE*'s jacket. He looks
back at his book.*

JULES, *possibly noticing* NATE*'s glance, begins to
withdraw her hands.*

> JOE:
> No! Don't take your hand away.

> NARRATOR:
> As previously stated, some of the lines of
> this play are verbatim, whereas some are
> paraphrases based on the best of Nate's
> recollection. Joe saying, "No! Don't take
> your hand away," is an instance of a sentence
> that Nate remembers, and will forever
> remember, verbatim.

JULES *cranes her neck slowly to see if* NATE *is still
looking over.* NATE *rigidly leans away from them, lasering
his eyes on his book.*

Satisfied, JULES *leans back toward* JOE *and resumes her
under-jacket activity.*

Sound cue: NATE*'s inner monologue:*

> *"NO NO NO NO NO. Not possible. You're
> imagining it, Nate. She's probably just*

giving him a leg massage. Stop being so
judgmental! Stop assuming that other people
are—"

NATE's *monologue is cut off by the sound of* JULES's *hand*
hitting the underside of the tray table in a rhythmic
THUMP THUMP THUMP.

                    NARRATOR:
At that moment, Nate was certain that the
thump thump thump of the tray table was the
worst noise that he had ever heard in his
life. But that was only because he hadn't yet
heard the noise Joe was about to make, which
sounded like the happy moans of a little boy
enjoying a piece of watermelon saltwater
taffy.

                    JOE:
Mmm. Ymm. Mmm. YmmMmmMmmYmmmmmmmm.

Sound cue: NATE's *inner monologue:*

     "*NO NO NO NO NO. Book must read book just*
     focus on book."

                    ISAAC ASIMOV, reading:
"Chapter 9. A positronic robot—"

Sound cue: NATE's *inner monologue:*

"Nope, sorry, Isaac Asimov, can't focus on positronic robots right now."

ISAAC ASIMOV:

It's okay. I get this. Weird stuff happening over there. *Humans, am I right?*

Sound cue: NATE's inner monologue:

"This can't be happening. I can figure this out with logic. What do I know to be true? One, Joe said, 'Don't take your hand away.' Two, Jules appeared to look at me, to see if I was watching. Three, the gyration of the tray table in sync with a rhythm common to masturbation. Conclusion: A thirty-nine-year-old lezzie is giving a hand job to a semi-senile octogenarian she just met. On an airplane. Next to me. But there must be another explanation?"

JULES *leans over and takes a sip of her Bloody Mary through a straw while continuing her hand activity.*

Sound cue: NATE's inner monologue:

"Two strangers equals a hand job on a plane? Does not compute."

ISAAC ASIMOV:

Does not compute!

NARRATOR:

Despite the evidence, Nate continued to
refuse to believe it was possible. He stared
at the pages of his book so hard it was in
danger of catching fire. He wasn't sure
how much time passed as he waited for the
thumping to stop. Maybe five minutes. Maybe
twenty. At last, in his peripheral vision, he
saw Joe get up.

JOE *moves aside the tray table, keeping the jacket
wrapped around his waist, and exits down the aisle.*

JULES *finishes drinking her Bloody Mary, then begins
sipping from JOE's drink.*

A *beat.*

Then, JULES *punches* NATE *in the shoulder.*

JULES:
Man, why do I always get the crazy ones?

NATE:
Oh. Yep.

NATE *turns away from JULES and looks at his book.*

JULES *opens her mouth to speak to NATE again, but then
stops herself. She produces an eye mask from her pocket*

and puts it on. She crosses her arms and attempts to
sleep.

A beat.

>   ISAAC ASIMOV, reading:
> "Chapter 9. A positronic robot. Chapter 9.
> A positronic robot. Chapter 9. A positronic
> robot." Um, Nate? I think you are just reading
> the same sentence over and over again?

JOE returns to his seat.

>   JOE:
> How ya doing there, kid?

>   NARRATOR:
> "Kid." Again, poor word choice, Joe.

JOE sits for a moment, as if deciding whether he should
wake JULES up or not.

Sound cue: NATE's inner monologue:

> *"I'm crazy. That must be it. I'm crazy.*
> *Nothing happened. I imagined it. The evidence*
> *is circumstantial, it's not like I ever*
> *actually saw—"*

JOE leans over and places his hand squarely on JULES's
groin. NATE's mouth drops open at what he is seeing.

JULES *wakes with a start, pulling her mask up to look at* JOE *as she quickly pulls his hand away.*

                         JOE:
        No?

                     NARRATOR:
        Like a confused adolescent who had just
        received his first sexual favor and knew he
        should return the gift but was unsure in the
        etiquette of the exchange.

JULES *turns to* NATE. *They make eye contact.* NATE's *mouth is still open. He closes his mouth and turns away.*

Still holding JOE's *arm where she grabbed him,* JULES *now gently returns* JOE's *arm to his own lap. She pulls her mask back down and resumes sleeping.*

JOE *closes his eyes and also tries to sleep.*

NATE *looks around. He is now the only person awake on the aircraft. He desperately wants to make eye contact with somebody else to verify what he saw.*

                  ISAAC ASIMOV:
        Hey, don't look at me man, I'm just a
        storytelling device.

NATE *stands. He now expresses his inner monologue out loud, rather than through the prerecorded audio.*

NATE:

What the fuck just happened? He just planted
his hand on her crotch and I definitely did
not imagine that!

NARRATOR:

Maybe you just witnessed a sexual assault.
Maybe you should say something.

NATE:

I don't know. I think the only way an old
man would be so audacious as to place his
arthritic hand on a stranger's groin would be
if she had just . . . I mean, the table was
thumping like . . . I don't know.

NARRATOR:

This is really hard for you to wrap your mind
around, huh? What's so tough to understand,
Nate? People wank each other off sometimes.
What's the big deal?

NATE:

What's the big deal? The big deal is that
two strangers just . . . I mean, people just
don't do stuff like this!

NARRATOR:

Are you sure you don't mean that *you* don't do
stuff like this?

NATE:

I can't even process what "this" was.

NARRATOR:

Well, you've still got five hours left on
this flight. Plenty of time to process.

NATE *considers this.*

NATE:

No, I don't think so. I'm never going
to think about this again. I'm going to
read *I, Robot*. I have to read *I, Robot*.
It is very important that I finish *I,
Robot* before this flight lands. That is my
primary directive now, no other thinking
necessary.

NATE *returns to his seat and picks up his book.*

NARRATOR:

And that's what Nate did. While everyone else
on the plane slept, he read as fast as he
could.

ISAAC ASIMOV, reading:

"Chapter 9. I've got my license, sir, but at
last reading it didn't say anything about
hyper-engines or warp-navigation."

                        NARRATOR:

But despite his best efforts to stay focused
on the book, Nate found his mind wandering.
He kept playing back the events of the flight
in his mind. Jules had asked him to switch
seats with her. What if he'd been a kind
human and done a favor to a stranger? How
would that have altered the time line?

Lights down to black. Lights up: NATE *and* JULES *have
switched seats and* NATE *is giving* JOE *a hand job.*

*Sound cue: Montage music plays during the following
sequence of quick scenes.*

                        NARRATOR:
Would Nate have given Joe a hand job?

                          NATE:
Why am I doing this?!

                          JOE:
I don't know, but don't take your hand away.
I haven't ejaculated in thirty years.

Lights down to black. Lights up: JOE *is asleep and* JULES
is now giving NATE *a hand job.*

                        NARRATOR:
Or maybe Jules would have given Nate a hand
job?

NATE:

I just wanted to read my book!

JULES:

I've got a plastic weapon in my carry-on that
can disable you in two hits, so just shut up
and enjoy the handie, brother!

Lights down to black. Lights up: Everyone in their
original seats, back to the start of the flight.

NATE *seems visibly relieved that he is now not involved in*
giving or receiving a hand job, but he is still on edge.

NARRATOR:

Or what if Nate had said yes to Jules's
invitation to drink with them?

NATE:

You know what? I actually could use a
whiskey.

PAUL:

Okay, we'll drink, too.

TACO:

Sure, what the heck, we'll drink, too.

NARRATOR *tosses everybody a single-shot whiskey bottle.*
Everyone downs their drinks, then immediately form a
chain, all jerking each other off.

PAUL:

This is quite fun, actually.

TACO:

Yes, it is quite fun.

PAUL:

You know, Taco, having a gay couple in
this one-act play about a hand job was a
misdirect.

TACO:

That is true, actually. It seems that we
would have been the ones most likely to be
involved in a hand job.

PAUL:

Ooh, that is quite funny, actually.

TACO:

Yes, quite funny.

NARRATOR:

Hey, how about one more just for fun?

*Lights down to black. Lights up: The entire cast is now
jerking off* ISAAC ASIMOV.

ISAAC ASIMOV:

Ro . . . ro . . . ROBOTS!!!

NARRATOR:

But of course, none of that happened.

Lights up: Back to night-mode lighting and the actual
time line as the montage music ends.

NARRATOR:

All that happened was five hours of Nate
reading in silence, punctuated only by the
occasional . . .

JOE:

You awake, kid? Hey there? You awake? Such a
nice young girl.

NARRATOR:

Of course, Nate never looked over at the
confused old man. He did not risk some sort
of awkward interaction, no. Nate just kept
reading his book.

ISAAC ASIMOV, reading:

"Chapter 10. It's the personal initiative
factor that's giving us the trouble. And it's
just during emergencies in the absence of a
human being that personal initiative is most
strained."

The warm orange light of morning begins to fill the
cabin, reflecting off the wire-frame windows.

                        NARRATOR:
        At last, orange dawn began to shine in
        through the window cracks. The flight
        attendants serve coffee and orange juice.

NARRATOR *brings over a tray full of coffee and orange*
juice as he says this.

                          JOE:
        Breakfast! Wake up, kid! Time for breakfast!

JOE *nudges* JULES *until she wakes.*

                         JULES:
        Ah, good morning, brother. Good morning,
        Paul! Good morning, Taco!

                          PAUL:
        Good morning!

                          TACO:
        Yes, good morning!

JULES *glances in* NATE*'s direction but does not say good*
morning to him.

                        NARRATOR:
        And as before, these four strangers started a
        conversation.

JULES:

My wife and I were thinking about heading to
Amsterdam to do some 'shrooms. Think you two
would care to join us?

PAUL:

Oh sure. 'Shrooms are fun.

TACO:

They are quite fun actually.

JULES:

Excellent. Here's my card. Give me a call.

JULES *gives* PAUL *a card from her pocket.*

JOE:

Oh, can I get one of those?

JULES:

That was my last one, brother.

JOE:

Oh. Well, here's mine. Give me a call, but be
careful. My wife might answer.

JULES:

Hah! Okay, I'll be careful.

JULES *winks at* PAUL *and* TACO.

Sound cue: NATE's *inner monologue:*

> " 'Be careful, my wife might answer.' What—why
> would he say that unless . . . unless . . .

NARRATOR:

At this point, why was Nate still collecting
evidence? Seems pretty obvious what
happened, right? Why was it so hard for Nate
to grasp that two strangers might engage in
some sort of substantive interaction? Well,
Nate, why?

The cast turns to NATE. NARRATOR *walks out from behind
podium.* NATE *stands, walking away from their collective
gaze.*

NATE:

Because . . . to me, the ideal seat partner
is one who keeps to himself. So, I assume
that's what other people want.

NARRATOR *gets up in* NATE's *face.*

NARRATOR:

How do you know what other people want, Nate?

Sound cue: PILOT *over PA:*

> "Flight attendants, prepare for landing."

JOE *and* JULES *hold hands and close their eyes.*

Sound cue: The noises of the plane landing and touching down back to earth.

> JOE:
>
> Such a nice young girl. I'll miss you. Best flight of my life. (*Points to window.*) What's that?

> JULES:
>
> That's the ground. We landed. We made it, brother! Told you we'd get through this together.

JULES *pats* JOE's *hand with her other hand, then releases it.*

> JOE:
>
> Such a nice young girl. Such warm hands.

> NARRATOR:
>
> He really said that. "Such warm hands." Nice for hand jobs and also nice for hand holding.

> JOE:
>
> What are you reading, Nate?

> NARRATOR:
>
> This was the first time that Joe had addressed Nate directly.

NATE:

I, Robot.

JOE:

Oh. Can I have it?

NARRATOR:

He didn't ask to look at it. He asked if he
could have it.

JULES:

Joe, I think Nate is still reading it. Aren't
you, brother?

NATE:

I am, but just one page left, actually.

JULES:

Oh, great! Well, finish it, *then* give it to Joe.

NATE:

Okay.

NARRATOR:

And as he had set out to do, Nate fulfilled
his primary directive. He finished the book.

ISAAC ASIMOV, reading:

"And just for a moment he forgot, or didn't
want to remember, that other robots might be

more ignorant than human beings. His very
superiority caught him."

NATE *closes the book, takes a breath in, then hands it
over to JOE.*

Sound cue: The ding *that lets everyone know they can now
stand up.*

The entire cast except for NATE *gets up and begins to
exit down the aisle.*

> NARRATOR:
> And the cathartic completion of reading the
> book combined with saying yes to a request
> from a stranger stirred something in Nate.
> He felt like he had been a part of a shared
> experience, the intertwining paths of five
> strangers, like some overly ambitious
> ensemble drama.

*Sound cue: Aimee Mann's "Wise Up," as made famous in the
movie* Magnolia.

The cast stops in the aisle. They turn back to face NATE
and begin to sing.

> JOE, singing to audience:
> "It's not / What you thought / When you first
> began it."

                    JULES, singing to JOE:
"You got / What you want / You can hardly
stand it though / By now you know."

                    Full Cast, singing:
"It's not going to stop / It's not going to
stop / It's not going to stop—"

*The music ends abruptly, and the cast returns to
exiting.*

                    NATE, singing to self:
"Till you wise up."

                         NARRATOR:
But actually, Nate hadn't been a part of the
experience.

NARRATOR *emerges from behind the podium and walks toward*
NATE *as he delivers his speech.*

                         NARRATOR:
As in almost every other moment of his daily
life—listening to a podcast on the subway,
avoiding a stranger's eyes on the sidewalk,
ignoring someone begging for change—Nate had
kept to himself and observed from a distance
great enough to avoid getting entangled,
sitting coldly and analytically on the side.
In the end, the real misdirect was Nate
himself. He was the monster all along. The

creepiest person on the plane wasn't the
one giving or receiving a hand job, but the
deviant watching off to the side, tweeting,
memorizing, cataloguing, and eventually
writing a one-act play about it, studying the
interaction instead of interacting, like some
sort of, yes, robot.

A beat.

               ISAAC ASIMOV:
Oh, snap.

Black out.

                  THE END

Acknowledgments

Thank you to the Upright Citizens Brigade Theatre in New York City for being my first comedy home, and to Funny or Die in Los Angeles for being my current one.

Thank you to past, present, and future members of my college improv group, the Immediate Gratification Players, for being the entity that made me strongly consider trying to do comedy instead of applying to law school.

Thank you to my book agent, Rob Weisbach, who gave me valuable notes and encouragement when this collection was at its early stages. Without him the book you're reading would have never become a physical thing that strangers like you can look at, which is funny to think about, don't you agree?

My manager, Cory Richman, was supportive when, after I finished reading B. J. Novak's story collection *One More Thing*, I sent an email saying, "Cory, I loved this book and I'd like to publish something like it. Can you help?" I mean, that's an insane thing to ask someone, but Cory treated it like it was a reasonable request and helped make it happen.

My editor at Simon & Schuster, Ben Loehnen, offered me incredible guidance on all bookish matters and has been a delight to work with from the very beginning. I hope that this collection does at least well enough for Ben not to be reprimanded in any way.

Thank you to my friends, coworkers, bosses, teammates, various editors at large, and multi-hyphenates therein who have given me feedback on my writing and otherwise helped make this book happen, including but not limited to: Polly Watson, Dan Abramson, Emma Allen, Christopher Monks, Jonah Ogles, Adam Laukhuf, Brian McManus, Tony Tulathimutte, Michael Backus, Shamus Khan, Zack Poitras, Pat O'Brien, Ben Wietmarschen, Langan Kingsley, Matt Klinman, John Harris, Mike Scollins, Cirocco Dunlap, Melinda Taub, Matt Mayer, Jenny Nelson, Kady Ruth Ashcraft, Nathan

Maggio, Jason Flowers, Rob Hatch-Miller, D'Arcy Carden, Jason Carden, Arthur Meyer, Colin Elzie, Michael Kayne, Natasha Vaynblat, Aaron Jackson, Zhubin Parang, Josh Sharp, Tracey Wigfield, Nicholas Stoller, Ryan Hunter, Abbi Jacobson, Megan Amram, Will Hines, Anthony King, Todd Bieber, Julie Gomez, Shannon O'Neill, Isaac Ravishankara, and Chris Graf.

Thank you to my sister, Courtney, for being my sibling and tribal counterpart. You are funnier, smarter, and a better sleeper than I am. To that last point, this seems like as good a space as any to say that I have a video of me sticking a crayon into Courtney's nose while she is sleeping and, somehow, *she does not wake up*. I have been told by Courtney that I am forbidden from releasing this video to the public until I am able to arrange a meeting between Courtney and Michael Cera. If anyone has any connections that could help make this happen, please let me know. The video is pretty funny, I'd say, and might be worth the trouble.

Thank you to my parents, Rhonda and Michael. You have supported me in every conceivable way since I was a small child demanding attention. You're both hilarious and hardworking and I've learned so much from each of you. I love you, and that's no joke.

Thank you to my wife, Miranda. To be precise, as of this exact writing, you are my fiancée. But between the deadline for this acknowledgment section and when the book is scheduled to come out, we have a wedding planned. So, unless you *Runaway Bride* me or something, you will be my wife at the time these words are readable for a general audience. Huh, this part is starting to feel like the "HonestJuice" chapter. I guess I'm all out of ideas, which is for the best because this is the end of the book. Well, Miranda, you're my best friend and I love you and every moment I spend with you I can't believe how lucky I am to be with someone who makes me as happy as you do. Life is beautiful and funny and I'm glad I get to spend it with you.

Last, thank you to Kurt Vonnegut, Flannery O'Connor, Philip K. Dick, and George Saunders.

Previously Published Work

Before We Begin Our Yoga Practice, a Few Words About Our Other Offerings and That Hissing Sound
The New Yorker, Daily Shouts
http://www.newyorker.com/humor/daily-shouts/before-we-begin-our-yoga-practice-a-few-words-about-upcoming-workshops-and-that-hissing-sound

Flora and Their Corresponding Holiday Ritual Call to Action, If Encountered
McSweeney's, Internet Tendency
https://www.mcsweeneys.net/articles/flora-and-their-corresponding-holiday-ritual-call-to-action-if-encountered

Personal Wi-Fi Terms and Conditions
The Occasional
http://www.theoccasional.com/content/my-personal-wifi-terms-conditions

I Like All Types of Music and My Sense of Humor Is So Random
The New Yorker, Daily Shouts
http://www.newyorker.com/humor/daily-shouts/i-like-all-types-of-music-and-my-sense-of-humor-is-so-random

Bruce Lee Novelty Plate
The Occasional
http://www.theoccasional.com/content/phone-call-with-the-dmv-about-a-license-plate-which-by-chance-spelled-out-bruclee

The Scientist Who Named It "Global Warming" Would Like to Apologize
Funny or Die
http://www.funnyordie.com/articles/44d2ccb862/the-scientist-who-named-it-global-warming-would-like-to-apologize

As the Toothbrush You Just Threw Away, I Have Some Questions About the Seven 12-Ounce Mountain Dews in Your Trash
McSweeney's, Internet Tendency
https://www.mcsweeneys.net/articles/the-toothbrush-you-just-threw-away-has-some-questions-about-the-seven-12-oz-mountain-dews-in-your-trash

HonestJuice Juicery
The Occasional
http://www.theoccasional.com/content/our-our-philosophy-poster-poster

An Intrepid Explorer Discovers a Man Cave
McSweeney's, Internet Tendency
https://www.mcsweeneys.net/articles/an-intrepid-explorer-discovers-a-man-cave

Only Six of My Seven Kids Have Whooping Cough, So I'm Staying Anti-Vax
Funny or Die
http://www.funnyordie.com/articles/6ba20bd4c1/only-6-of-my-7-children-have-whooping-cough-so-i-m-staying-anti-vax

It's Not You, It's Your Man Bun
The New Yorker, Daily Shouts
http://www.newyorker.com/humor/daily-shouts/its-not-you-its-your-man-bun

The Transformation
The Occasional
http://www.theoccasional.com/content/the-transformation

I'm Not an Asshole, I'm Just an Introvert
The New Yorker, Daily Shouts
http://www.newyorker.com/humor/daily-shouts/im-not-an-asshole-im-an-introvert

Letter to Christopher Columbus from Leif Eriksson
Funny or Die
http://www.funnyordie.com/articles/f75c1827b9/a-letter-to-christopher-columbus-from-leif-erikson

About the Author

NATE DERN grew up in the mountains of Evergreen, Colorado, where he enjoyed running on dirt trails and reading Kurt Vonnegut. Former artistic director at the Upright Citizens Brigade Theatre and head writer at Funny or Die, Dern is head creative of Comedy Central's Creators Program.